CURBING UNETHICAL BEHAVIOR IN GOVERNMENT

CURBING UNETHICAL BEHAVIOR IN GOVERNMENT

Joseph Zimmerman

Contributions in Political Science, Number 348
Bernard K. Johnpoll, Series Editor

GREENWOOD PRESS
Westport, Connecticut · London

Library of Congress Cataloging-in-Publication Data

Zimmerman, Joseph Francis.
    Curbing unethical behavior in government / Joseph Zimmerman.
        p.   cm.—(Contributions in political science, ISSN 0147–1066
; no. 348)
    Includes bibliographical references and index.
    ISBN 0–313–28608–6 (alk. paper)
    1. Political corruption. 2. Political ethics. I. Title.
  II. Series.
  JF1081.Z56   1994
  364.1′323–dc20   94–7615

British Library Cataloguing in Publication Data is available.

Library of Congress Catalog Card Number: 94–7615
ISBN: 0–313–28608–6
ISSN: 0147–1066

First published in 1994

Greenwood Press, 88 Post Road West, Westport, CT 06881
An imprint of Greenwood Publishing Group, Inc.

Printed in the United States of America

♾™

The paper used in this book complies with the
Permanent Paper Standard issued by the National
Information Standards Organization (Z39.48–1984).

10 9 8 7 6 5 4 3 2 1

Contents

Preface

One of the most difficult governmental problems to solve is unethical behavior by public officers and employees. The most serious ethical problem involves public officers who exercise broad discretionary authority, since the opportunities to do favors in exchange for gifts and gratuities are manifold. Ethical problems, however, are not limited to this type of egregious conduct. Public officers and employees do favors for friends and relatives, steal government equipment and supplies, use public motor vehicles for private purposes, refuse to provide government information to citizens without justification, lobby their former government agencies on behalf of clients for fees, and so on.

Ethical problems are associated with misfeasance and nonfeasance as well as malfeasance. The failure of a responsible officer to remove an incompetent public servant is a violation of the fiduciary duty of the officer. Similarly, holders of positions with no duties are sinecurists defrauding the taxpayers.

This book builds upon an earlier study, conducted for the International Union of Local Authorities in the Hague, which examined local governments' ethical problems in many nations and the corrective and preventive actions initiated by the concerned governments.

In this volume, particular stress is placed upon the importance of actions to ensure open government—the "glass house"—as a deterrent to improper conduct, a facilitator for its detection, and a promoter of a moralistic political culture. Open government has the additional advantage of promoting citizen participation in policy-making and implementation.

Continuing ethical education for public servants is highlighted as well as the need for a board to provide advice to public servants who are uncertain of the propriety of a contemplated action. The recommended board also should be assigned the duties of receiving and auditing all required financial statements filed by candidates for elective office, lobbyists, and public employees; and conducting investigations of allegations of unethical behavior.

There are many books on the subject of government ethics—some are philosophical, others are practical handbooks, and still others are confined to one plane or branch of government or public administration. This prescriptive book is distinguished from others by two features. First, it examines in a comprehensive manner the various actions taken by legislative bodies and administrators to promote ethical governance, and it assesses their effectiveness. Second, the book presents a model for promoting ethical conduct by elected and appointed public servants, to achieve the ideal expressed in the Roman maxim *Salus Populi Suprema Lex Est*—"let the welfare of the people be the supreme law."

It is impossible to acknowledge the many individuals and organizations whose contributions are reflected in this volume. Ancient philosophers and current researchers have influenced the author, and their contributions are listed in the bibliography. I owe a particular debt of gratitude, however, to Peggy Zimmerman for editorial assistance and to Addie Napolitano for preparing the manuscript.

CURBING UNETHICAL BEHAVIOR IN GOVERNMENT

Chapter 1

Ethics in the Public Service

Organized societies since the beginning of recorded history have established rules of conduct for the guidance of citizens and public officials. Although a code of ethics was enshrined in the decalogue in the Old Testament of the Bible, ethical standards need not be associated with a religion. Derived from a Greek word meaning "custom," ethics is the science of morals.

Ideally, a public officer's relationship to citizens should be a fiduciary one, with the official acting as a trustee to promote the public good. The Philippines Constitution, for example, declares "public office is a public trust. Public officers and employees shall serve with the highest degree of responsibility, integrity, loyalty, and efficiency, and shall remain accountable to the people."[1]

Prior to assuming office, most government officers in the United States swear or affirm that they will faithfully and impartially discharge and perform all the duties of their respective offices to the best of their ability. If the oath or affirmation is kept strictly, there should be no ethical problems. Unfortunately, the types of unethical behavior engaged in by certain government officers and employees appear to be limited only by the ingenuity of the human mind.

If improper behavior becomes common in a government, the burden placed on taxpayers will become a significant one. Such behavior, furthermore, will undermine citizen support of the government, and public policies will be implemented without the cooperation or with the opposition of citizens. As a result, the effectiveness of the policies will be weakened and the costs of implementation increased.

Similarly, democratic government is premised upon active citizen participation. Unethical behavior by government officers and employees will discourage citizen participation because the good citizen will not wish to be associated with a government that has a reputation for being corrupt. In addition, highly qualified individuals will be reluctant to accept a position in a government viewed as corrupt.

It is incumbent upon governments to remove incentives and opportunities for public officers and employees to make private gains from their government service, educate public servants relative to their fiduciary duties, provide clear guidance with respect to acceptable and unacceptable conduct, and initiate actions to detect and punish individuals who violate the ethical precepts.

The extent and nature of ethical problems in government are related to the prevailing political culture, which also creates barriers to the initiation of measures to solve the problems.

POLITICAL CULTURE AND ETHICAL VALUES

Cultural norms—ethos—differ to an extent from nation to nation and from state to state in the United States. An action that is acceptable in one nation may be a major crime in another nation. Relative to governments, the prevailing cultural norms tend to define acceptable conduct regardless of whether aspects of the conduct are legal. Furthermore, each sizable governmental department or agency has an organizational culture that may contain tenets at variance with legal standards of employee behavior.

Daniel J. Elazar developed a typology of political cultures that is helpful in promoting an understanding of ethical values and the types of unethical action most apt to be encountered in a particular government.[2] Defining the individualistic political culture as one emphasizing "the conception of the democratic order as a marketplace," Elazar added that the "bureaucratic organization is introduced within the framework of the favor system; . . ."[3] Although a merit system may exist for a substantial number of governmental employees, high-level officials are politically appointed and the merit system is bent "to meet political demands."[4] In this type of political culture, it is apparent that the culture makes the governmental system susceptible to unethical behavior.

Elazar's second type—moralistic political culture—defines a good government as one which "promotes the public good" and emphasizes "honesty, selflessness, and commitment to the public welfare. . . ."[5] This political culture fosters ethical actions by governmental officials and employees, and also encourages active participation by citizens in the formulation and implementation of governmental policies. As a result, problems of unethical behavior are less common where this type of political culture predominates.

The traditionalistic political culture, Elazar's third type, "is rooted in an ambivalent attitude toward the marketplace coupled with a paternalistic and elitist conception of the commonwealth."[6] This type values family and social connections, and "like the individualistic political culture, those active in politics are expected to benefit personally from their activity, although not necessarily by direct pecuniary gain."[7] This political culture, according to Elazar, is found primarily in societies retaining key features of a social order predating the industrial revolution. He noted that in the areas of the United States where this culture predominates today, "political leaders play conservative and custodial rather than initiatory roles unless pressed strongly from the outside."[8] In consequence, government does not play an active role and the opportunities for unethical behavior are more limited.

Ethical problems often are associated with gifts given to public officers and employees which may be viewed as bribes for specific decisions or rewards for past actions. A key question is whether public officers and employees should be allowed to accept gifts in a society where gift-giving and receipt are part of the cultural milieu. The Parliament of the United Kingdom answered this question by forbidding a civil servant to accept any gift or reward from an organization or citizen with whom the civil servant has official contact.[9]

The framers of the U.S. Constitution were fearful that an official of the national government might be bribed by a foreign nation and included a provision that no official may "accept of any present, emolument, office, or title, of any kind whatever, from any king, prince, or foreign state" without congressional approval.[10] The framers were aware that offense could be given to a foreign nation by the refusal of an officer to accept a gift. General approval of acceptance of certain gifts from foreign nations by officials has been granted by the Congress, which occasionally grants special permission to a named official to accept a gift.[11] The gift problem is addressed in detail in Chapters 2 and 3.

NATURE OF ETHICAL PROBLEMS

Opportunities for unethical actions by public servants were limited when governments were relatively small, during the agrarian period, and performed few major functions. Nevertheless, Machiavelli advised the prince:

we should notice also how easily men are corrupted and become wicked, although originally good and well educated. . . . All this, if carefully studied by the legislators of republics and monarchies, will make them more prompt in restraining the passions of men, and depriving them of all hopes of being able to do wrong with impunity.[12]

Thomas Jefferson in 1782 pointed out that "in every government on earth is some trace of human weakness, some germ of corruption and degeneracy, which cunning will discover, wickedness insensibly open, cultivate, and improve."[13] James Madison highlighted, in the *Federalist Papers*, an ethical problem which he contended the proposed U.S. Constitution would address effectively:

Complaints are everywhere heard from our most considerate and virtuous citizens . . . that the public good is disregarded in the conflict of rival parties, and that measures are too often decided, not according to the rules of justice and the rights of the minor party, but by the superior force of an interested and overbearing majority.[14]

Protecting minority rights in a majoritarian governance system is an important but difficult ethical task.

John C. Bollens and Henry J. Schmandt identified two types of corruption—enhancement of the wealth of the officeholder and maintenance or expansion of the personal power of the officeholder:

Acts of bribery, kickbacks, influence peddling, and conflict-of-interests comes under the first classification, while election frauds, "dirty tricks," illegal campaign contributions, and abuse of administrative authority fall into the second category.[15]

They placed sexual favors in either category, "depending on whether their use is for the personal pleasure of the office holder or for gaining influence over others."[16] The office holder may be an elected one or a bureaucrat.

Elected Officers

Elected officers have special responsibilities to promote and uphold the highest ethical standards by serving as role models. Yet these officers often abuse their positions for personal gain.

Escalating election campaign costs for major offices prompts candidates to accept funds from many different individuals and organizations whose contributions may be rewards for past actions or based upon anticipation of special access or a quid pro quo in the future. The U.S. Supreme Court in 1991 reversed the conviction of a state legislator of extortion and stressed:

Whatever ethical considerations and appearances may indicate, to hold that legislators commit the federal crime of extortion when they act for the benefit of constituents or support legislation furthering the interests of some of their constituents, shortly before or after campaign contributions are solicited and received from those beneficiaries, is an unrealistic assessment of what Congress could have meant by making it a crime to obtain property from another, without his consent, "under color of official right."[17]

The Court noted that a conviction would require evidence that force, violence, or fear had been employed or contributions were made in exchange for a specific promise by the officeholder to perform a certain official act.[18]

Each house of a legislative body, however, possesses clear authority to discipline a member. A U.S. Senate Select Committee issued a report in 1991 which concluded Senator Alan Cranston of California "engaged in a pattern and practice of mixing fund raising and substantive legislative or regulatory issues. Although this practice was largely carried out by staff, Senator Cranston condoned, supervised, or participated in it."[19] The senator was reprimanded by the Senate for his behavior and did not seek reelection in 1994. Campaign finance is explored in more detail in Chapter 4.

Elected officers also may attempt to hide their financial activities in violation of mandatory disclosure laws or regulations. For example, U.S. Representative Geraldine A. Ferraro of New York, a vice presidential candidate in 1984, was investigated by the House Committee on Standards of Official Conduct. The committee's staff concluded that she "either failed to disclose or incorrectly disclosed a significant number of items relevant to her total financial concerns," and ten of the allegations made against her by the Washington Legal Foundation were supported by the evidence.[20]

Drawing the line between informing constituents, an important responsibility of a public representative, and electioneering is a difficult task. Similarly, state and local government agencies often use public resources to promote an affirmative referenda vote on proposed bond issues desired by the agencies and contend they simply are informing the voters.

Elected officers in some instances commit unethical acts by directing their staff to perform work for the officers' personal benefit such as typing private letters, photocopying private documents, preparing legal papers for private use, and so on. A more serious ethical violation involves the outside employment of an elected official, which produces a conflict of interest or representation of private parties before other governmental bodies for compensation.

In making appointments, elected officers must investigate fully the backgrounds of potential appointees to ensure that they are persons of the highest ethical standards and would not have a conflict of interest if appointed. In 1993, a newspaper investigation of the backgrounds of members of the New York State Occupational Safety and Health Hazard Abatement Board revealed that more than $3.5 million in grants during the previous three years had been made to individuals associated with board members.[21] The newspaper editorially was critical of the refusal of the governor's office to release information about the backgrounds of board members.

Bureaucrats have criticized the Congress for failure to serve as a role model by exempting itself from various ethics laws. In 1988, Assistant Attorney General William F. Weld pointed out, "actions that would be illegal if committed by someone in the executive branch were perfectly all right if committed by a member of Congress."[22]

Bureaucrats

The "end justifies the means" rationale is commonly encountered in the public service, since laws and administrative rules and regulations are "bent" or broken and the violations are justified on the ground that the objectives of the actions are worthy and desirable. This rationale is reflective of cultural norms emphasizing achievement of goals benefiting the general public. The U.S. General Accounting Office in 1992 reported a related problem:

Widespread contract deficiencies result in part from an environment within agencies that too often stresses accomplishing the mission at the expense of cost-effective contract management. The cost to the taxpayer of such practices is enormous . . . the nation will be paying for many years for the results of DOE's [Department of Energy] contract mismanagement and emphasis on the production of nuclear material. DOE's cost estimates to correct environmental, safety, and health problems at DOE's nuclear weapons complex now stand at over $160 billion.[23]

The public's will, expressed by elected officers or referenda, should not be distorted deliberately by public servants who believe that they know what is best for the public. Anti-innovationism tends to be a characteristic of many public bureaucracies and procrastination can be the equivalent of nonfeasance of duties. In some instances, bureaucrats attempt to prevent change by employing what Jeremy Bentham labeled the "Snail's-Pace Argument, or 'One Thing at a Time.' Slow and Sure."[24] Serious bureaucratic resistance, edging on sabotage, to change ordered by the legislative body or the chief executive is insubordination, no matter how the resisting officers rationalize their opposition.

A perennial problem is the ultra vires problem (i.e., officials exceeding their legal authority through ignorance or deliberately). Internal and external controls, described in Chapter 7 are helpful in ensuring that government officers and employees do not exceed their authority.

The deliberate use of faulty methodology or manufactured data to support a policy position by bureaucrats clearly is unethical as are the failure to search for all available information and the withholding of information from superiors and the public.

Similarly, an attempt to distort the policy established by a legislature by drafting rules and regulations not in compliance with the intent expressed in the enabling statute is a problem which has become more serious with the growth of administrative law in the United States. This problem is reflected in the enactment of statutes by a number of state legislatures providing for a committee to review administrative rules and regulations and veto ones not in conformance with legislative intent, or to report such rules to the legislature for its action.

Ethical violations by bureaucrats are apt to occur during political campaigns, particularly if the bureaucrats are political appointees. In 1992, for example, two politically appointed officials of the U.S. Department of State searched the department's Passport Office files in an attempt to locate information on presidential candidate William J. Clinton that could be employed against him in the election campaign. On the surface, there was a violation of the Privacy Act of 1974, which is explained in Chapter 5.

Bias in policy making and administration often is difficult to detect. All citizens—regardless of ethnic, racial, religious, social backgrounds—must be accorded equal protection of the laws, due process of law, and equal access to and treatment by government officers. The latter, however, consciously or unconsciously, may favor members of certain groups.

A serious ethical problem involves deliberate attempts by bureaucrats to "co-opt" citizens—the product of a natural desire to want citizen support for government programs. Co-optation, the deliberate manipulation of citizens to win their support for a government program, is unethical.[25] If there is a legal requirement for citizen participation in a program, it is incumbent upon officials to provide citizens with full information and accord them the opportunity to participate in the decision-making process from the alpha to the omega.

More Recent Problems

The nature of ethical problems and the magnitude of the problems have changed over time. Most eighteenth- and early nineteenth-century ethical problems generally were addressed adequately by conflict-of-interest statutes which clearly identified unacceptable conduct (see Chapter 2). With industrialization and urbanization, however, a great growth in the number of governmental programs, including regulatory ones, occurred, and opportunities for unethical behavior became widespread. The technical nature of many types of governmental regulation necessitates the granting of broad discretionary authority to bureaucrats, thereby facilitating malfeasance for personal gain.

A large, gray area developed between what was clearly ethical behavior and what was clearly unethical behavior, and public officers and employees were faced with difficulties in distinguishing right conduct from wrong conduct. Responding to the inadequacies of the conflict-of-interest laws, legislative bodies commenced to enact codes of ethics containing guidelines for behavior by government employees and providing for a board of ethics empowered to issue advisory opinions in response to requests from employees for guidance on contemplated actions with ethical implications. Legislative bodies also have created committees to provide advice to members and their staffs (see Chapter 3).

Illustrative of the subtle nature of certain ethical problems is a case involving a supplier of groceries to the county jail in Georgia, who was elected to the County Commission. Should the newly elected commissioner stop selling groceries to the county jail even if his firm won the contract to supply the groceries through competitive bidding? The commissioner believed that such bidding would negate any potential conflict of interest, but wisely sought the advice of the Georgia attorney general. The latter opined that a conflict of interest would exist under such circumstances, since the County Commission is responsible for ensuring that the goods are delivered on a timely basis and are quality goods.[26]

Similarly, the new U.S. Environmental Agency Administrator, Carol M. Browner, learned in 1993 that Citizen Action, which employs her husband, opposed a proposed incinerator in Florida. As a consequence, she stopped a meeting convened to allow citizen activists to express their opposition to the proposed incinerator and requested the agency's ethics officer to determine the appropriateness of her participation in the meeting. As a consequence, she properly recused herself from participation in the matter.[27] Codes of ethics and boards or officers providing advice on ethical questions are examined in detail in Chapter 3.

The entrance of more women into the public service during the latter half of the twentieth century generated another ethical problem. Sexual harassment apparently was not a major problem in the national government in the United States when there were relatively few officers and employees and most, including clerks, were men. The changed situation for women and men is reflected in a 1981 report issued by the U.S. Merit Systems Protection Board, revealing "that sexual harassment is a problem for a large number of federal workers—approximately 294,000 women and 168,000 men. For many of the women, harassment occurred repeatedly and frequently lasting a relatively long time. The men . . . had similar experiences."[28] The forms of harassment were:

Actual or attempted rape or sexual assault;

Pressure for sexual behaviors;

Deliberate touching, leaning over, cornering, or pinching;

Sexually suggestive looks or gestures;

Letters, phone calls, or materials of a sexual nature;

Pressures for dates; and

Sexual teasing, jokes, remarks, or questions.[29]

The seriousness of the individual harassments obviously differed and, in some cases, approximately one percent of the total involved the commission of a felony as in the case of rape or attempted sexual assault. Other forms of sexual harassment were less serious but a violation of ethical standards. The frequency of harassment varied by agency, and workers are harassed most commonly by fellow workers, compared to supervisors.

The report noted a sharp difference between men and women relative to the frequency of the occurrence of actual or attempted rape or assault, with more than 50 percent of the men reporting frequent experience compared with 20 percent of the women who reported they experienced rape or sexual assault more than once.[30] The board emphasized the instances reported by men were surprising and "the sharp difference between men and women may reflect a difference in perceptions about what constituted attempted rape or sexual assault."[31]

Extensive privatization of traditional governmental functions in the United States involves governing bodies entering into contracts with business firms for the provision of services and necessitates close legislative oversight of contract auditing. Lack of thorough and timely contract auditing opens the government to vulnerability for fraud, abuse, and waste. Cost plus or cost reimbursable contracts must be examined thoroughly on a regular basis to ensure that reported costs were incurred. In particular, great opportunities exist for fraud relative to indirect or overhead costs which may not be allocated properly to a specific government contract.

Media attention tends to focus upon the large governments—national, state, and municipal—and to neglect the low-visibility units. Hence, the impression is given that large size is associated positively with unethical behavior. Whether there is a positive correlation between size and the amount of unethical behavior has not been determined. However, limited evidence suggests that unethical behavior may be a serious problem in low-visibility units (e.g., small municipalities and special district governments).[32] The latter generally receive little media attention unless a major problem develops, and many special district governments are exempt from civil service requirements.

THE REFORM MOVEMENTS

Corrupt and unresponsive governments in the nineteenth century spawned several reform movements. Public disgust with the spoils system led to the adoption of constitutional and statutory provisions establishing a merit system for the selection and promotion of most employees in the executive branch of a government. Civil service reformers continue their efforts today to strengthen the system, and advocate a rigorous applicant screening process to reduce the number of employees with a proclivity for unethical behavior.

The municipal reform movement at the turn of the century, aided by the muckrakers, sought to eliminate corruption in government and promote the provisions of municipal services in the most economical and efficient manner. These reformers desired to restructure a municipal government to make its operations clearly visible to voters who thereby would be able to hold the appropriate governmental officer(s) responsible for unethical actions and failure to achieve goals. To make governments more visible, they recommended replacement of the large, ward-elected, bicameral city council by a small unicameral one elected at large. In addition, the reformers recognized the relationship between organizational structure and opportunities for unethical behavior. Hence, they sought the elimination of independently elected executive branch boards and officials, and the centralization of all executive authority in an appointed professional city manager.[33]

The opportunities for unethical conduct are related in part to the extent to which authority in the executive branch is centralized in a single chief executive or dispersed widely among elected officers. Two competing theories have influenced the organization of the executive branch of governments in the United States. One paradigm reflects distrust of a strong chief executive and is reflected in the constitutions of the original thirteen states except Massachusetts. The 1777 New York Constitution, for example, did not confide the appointment power in the governor. As governments commenced to perform more functions in the nineteenth century, Jacksonian democracy became the dominant movement determining the organization of the executive branch, and the result was the creation of new departments and boards with executive officers elected for short terms.

The other paradigm is based upon the belief that high ethical standards and provision of services in the most economic and efficient manner will be promoted if all executive power is delegated to a single chief executive with adequate authority to monitor closely executive branch activities on a continuous basis.

Tracing its origin to President William Taft's Commission on Economy and Efficiency in Government, the administrative reorganization movement in the first two decades of the twentieth century focused upon the reorganization of the executive branch of state governments. The movement sought to centralize authority in the governor, organize the executive branch by major function to improve economy and efficiency, and establish internal control systems to ensure that governmental policies were executed honestly in the most economic and efficient manner.

Many individuals active in the municipal reform movement and the administrative management movement also were promoters of the short ballot, which would reduce the burden placed upon voters at elections by concentrating all executive power in a single chief executive officer—the governor, the mayor, the city manager.[34] As noted, the diffusion of responsibility among numerous elected officials under Jacksonian democracy made it extremely difficult for the electorate to hold the officers accountable for their actions.

LEGISLATING ETHICS

There is a general consensus that governmental affairs cannot be conducted according to the same standards that prevail in the business world. The law of the market place—*caveat emptor*—is not accepted completely today in the business world and, obviously, is an unsatisfactory guide or standard for elected official and civil servant behavior. This fact has long been recognized by legislative bodies which enacted laws making illegal the bribery of public officers, embezzlement of government funds, fraudulent actions involving the government, and misuse of public equipment and supplies. In addition, macing and sinecures have been made illegal. The former involves continuing contributions to a political party as a condition for obtaining and keeping a public job. The latter refers to paid governmental positions that have no duties.

While conventional wisdom holds that ethics cannot be legislated, lawmaking bodies throughout the world enact statutes designed to ensure that all governmental actions are ethical in nature. As noted, governments have enacted conflict-of-interest statutes and codes of ethics. In addition, many governments have enacted one or more sunshine laws—mandatory disclosure laws, freedom of information laws, and open meeting laws. These laws seek to enable citizens to obtain information that will assist them to monitor the performance of governments and civil servants, thereby reducing the opportunities for unethical behavior. Sunshine laws are helpful in promoting ethical behavior by public officers and employees. Aristotle stressed the importance of an educated citizenry in the following terms:

But if the citizens of a state are to judge and to distribute offices according to merit, then they must know each other's characters; where they do not possess this knowledge, both the election to office and the decisions of lawsuits will go wrong.[35]

Not all legislative efforts to raise ethical standards pass constitutional muster. Candidates for elective office on occasion defame the character of opponents by making charges against them with knowledge the charges are not true, and/or they engage in other unethical campaign practices. Publicity about "dirty" campaign tricks following the Watergate scandal led the New York State legislature to direct the State Board of Elections to issue a "Fair Campaign Code." Promulgated in 1974, the code established ethical standards for election campaigns and specifically prohibited "political espionage and other political practices involving subversion of the political parties and process."[36]

The U.S. District Court ruled in 1975 that the code's prohibition of personal attacks on the ethnic background, race, religion, or sex of a candidate for public office violates the First Amendment to the U.S. Constitution, and the decision was upheld unanimously by the U.S. Supreme Court.[37] This decision, however, does not prevent an injured party from suing the perpetrator for defamation of character.

Governments have an obligation to adopt ethical standards applicable to all public officers and employees, and special standards applicable to officers and employees authorized to exercise broad discretionary authority. Adoption of such standards will not ensure that officers and employees will be guided by right conduct. It is essential that copies of the standards be provided to officers and employees and updated as needed, with meetings held to explain the standards.

Donald C. Menzel surveyed employees of a Florida city and county, and discovered that less than one-half of those surveyed were aware their conduct as government employees is governed by Florida law.[38] Nearly 30 percent of the respondents reported they had observed unethical behavior by at least one government employee during the previous year, and approximately 20 percent of the city employees believe it is proper to accept "gifts from the public or persons who do business with their government."[39] Most interestingly, Menzel discovered that "large numbers of employees perceive themselves to have very high ethical standards. Asked to rate the ethical standards of their co-workers, most assigned a lower rating."[40]

Similarly, James S. Bowman surveyed a random sample of government administrators who are members of the American Society for Public Administration and reported that "just over half of the sample concedes that supervisors are under pressure to compromise personal standards" and "nearly one-fourth . . . believe that institutions have a reactive, negative, primitive, 'low road' approach to ethics, one that reinforces popular suspicions and focuses on wrongdoing."[41]

AN OVERVIEW

The following eight chapters describe and analyze actions that have been initiated by governments to ensure that private interests do not benefit at the public's expense. The oldest legal approach to ethical governance— conflict-of-interest statutes—is the subject of Chapter 2. These statutes make illegal egregious behavior by public officers and employees, but are ineffective in addressing subtle unethical actions.

Codes of ethics, the subject of Chapter 3, provide guidance to public servants relative to a variety of situations with ethical overtones and typically establish a board of ethics to provide advice to officers and employees who are uncertain as to whether a contemplated official action would constitute a conflict of interest.

Complementary mandatory-information-disclosure laws are outlined and evaluated in Chapter 4. The purpose of these "sunshine" laws—applicable to candidates for elective office, lobbyists, and government officers and employees—is to make public information which can be utilized in an investigation of unethical behavior. In part, these laws have a deterrent effect on individuals required to make the disclosures.

Chapter 5 focuses on freedom of information statutes which are "sunshine" laws closely related to mandatory disclosure laws. The former guarantee citizens ready access to most government information, thereby facilitating citizen input into the decision-making process and their evaluation of the performance of elected and appointed officials, as well as making available information that may reveal nefarious behavior. Care, however, must be taken by legislatures to ensure that the freedom of information laws do not invade personal privacy.

The subject of Chapter 6 is open meeting laws which also seek to shed "sunshine" on governments by opening up to the public the decision-making process engaged in by legislative bodies and administrative agencies. In common with freedom of information statutes, care must be exercised in the framing of an open meeting statute to protect personal privacy.

Although conflict-of-interest and "sunshine" statutes can promote ethical behavior and deter iniquitous actions by public servants, the statutes are not self-enforcing. Chapter 7 highlights the importance of systems of internal and external controls in curbing unethical behavior in government. The former controls are implemented by each agency in contrast to external controls which are implemented by outside bodies—legislatures, auditors, special prosecutors, and ombudsmen.

The elimination of improper comportment by public servants can be facilitated by whistleblowing, the subject of Chapter 8. In general, government officers and employees have the most knowledge of wrongdoing, but may be deterred from reporting it by peer pressure and fear of retaliation. To encourage whistleblowing, legislatures have enacted special protection laws.

Chapter 9 examines the need for postgovernment service restrictions and the revolving door problem—public officials resigning their positions to join a private firm that they may have been regulating or a firm holding a government contract that they have been overseeing. Although not a universal problem, it is a major one for the U.S. Department of Defense and many regulatory agencies.

The concluding chapter contains a model for ethical government incorporating key elements of actions, described in Chapters 2 through 9, to curb improper behavior by public servants and notes the importance of developing a moralistic political culture.

NOTES

1. Constitution of the Republic of the Philippines, art. XIII, § 1.

2. Daniel J. Elazar, *American Federalism: A View from the States*, 3d ed. (New York: Harper & Row, 1984), pp. 114–22.

3. Ibid., pp. 115–16.

4. Ibid., p. 117.

5. Ibid.

6. Ibid., p. 118.

7. Ibid., p. 119.

8. Ibid.

9. *United Kingdom Prevention of Corruption Act*, 1906.

10. The Constitution of the United States, art. I, § 9.

11. Foreign Gifts and Decorations Act of 1966, 80 Stat. 952, 22 U.S.C. § 804 (1990); Mutual Educational and Cultural Exchange Act, 75 Stat. 527, 22 U.S.C. § 2451 (1990).

12. Niccolo Machiavelli, *The Prince and the Discourses* (New York: The Modern Library, 1940), p. 226.

13. Paul L. Ford, ed. *The Works of Thomas Jefferson* (New York: G. P. Putnam's Sons, 1894), p. 64.

14. *The Federalist Papers* (New York: New American Library, 1961), p. 77.

15. John C. Bollens and Henry J. Schmandt, *Political Corruption: Power, Money, and Sex* (Pacific Palisades, Calif.: Palisades Publishers, 1979), p. 17.

16. Ibid.

17. *McCormick v. United States*, 111 S.Ct. 1816 (1991).

18. Ibid.

19. *Investigation of Senator Alan Cranston. Report of the Select Committee on Ethics, United States Senate Together with Additional Views* (Washington, D.C.: The Committee, 1991), vol. I, pp. 57–58.

20. *In the Matter of Representative Geraldine A. Ferraro. Report of the Committee on Standards of Official Conduct, United States House of Representatives* (Washington, D.C.: United States Government Printing Office, 1985), p. 28.

21. "Raise Safety Board Ethics," *Times Union* (Albany, New York), April 12, 1993, p. A–6.

22. Remarks of William F. Weld, Assistant Attorney General, Criminal Division, United States Department of Justice at the Morning Newsmaker. The National Press Club, Washington, D.C., March 8, 1988, p. 9.

23. *Federal Contracting: Cost-Effective Contract Management Requires Sustained Commitment* (Washington, D.C.: United States General Accounting Office, 1992), p. 13.

24. Harold A. Larrabee, ed., *Bentham's Handbook of Political Fallacies* (Baltimore: Johns Hopkins University Press, 1952), p. 131.

25. The classic study of co-optation is Philip Selznick's *TVA and the Grass Roots* (Berkeley: University of California Press, 1949).

26. *Opinions of the Attorney General of Georgia*, Opinion no. U-83-8 (1983).

27. Letter from Administrator Carol M. Browner of the United States Environmental Protection Agency to all Agency employees, dated January 27, 1993.

28. United States Merit System Protection Board, *Sexual Harassment in the Federal Workplace: Is It a Problem?* (Washington, D.C.: United States Government Printing Office, 1981), p. 33.

29. Ibid., p. 34.

30. Ibid., p. 38.

31. Ibid.

32. The most comprehensive book on public authorities is Donald Axelrod's *Shadow Government: The Hidden World of Public Authorities and How They Control over $1 Trillion of your Money* (New York: John Wiley and Sons, 1992).

33. See Richard S. Childs, *The First Fifty Years of the Council-Manager Plan* (New York: National Municipal League, 1965).

34. Richard S. Childs, *The Short Ballot: A Movement to Simplify Politics* (New York: The National Short Ballot Organization, 1916).

35. Benjamin Jowett, trans. *Aristotle's Politics* (New York: Carlton House, n.d.), p. 288.

36. Official Compilation of Codes, Rules, and Regulations of the State of New York, subtitle V, Part 6201 (1974).

37. *Vanasco v. Schwartz*, 401 F.Supp. 87 (1975); and *Vanasco v. Schwartz*, 423 U.S. 1041 (1976).

38. Donald C. Menzel, "Ethics Attitudes and Behaviors in Local Governments: An Empirical Analysis," *State and Local Government Review*, Fall 1992, p. 96.

39. Ibid., p. 97.

40. Ibid., p. 101.

41. James S. Bowman, "Ethics in Government: A National Survey of Public Administrators," *Public Administration Review*, May/June 1990, p. 347.

Chapter 2

Conflicts of Interest

The English common law, especially the rules of trust, is the original source of conflict-of-interest provisions governing the behavior of public officers and employees. Under the common law, a government officer has a fiduciary obligation, may have neither a direct nor an indirect interest in a governmental transaction, and must act solely in the public interest. The common law utilizes inconsistency with the public good regardless of whether the public officer receives a private benefit or a personal pecuniary gain. Whereas the common law generally deals with public officers involved in a transaction, subsequent statutory provisions typically include coverage of all officers and employees, regardless of whether they are involved with a given transaction.

Until the latter part of the nineteenth century, governmental functions in the United States were limited, the number of civil servants was relatively small, and ethical questions focused primarily upon legislators. The traditional protections against conflicts of interest contained in the common law proved to be inadequate in the nineteenth and twentieth centuries as governmental intervention into private affairs became more pervasive and governments increased in size and complexity. As a result of these developments, legislatures commenced to enact conflict-of-interest statutes based chiefly upon common law principles. In general, the nineteenth-century statutory supplements to the common law were limited ones aimed at preventing specific abuses.

Congress in 1853, for example, enacted a law prohibiting an officer of the United States to act as an attorney in prosecuting a claim against the

United States and stipulating no officer "shall receive any gratuity, or share of, or interest in any claim against the United States with intent to aid or assist, or in consideration of having aided or assisted, in the prosecution of such claim. . . ."[1] Complex conflict-of-interest statutes date to the twentieth century.

The statutes recognize that no person, upon assuming a public office, can dissociate himself/herself completely from his/her private activities. Hence, the major purpose of the statutes is to provide guidance to public officers and private firms that deal with governments relative to prohibited activities. The statutes, however, also contain criminal penalties designed to deter venal conflicts of interest.

In addition to the general conflict-of-interest statutes, there are specific conflict-of-interest statutes for named officials. Similarly, the statutes recognize that the nature of conflicts of interest of executive officers and legislators are not identical.

Conflict-of-interest provisions are found in state constitutions as well as in statutes. The New York State Constitution forbids a public officer to "receive or consent to receive, directly, or indirectly, anything of value or of personal advantage, or the promise thereof, for performing or omitting to perform any official act, or with the express or implied understanding that his official action or omission to act is to be in any degree influenced thereby. . . ."[2] The Constitution also provides that any person offering a bribe to a public officer is guilty of a felony.[3]

Although most prohibitions of conflicts-of-interest provisions are contained in state statutes, a governor may establish additional prohibitions subject to the powers granted to him/her by the state constitution or statutes. The New York State Court of Appeals, the highest state court, in 1978 opined that the governor may forbid appointees serving at his pleasure to engage in transactions or business associations that have the potential for conflicting with their official duties, but he may not impose such prohibitions upon civil service employees or gubernatorial appointees serving for fixed terms who cannot be removed from office without just cause.[4]

Conflict-of-interest prohibitions can have a deterrent effect upon the recruitment of public officers. The problem tends to be the greatest in small local governments since the most competent individuals tend to be professionals and members of the business community. If they are required to divest their professional and/or business interests in order to become a public officer, they are apt to conclude that the burden associated with public office-holding is too great and refuse to serve.

The effectiveness of conflict-of-interest provisions is dependent upon education of public officers and employees and a system of internal controls to detect conflicts (see Chapter 7).

MAJOR PROVISIONS

Constitutional statutory conflict-of-interest provisions address the scope of their coverage, definition of interest, dual office-holding, contracts, bribes, gifts, disclosure of confidential information, representing private parties before public bodies, outside employment, and post-employment restrictions, and provide penalties for violations.

Coverage

Statutes in several states make a distinction between public officers and public employees based upon one or more of the following factors:

1. Creation of the position by constitution or statute,
2. Powers and duties involving an exercise of a portion of the sovereign power,
3. Regular and continuous service as opposed to those limited to a particular transaction,
4. A fixed tenure of office,
5. Necessity of an oath,
6. Liability to account for misfeasance or nonfeasance,
7. Compensation for services, and
8. The importance, dignity, and independence of the official.[5]

The Washington Supreme Court in 1944 identified five elements which make public employment a public office:

1. It must be created by the Constitution or by the Legislature or created by a municipality or other body through authority conferred by the Legislature;
2. It must possess a delegation of a portion of the sovereign power of government to be exercised for the benefit of the public;
3. The powers conferred and the duties to be discharged must be defined, directly or impliedly, by the Legislature or through legislative authority;
4. The duties must be performed independently and without control of a superior power, other than the law, unless they be those of an inferior or subordinate office created or authorized by the Legislature and by it placed under the general control of a superior office or body; and

5. It must have some permanency and continuity and not be only temporary or occasional.[6]

In some states, a number of "officers" have been termed "employees" even though they perform the duties of an "officer." Kaplan and Lillich in 1958 noted, "many public officers perform ministerial functions, and many public employees are given wide discretionary powers."[7]

Governments today rely heavily upon consultants for expert assistance in solving various problems. These consultants may work only one or two days a month for the government and provide a type of assistance which the government otherwise could not obtain. A 1961 study pointed out:

Existing statutes now in force make it extremely difficult for the Government to secure the services of certain types of consultants. If these laws were strictly enforced, and if more persons were aware of them, their deterrent effect would be greater still.

The heart of the difficulty lies in the failure of present-day law to recognize the special problems of the occasional consultant.

Take, for example, the statutes prohibiting outside compensation for government employees. A consultant working for the government a week or two a year can scarcely sever his economic ties with his regular business or profession. This being so, the legal restrictions against outside compensation are either ignored in practice or else bypassed through erratic and improvised exemptions.[8]

A related problem involves political party officers. The chairman of the political party controlling a county government, for example, may be able to influence the decisions of the governing body to favor the chairman or the chairman's spouse. In 1992, it was revealed that the wife of the Rensselaer County, New York, Democratic chairman had been paid $434,000 in commission for co-brokering the county's insurance contract in the period from 1986 to 1992.[9]

Definition of Interest

A broad definition of interest is contained in Rule 56 issued by the treasury department in the United Kingdom.

The first duty of a civil servant is to give his undivided allegiance to the state at all times and on all occasions when the state has a claim on his service. . . . But to say that he is not to subordinate his duty to his private interests, nor to make use of his political position to further those interests, is to say no more

than that he must behave with common honesty. A civil serv
subordinate his duty to his private interests; but neither is he to p
position where his duty and his interests conflict. . . . These obli₅..
do not doubt, universally recognized throughout the whole of the service, ..
were otherwise, its public credit would be diminished and its usefulness to the
state impaired.

Conflict-of-interest acts prohibit an officer to have a direct or indirect
interest in a transaction and also stipulate that certain family members with
pecuniary interests in a pending governmental matter are considered to be
part of the public officer's interest if he/she is aware of the family members'
interests.

A direct interest refers to situations where an officer is the owner,
partner, or a major shareholder of a firm entering into a transaction with
the government and the officer will be the beneficiary of the profits of
the firm under the contract. At common law, an officer was acting
illegally if his/her actions were inconsistent with promotion of the public
interest. Statutory conflict-of-interest provisions, however, apply only if
the officer has a financial interest in a transaction and include a prohibition of indirect interest under the principle that the officer's loyalty
should be totally to the public weal and he/she should have no type of
interest in a transaction. There is, however, a tendency for statutes to
permit a government officer to have an interest in a contract with the
government, provided the interest is disclosed publicly in advance and
the officer refrains from voting on the award of the contract.[10]

An indirect pecuniary interest is defined as an interest a government
officer has in his/her company, employer, partner, or similar entity that
has a pecuniary interest in a matter pending before the governmental
body. To be effective, the definition of a business must be broad. The
Model State Conflict-of-Interest and Financial Disclosure Law defines
"business" to mean:

any entity operated for economic gain, whether professional, industrial, or
commercial, and whether established to produce or deal with a product or a
service, including but not limited to, entities operated in the form of sole
proprietorship, as self-employed persons, partnership, corporation, joint stock
company, joint venture, receivership or trust, and entities which for purposes of
taxation are treated as nonprofit organizations.[11]

Similarly, it is important to define "business with which a person is
associated." The commentary on the Model Law stresses that such a

definition "is intended to delineate business relationships that involve some measurable element of close and continuing association and economic interest which might lead to a conflict of interest."[12] The definition excludes relationships that are simply formal such as the relationship between an insurance company and a person the company insures, and also excludes a relationship involving an officer owning a small number of shares of stock in a large corporation whose shares are traded publicly. In the latter case, it is apparent that the ownership interest is too small to tempt a public officer to promote the interests of the corporation.

"Interest in Real Property" is defined by the Model Law as including "any leasehold, beneficial interest, ownership interest, or an option to acquire any such interest in real property."[13] Interests other than ownership of the legal title to property can create a conflict of interest.

Courts probe closely to determine whether there is an indirect interest and place the burden of proof upon the public officer.[14] In 1934, the California Supreme Court opined it "is not concerned with the technical relationships of the parties, but will look beyond the veil which enshrouds the matter to discern the vital facts."[15]

If an interest is shared with numerous citizens, it is not prohibited.[16] Similarly, a personal interest is not involved if the officer is a member of a nonprofit organization promoting the general welfare.[17] The California Government Code specifically stipulates that there is no conflict of interest if the public officer is a nonsalaried officer of a nonprofit corporation.[18]

In 1940, the New York State Supreme Court, a general trial court, employed the company prosperity theory and opined that an officer had a financial interest in a company even though the officer worked for the company without compensation.[19] This decision was based upon the theory that the officer may benefit upon leaving the public service, provided the company prospers.

Conflict-of-interest statutes and court interpretations are inconsistent in defining an indirect conflict. Critics maintain that "intention and motives rather than the external act should be the basic consideration" in determining whether there is an indirect interest.[20] The inadequacy of the statutory provisions on indirect interests is a strong argument in favor of a code of ethics, a topic explored in detail in Chapter 3.

Conflict-of-interest statutes require public officers and employees to disclose publicly whether they have a pecuniary interest that would benefit from a proposed governmental action (see Chapter 4). If a public servant has such an interest, the official is required to abstain from participating in the decision-making process. A 1929 Irish government circular stipulates that "a civil servant, who in the course of his official duties comes into contact with any matter affecting a business organization in which he has an interest, should immediately disclose the measure of his interest to the Head of his Department so that some other officer may, if the Head of the Department considers it necessary, be asked to deal with the matter."[21] A pecuniary interest relates to money, but does not have to involve cash. Unrealized gains or losses, capable of being measured in money, are pecuniary interests.

Family Members. Conflict-of-interest acts stipulate that certain family members with pecuniary interests in a pending governmental matter are considered to be part of the public officer's interest if he/she is aware of the family members' interests. Typically, the list of family members includes the official's spouse or common law spouse, parents, and children regardless of where they are domiciled. Only relatives specified in the statute are considered to be covered by the statute.

The Model State Conflict-of-Interest and Financial Disclosure Law defines "Member of Household" to include:

1. A person who is another person's spouse, child, ward, parent, or other relative, or the child, ward, parent, or other relative of such person's spouse, and who shares such other person's legal residence; or

2. A person who is another person's spouse, child, ward, parent, or other relative of such person's spouse, and over whose financial affairs and holdings such other person has legal or actual control, whether or not they share a legal residence.[22]

The definition is broad because the public officer may not only take action to benefit directly a member of his/her household, but also may take an action that in the future will benefit him/her directly; such as inheriting the estate of a member of the household. In common with the public officer, a member of a household may have an exempt or remote interest, as explained in subsequent sections.

A more difficult question to address by statute is a possible conflict of interest involving an intimate friend of a government official. Statutes presume that a public officer may act to benefit a member of his/her family, but often are silent relative to close friends of the official.

The Exempt Interests. Recognizing that certain interests cannot cause harm to the public weal, the conflict-of-interest statute specifies exemptions from its coverage. Typically, the following exemptions are included in the statute:

- Purchasing bonds issued by the federal, state, or local government.
- Being entitled to receive a service, loan, subsidy, or other benefit offered by the government on the same terms to other citizens.
- Being a member of a volunteer fire company.
- Provision of electrical, water, or other utility services by a municipal government on the same terms as provided to the general public.
- Possessing a total value of an involved interest less than a specified amount.

The Remote Interest. A conflict-of-interest statute may allow a public officer to retain a private interest during the conduct of government affairs, provided the private interest is remote and is disclosed. A public officer is not considered to have a conflict of interest if his/her interest is so insignificant or remote in nature that it could not be regarded as apt to influence the officer's decisions. While the principle of the remote or *de minimis* interest exclusion is easy to describe, applying the principle is difficult. Assuming a public officer has a financial interest in a business entity that receives a state contract, what degree of association of the officer with the business firm is sufficient to disallow the contract because of a conflict of interest?

The exemption for "remote interest" in conflict-of-interest statutes typically provides that the concerned officer must make a full disclosure of the nature and extent of the interest, a contract must be approved after recording of the disclosure, and the officer with the remote interest must not attempt to influence another officer to enter into the contract.[23] Statutory prohibitions of participation by an officer with a conflict of interest in awarding a contract are designed to ensure that members of the body making the award do not engage in reciprocal favors or back-scratching.

The California State legislature defined a remote interest to include:

1. That of a nonsalaried officer of a nonprofit corporation;
2. That of an employee of the contracting party if such contracting party has ten or more other employees and if the officer was an employee of said contracting party for at least three years prior to his initially accepting an office;
3. That of a parent in the earnings of his minor child for personal services;
4. That of a landlord or tenant of the contracting party;
5. That of an attorney of the contracting party; or
6. That of a member of a nonprofit corporation formed under the Agricultural Code or a nonprofit corporation formed under the Corporations Code for the sole purpose of engaging in the merchandising of agricultural products.[24]

States with remote interest statutory provisions differ relative to whether the information disclosed by the officer must be disclosed to the public. New York has such a requirement, but Texas and Washington only require that the report be filed with the secretary of state and be available to the officers awarding the concerned contract.[25] The latter type of provision appears to be the most desirable, since the public interest will be protected by allowing officers awarding a contract to read the disclosed information and simultaneously protecting the privacy of the officer making the disclosure.

Relative to holding shares in a corporation, a public officer is deemed by statute to have a remote interest if he/she owns less than a specified percent—ranging from 3 percent to 10 percent—of the shares of a corporation which is seeking the award of a government contract.[26]

Remote interest provisions also allow the government to purchase equipment and supplies from a company in which an officer has an interest, provided the amount is under a specified sum in a single purchase or during the course of a year.[27]

Dual Office-Holding

At common law, dual office-holding is permitted, provided the offices are not incompatible. If the offices are not compatible, an individual forfeits or must resign his/her first office upon acceptance of the second office. A state legislator at common law, for example, is not prevented from holding a municipal office, even though the municipality lobbies the state legislature for the enactment or defeat of specific bills, provided the municipal office held by the state legislator is not involved in the lobbying effort. The state legislature, of course, can override the common law by statute.

The prohibition of dual office-holding can be traced to the new testament of the bible which advises, "no man may serve two masters, for either he will hate the one and love the other; or else he will hold to the one and despise the other."[28] Nizan Al-Mulk wrote a book of rules for Persian kings advising against dual office-holding:

When two appointments are given to one man, one of the tasks is always inefficiently and faultily performed; and in fact you will usually find that the man who has two functions fails in both of them, and is constantly suffering censure and uneasiness on account of his shortcomings.[29]

In effect, Al-Mulk warned that the duties would conflict in terms of the amount of time that would be devoted to one office or to the other office.

State constitutions and statutes, and local government charters and ordinances often contain a provision against dual office-holding. The New York County Law, for example, forbids a county judge, family court judge, surrogate, district attorney, sheriff, county clerk, or any elective county officer to serve simultaneously in any other elective county or town office.[30] In 1990, the Alabama attorney general issued an opinion that an individual may not serve simultaneously on a county board of registrars and as a member of a city council since "both positions are offices of profit."[31]

The purpose of the prohibition of dual office-holding is to prevent a situation in which an officer must choose between executing the duty of one office instead of the duty of a second office. Relative to the common law doctrine of compatibility of office, a public officer may seek election to an office with incompatible duties while holding the first office, but must resign the first position if elected to the second office.[32] A statute, however, could prohibit a person holding a public office from being a candidate for election to a second office. In 1991, the New York State attorney general issued informal opinion 91-57 that the state election law prohibits a person from simultaneously running for two public offices if he/she would be prohibited by law from holding both offices at the same time.

If the state constitution and statutes do not address the question of dual office-holding, an individual may hold two or more offices unless such holding violates the doctrine of incompatible offices. The New York State Court of Appeals in 1874 opined that two offices are incompatible if one is subordinate to a second office or an inherent inconsistency exists between the two offices.[33] Relative to the subordinate statute, an officer cannot hold a second office which reports to the first office. An inconsistent office is one that involves a potential conflict of duties with respect to a second office, such as the position of auditor and the position of finance director. The Washington State Supreme Court held, in 1957, that "offices are incompatible when the nature and duties of the offices are such as to render it improper, from considerations of public policy, for one person to retain both."[34]

The New York State attorney general in 1989 issued an informal opinion that a village attorney may serve as a village court justice provided he does not represent the village in court.[35] In the same year, the attorney general opined that "the positions of village planning board member and town code enforcement officer are compatible."[36] All villages in New York State are located within towns, and questions arise whether a town employee who is a member of a village board of trustees may vote on matters before the board affecting the town. In 1989, the attorney general advised that the village trustee should recuse himself from participating in any matter involving the town.[37] Similarly, he advised in informal opinion 90-12 in 1990 that a woman town council member may not participate in any matter relating to the operations of the town highway department that involves her husband, who is superintendent of highways.

State laws commonly prohibit certain public officials from holding a specified second public office even though such office-holding may be compatible under the common law. The Washington Revised Code, for example, allows an individual to serve both as municipal clerk and a municipal treasurer under certain conditions.[38]

Contracts

The oldest constitutional and/or statutory conflict-of-interest provisions forbid public officers to enter into a contract with his/her government. Under the typical broad statute, a member of a board that awards a contract who has a conflict of interest voids the contract and also makes the officer subject to criminal penalties even if the officer did not participate in the awarding of the contract.[39]

The Alabama attorney general in 1990 issued an opinion that a municipality may not enter into a contract with a corporation if one of the owners is employed as a part-time reserve police officer.[40] On the other hand, the attorney general held that a municipality may do business with a corporation provided the spouse of a municipal employee owns less than half of the stock of the corporation.[41]

Conflict-of-interest provisions normally have *de minimis* exceptions. For example, a Massachusetts statute authorizes a legislator to hold a state contract, other than one with the General Court (state legislature), "if his direct and indirect interests and those of his immediate family in the corporation . . . with which the contract is made do not in the aggregate amount to ten percent of the total proprietary interests therein, and the contract is made through competitive bidding and he files with the State Secretary a statement making full disclosure of his interest. . . ."[42] Any legislator possessing a financial interest other than one under the above conditions is subject to a $3,000 fine or two years imprisonment, or both (a stock interest of less than 1% is exempted).

The Massachusetts law also provides additional remedies, including cancellation of the contract if there is a demonstration of actual influence, recovery of profits of the contract or five hundred dollars, whichever is greater, and civil damages double the profit, provided there has been no conviction or acquittal in a criminal action.[43]

A note in the *Harvard Law Review* commented on the Massachusetts law:

The Massachusetts rule may be a surprisingly harsh reaction to past abuses, but in States where passage is politically feasible, where the ineligibility of a number of business firms would not hinder the State's procurement processes, and where the elimination of a number of prospective legislative candidates would not cause a serious shortage, the disqualifications of legislators as state contractors seems a desirable prophylactic measure and in some States may be a necessary step to the elimination of present or apparent conflicts.[44]

In several states, the penalty is more severe, as conviction of a violation of the constitutional or statutory provision results in the vacating of the office.

The Revised Code of Washington stipulates:

No municipal officer shall be beneficially interested, directly or indirectly, in any contract which may be made by, through, or under the supervision of such officer, in whole or in part, or which may be made for the benefit of his office, or accept, directly or indirectly, any compensation, gratuity, or reward in connection with such contract from any other person beneficially interested therein. . . .[45]

Note that this section does not prohibit an officer from having an interest in all municipal contracts, since the prohibition applies only to contracts partially or totally subject to his/her control. In 1902, the Washington State Supreme Court invalidated a contract under which a mayor subcontracted with a prospective prime contractor to provide materials. The court emphasized, "however devious and winding the chain may be which connects the officer with the forbidden contract, if it can be followed and the connection made, the contract is void. . . ."[46]

There are five exceptions allowed by certain conflict-of-interest statutes relative to a public officer having a current interest in a contract. First, the public utility exception exempts the officer from the prohibition, since the utility's contract with the government is determined by law and the officer cannot add provisions to the contract to advance the officer's interest.[47]

Second, the statutes provide that contracts entered into as the result of a bona fide emergency are exempt from the conflict-of-interest provision.[48] In *Crass v. Walls*, the Tennessee Court of Appeals noted that the exception only applies to a situation "where there is an immediate necessity for the contract and it is shown that there was no one other than the city officer with whom it could have been made."[49]

Third, a more recent development has been the enactment of statutes allowing a public officer to contract with the government provided the contract is awarded by competitive bidding.[50] This type of provision is a deviation from the common law which clearly prohibits such an interest in a contract. These statutes require the concerned officer to disclose the interest in the contract in advance and contain a number of restrictions. Hence, the statutes widen the pool of eligible government officers by allowing private businessmen the opportunity to serve the public while their firms continue to enter into contracts with the government.

The competitive bidding statute, however, typically provides that the award must be made to the lowest responsible bidder. The New York State Finance Law is quite specific:

Contracts . . . shall be let to the lowest responsible bidder, as will best promote the public interest, taking into consideration the reliability of the bidder, the qualities of the articles proposed to be supplied, their conformity with the specifications, the purposes for which required and the terms of delivery; provided, however, that no such contract shall be let to a bidder other than the lowest responsible bidder without the written approval of the [State] Comptroller.[51]

It is apparent that this type of statute affords the administering officer considerable discretion in the award of a contract. Furthermore, a government agency, through an affiliated nonprofit corporation, may be able to avoid the competitive bidding requirement. The New York State Division of Substance Abuse Services, for example, awarded contracts through its nonprofit corporation—Narcotic and Drug Research, Incorporated—to friends and business associates of senior division officials, including the director.[52]

Fourth, a public officer may be allowed to have an interest in a contract provided "the compensation might be so slight or the officer's employment so transient that there would arise no conflict of interest."[53]

Fifth, the New York Public Officers Law exempts from its conflict-of-interest provisions the uncompensated members of the State Board of Regents.[54]

The statutes are clear that an officer, with the exceptions noted, may not participate in a transaction while in office, but difficult problems of interpretations of the statutes arise relative to the question of when an interest was acquired. With respect to contracts, the key time is the time when the government awards a contract. Unless a statute contains a provision to the contrary, a contract awarded before the government employs an officer or subsequent to the officer's departure from government service is exempt from the conflict-of-interest provision.

If a public officer entered into a contract with his/her government prior to assuming public office, the existence of the contract does not cause the public officer to have a conflict. However, if the contract is still being performed when the officer assumes office, the conflict-of-interest provision may apply.[55] To avoid violating the statute, the officer should divest his/her interest in the contracting firm prior to assuming office. Furthermore, he/she should divest the interest in a firm after assuming office if the firm is apt to continue to enter into contracts with the government.[56]

The statutes do not forbid an individual to resign from office in order to enter into a contract with the government, provided he/she was not involved in the awarding of the contract.[57] Similarly, the statutes do not forbid an individual to enter into a contract with the government after the individual's public service has ended.[58] However, a few state constitutions and statutes forbid the former officer to contract with the government for a stated period subsequent to the end of the officer's service.[59]

A public officer may acquire an interest in a contract subsequent to its award by investing in the contracting firm, entering into a subcontract with the contracting firm, or obtaining a position in the firm. A small number of statutes make it illegal for the officer to profit from a government contract.[60] The Iowa Supreme Court upheld a court order stopping an officer's subsequent acquisition of an interest in a contract on the ground the interest conflicted with his duty of unquestionable loyalty.[61] Nevertheless, courts generally have allowed the acquisition of an interest in a contract by an officer after its letting if the interest was acquired in good faith and no a priori arrangement had been made.[62]

Bribes, Loans, Gifts, and Rewards

The traditional conflict-of-interest statutes view gifts as bribery and extortion. The Massachusetts statute specifically prohibits the soliciting or accepting of any item of value in exchange for:

1. Being influenced in his performance of any official act or any act within his official responsibility, or

2. Being influenced to commit or aid in committing, or to collude in, or allow any fraud, or make opportunity for the commission of any fraud, on the Commonwealth or on a state, county, or municipal agency, or being induced to do or to omit to do any acts in violation of his official duty.[63]

Corrupt intent must be proven in order to convict a public officer or employee of violation of the above provisions. In general, if a private party and a public officer agree that the bribe or gift will result in a specific course of action by the officer, corrupt intent is proven.

The item of value need not be money, and the public employee need not be the recipient of the item of value. The latter can involve home improvements or trips to resorts, and the recipient may be a family member or personal friend. The United States Code forbids executive branch employees to accept travel and related expenses from nonfederal sources, except under conditions prescribed in regulations promulgated by the Administrator of General Services Administration in consultation with the Director of the Office of Government Ethics.[64]

Although a national government employee is forbidden to give a gift to a superior, the Ethics Reform Act of 1989 authorizes the Office of Government Ethics to promulgate regulations exempting from the prohibition "voluntary gifts or contributions that are given or received for special occasions such as marriage or retirement or under other similar circumstances."[65]

Is a campaign contribution given by a contractor to an elected official a bribe? This question, examined in greater detail in a subsequent section, is difficult to answer unless there is proof that the contribution was given in anticipation of the award of a government contract.

Conflict-of-interest laws also make it a crime for a person to give and a public officer to accept a bribe in exchange for an appointment to a public office.[66] Among other purposes, the laws seek to end the practice of macing; that is, an agreement that an individual will be appointed to a government position in exchange for a promise to contribute a percentage of his/her salary to the political party controlling the government.

The New York State Court of Appeals in 1977 affirmed the decision of a lower court dismissing a bribery charge on the ground the public servant accepting the bribe lacked authority to carry out the aim of the bribe.[67] The court labeled the behavior of the civil servant "reprehensible," but added that current law did not prohibit such an action. In 1986, the New York Penal Law was amended by the state legislature to authorize prosecution of corrupt officers regardless of whether the actions requested by the person offering the bribe are within the official authority of the corrupt official.[68]

The New York State General Municipal Law forbids a municipal officer or employee to solicit or accept a gift valued at seventy-five dollars or more, "whether in the form of money, service, loan, travel, entertainment, hospitality, thing or promise, or in any other form, under circumstances in which it could reasonably be inferred that the gift was intended to influence him, or could reasonably be expected to influence him, in the performance of his official duties or was intended as a reward for any official action on his part. . . ."[69] An identical provision is contained in the New York Public Officers Law.[70]

A bribe giver seeks to subvert the normal governmental processes in order to obtain special benefits. It is no defense that the same governmental action would have been initiated in the absence of a bribe. Crimes have been committed when an agreement is made that a bribe will be given in exchange for a stipulated action, regardless of whether money or other material assets are exchanged.[71]

When detected, bribe givers and receivers typically describe the money exchanged as a loan subject to repayment. In 1992, the former county executive of Albany County, New York, was convicted of accepting a bribe from the architect selected to design the county-owned Knickerbocker Arena. The former county executive and the architect maintained the money was a loan, but it was channeled through an attorney who later prepared and back-dated a loan agreement.[72]

The New York City Charter forbids a public employee to enter into any business or financial relationship with a city employee who is a superior or subordinate of the former.[73] The purpose of the prohibition is to protect the public against business relationships of city officials with each other that would affect adversely the professional relations between the officials. A superior, for example, might not discipline or fire a subordinate if they have a business relationship such as a joint real estate venture.

A 1992 investigation revealed that there was an unlawful financial relationship between the executive director of the New York City Division of School Safety and the division's chief of operations.[74] The executive director initially denied the financial relationship when questioned by the school chancellor by maintaining it was an interest-bearing loan.[75] Nearly one year later, he admitted that he held ownership interest in the Florida property in his Board of Education "Report of Finance Interest." One year later, he denied the ownership interest and maintained the transaction was an interest-free loan.

Whereas the purpose of a bribe is to influence the action of a public officer in the future, a reward has the purpose of compensating an officer for past misconduct. The New York State Penal Law, for example, declares, "a person is guilty of giving unlawful gratuities when he knowingly confers, or offers or agrees to confer, any benefit upon a public servant for having engaged in official conduct which he was required or authorized to perform, and for which he was not entitled to any special or additional compensation."[76]

Disclosure of Confidential Information

Governments generate and collect information and data that must be kept confidential if the public interest is to be protected. Release of such information and data can damage the reputations of individuals and also advance the personal or pecuniary interests of a government official or employee. To protect the former, privacy laws, examined in Chapter 5, have been enacted by the Congress and state legislatures.

The term *honest graft* sometimes is used by public officers to describe unethical gains which do not render the recipient liable to legal penalties; for example, gains resulting from the purchase of property about to be taken by eminent domain for a public purpose and profiting from its subsequent appreciation in value.

Federal statutes contain general and specific prohibitions of the revelation of confidential information, including results of bank examinations, crop information, and farm credit.[77] The New York State General Municipal Law forbids a public officer or employee to disclose confidential information or use it to promote his/her personal interests.[78] The New York Public Officers Law contains a similar provision and also forbids an officer or employee to "accept employment or engage in any business or professional activity which will require him to disclose confidential information which he has gained by reason of his official position or authority."[79]

Recognizing that a blanket prohibition of disclosure of confidential information is difficult to enforce, codes of ehtics have been adopted and advisory opinions have been issued by boards of ethics to provide guidance relative to what constitutes confidential information, a subject examined in Chapter 3.

A particularly difficult problem arises when a chief executive or high executive officer uses the cloak of confidentiality to frustrate legislative oversight of executive actions. The recent Iran-Contra affair illustrates the withholding of information from Congress on covert operations required to be disclosed to congressional intelligence committees. During the Cuban missile crisis, Secretary of Defense Robert McNamara denied at a congressional hearing that there were undisclosed agreements with the Soviet Union when the United States had agreed to withdraw Jupiter missiles from Turkey.

The Representation Problem

Should a public officer be permitted to represent a private party for gain before a governmental official or body? A federal law forbids federal officers, including members of Congress, to be compensated

for any services rendered or to be rendered, either by himself or another, in relation to any proceeding, contract, claim, controversy, charge, accusation, arrest, or other matter in which the United States is a party or directly or indirectly interested, before any department, agency, court martial, officer, or any civil, military, or naval commission. . . .[80]

Representing a party in a court, however, is exempt from the prohibition. The U.S. District Court has interpreted the provision relative to compensation as designed to eliminate the undue influence a member of Congress might bring upon executive officers.[81]

The Pennsylvania statute applies only to officers and employees of the executive branch, and their representing parties before executive agencies.[82] Hence, these officers may represent private parties before local governments, the state legislature, and the courts.

The New York Public Officers Law forbids an executive officer or employee or a member of the state legislature or employee to

receive, or enter into any agreement express or implied for, compensation for services to be rendered in relation to any case, whereby his compensation is to be dependent or contingent upon any action by such agency with respect to any license, contract, certificate, ruling, decision, opinion, rate schedule, franchise, or other benefits; provided, however, that nothing in this subsection shall be deemed to prohibit the fixing at any time of fees based upon the reasonable value of the services rendered.[83]

This prohibition is aimed at contingent compensatory arrangements and excludes payment of fees for services rendered independent of the agency's action. The New York State attorney general in 1954 advised in opinion 246 that a state officer who is an attorney may represent a client seeking adjustment of the compensation paid for lands taken by the State Thruway Authority provided the fees "are not dependent upon whether such adjustments are in fact made or the amounts thereof."

Unfortunately, the New York State statute allows public officers and employees to engage in such representation and to charge "fees based upon the reasonable value of the services rendered." This exception in particular creates the appearance of an impropriety whenever a state legislator appears before a state agency, since the state legislature can exercise various controls of an agency, including the appropriations for the agency.

The New York City Charter in 1957 contained a provision forbidding any paid officer or employee or member of the city council from representing a client in a litigation if the City was a party.[84] This prohibition made maintenance of a private law practice by a city official or employee difficult. A 1959 amendment to the charter allows members of the council to appear before a city department without compensation on "behalf of constituents or in the performance of public, official, or civil obligations."[85]

Outside Employment

Conflict-of-interest statutes restrict public employees relative to other employment in order to ensure that the public weal is protected, on the theory that no person may serve simultaneously two masters. The problem involves a public employee working for another person or business firm with interests parallel to the interests of the agency employing the public officer.

The prohibition typically is written in broad terms to prohibit any employee from seeking compensation or receiving compensation or representing anyone other than the government relative to any matter in which the government is a party or has a direct and substantial interest. The Massachusetts State Ethics Commission has explained that "the prohibition applies as long as some state agency has a direct and substantial interest in the matter; it does not matter whether your own agency has the interest."[86]

The Massachusetts statute defines a particular matter as

any judicial or other proceeding, application, submission, request for a ruling or other determination, contract, claim, controversy charge, accusation, arrest, decision, determination, finding, but excluding enactment of general legislation by the General Court and petitions of cities, towns, counties, and districts for special laws related to their governmental organizations, powers, duties, finances, and property.[87]

The Model State Conflict-of-Interest and Financial Disclosure Law forbids state officers and employees to seek outside employment and contains a correlative prohibition relative to business firms:

(a) No state official and no state employee shall seek employment with, or allow himself to be employed by, any business which is or may be regulated by a department or agency which he services. The term employment within the meaning of this section includes professional services and other services rendered by the state official or state employee whether rendered as an employee or as an independent contractor.

(b) No business shall employ a state official or state employee if the employment violates subsection (a) of this section.[88]

Postemployment Restrictions

Should a former government official be forbidden to represent a client before an agency in which the former official worked? In 1872, the Congress enacted the Civil Post-Employment Act prohibiting an employee of an executive department to act as an attorney or agent relative to the prosecution of a claim pending in the department while he was an employee for a period of two years after the termination of employment.[89]

The New York State Public Officers Law prohibits an officer or employee of a state agency, for a two-year period subsequent to termination of employment by the agency, to appear before it or receive compensation for services rendered on behalf of another person or firm "in relation to any case, proceeding, or application or other matter before such agency."[90] This prohibition was held by the New York Court of Appeals, in 1990, not to violate due process of law by preventing the concerned individuals from pursuing their professional careers because the restriction was related reasonably to the goal of the state legislature to restore public confidence in the integrity of the government.[91]

The Massachusetts conflict-of-interest statute contains a "forever ban" on a state or municipal employee acting as an agent or attorney for anyone other than the Commonwealth or the municipality relative to "any particular matter" in which the employee participated.[92] The statute also forbids a partner of a former state or municipal employee for a period of one year subsequent to the termination of the latter's employment by the government to engage "in any activity in which the former" employee is prohibited from engaging in.[93] Postemployment restrictions are examined in detail in Chapter 9.

LEGISLATORS' CONFLICTS OF INTEREST

Of all public officers, the legislator is the one most apt to encounter conflicts of interest because of the great variety of issues that are brought to the legislative forum for resolution and the influence that he/she may be able to exert over executive officers and agencies. Hence, it is essential to incorporate provisions in state constitutions and/or statutes to ensure that the spheres of the private activities of legislators are compatible with their legislative responsibilities in promoting the public interest. As noted, many conflict-of-interest statutes apply to all public officers and employees. Other statutes apply only to legislators because of the special ethical problems that may arise in the legislative forum.

It is apparent that legislators must be impartial in making decisions and not influenced by the possibility of personal gain. A special committee of the New York State legislature reported in 1964:

We recognize that members of the Legislature and legislative employees are required by the demands of their constituents to maintain frequent liaison with state agencies and to seek appropriate action with respect to countless administrative requests. We do not seek to discourage this traditional practice and consider it an essential part of their duties so long as it is done with propriety and without compensation.[94]

Personal ethics governing the behavior of legislators is influenced by the fact that most legislators in the United States devote only part of their time to their official duties and typically spend a significant portion of their time on other gainful activities. Lawyer-legislators are common, and the question is raised whether they should be allowed to represent private clients for compensation before regulatory agencies. Fear is expressed that such an appearance places undue influence upon the agencies which are dependent upon the state legislature or local governing body for funds.

The New York Public Officers Law allows a lawyer-legislator's firm to appear before a state agency provided the legislator "does not share in the net revenues, as defined in accordance with generally accepted accounting principles by the State Ethics Commission or by the Legislative Ethics Committee in relation to persons subject to their respective jurisdictions, resulting therefrom, or, acting in good faith, reasonably believed that he or she would not share in the net revenues as so defined. . . ."[95] Patrick J.

Dellay maintains that "permitting an exception in cases where the public official does not share in the profits creates a statute that is easily side-stepped and nearly impossible to enforce because it would necessitate inquiry into the division of fees among members of a firm."[96]

A complicating factor is the typical legislator's need for campaign funds. If a legislator becomes indebted to individuals or private business firms which made substantial campaign contributions, the potential for conflicts of interest is increased. In 1991, the Select Committee on Ethics of the United States Senate concluded that Senator Alan Cranston of California "engaged in improper conduct that may reflect upon the Senate, . . ."[97] The senator accepted campaign contributions totaling $850,000 from companies under the control of Charles H. Keating, Jr., and intervened on behalf of Mr. Keating's Lincoln Savings & Loan Association before the Federal Home Loan Board. The committee found that the senator had "engaged in an impermissible pattern of conduct in which fund raising and official activities were substantially linked."[98]

Many legislative bodies have established limits on speaking fees and other specified sources of outside income of members to ensure that private interests do not become entangled with the public's interest. On May 31, 1989, Speaker Jim Wright of the U.S. House of Representatives became the first Speaker to resign the office. He had been accused by the House Ethics Committee of sixty-nine violations of House rules, including the rule limiting speaking fees. Wright wrote a book, *Reflections of a Public Man*, and would waive a speaking fee if an organization would purchase a large number of copies of the book.[99]

Responding to the problem highlighted by Speaker Wright, the Congress enacted the Ethics Reform Act of 1989 which forbids employees of the U.S. Government to accept any honorarium defined as "a payment of money or any thing of value for an appearance, speech, or article by a member, officer, or employee, excluding any actual and necessary travel expenses incurred by such individual (and one relative) to the extent that such expenses are paid or reimbursed by any other person, and the amount otherwise determined shall be reduced by the amount of any such expenses to the extent that such expenses are not paid or reimbursed."[100]

Many U.S. government employees objected to the ban on accepting honoraria for articles. On March 30, 1993, the U.S. Court of Appeals for the District of Columbia Circuit ruled the ban on honoraria was "unduly overinclusive" because it applied to speaking or writing on subjects not related to the employee's job.[101]

A basic question is whether a legislator should disassociate h
self from all bills affecting his/her business or profession, or sh
lead the debate on the bills because of personal familiarity wiս ....
Rule 151 of the House of Commons in the United Kingdom answers this
question by stipulating, "a member may not vote on any question in which
he has a direct pecuniary interest. If he votes on such questions, his vote
may, on motion, be disallowed."

As noted in an earlier section, an appearance of impropriety is created
whenever a legislator appears before an executive agency on behalf of a
client. Although thirty-two states restrict such appearances, there are
exceptions. Commonly, a legislator is authorized to make an inquiry on
behalf of a constituent provided no fee is involved.[102] Furthermore, a
legislator in several states may represent a client before an agency if the
involved matter is ministerial in nature.

The common law and the early conflict-of-interest statutes do not
contain specific provisions relative to detection of violations and enforcement of the prohibitions. Reliance was placed upon members of a legislature to police the interests of the members. Any member may challenge
the right of another member to participate in a debate on a matter and to
vote on the matter on the ground of a conflict of interest. Similarly, reliance
was placed upon the voters to address the problem of conflicts of interest
by refusing to cast ballots for candidates who have such conflicts. In a
one-party area, however, many voters will cast ballots only for candidates
of their party, regardless of the fact that a number of these candidates have
conflicts of interest.

The courts typically play a small role relative to legislative conflicts of
interest. The reluctance of the courts to become involved is based in part
upon a typical constitutional provision that each house of the state legislature is "the judge of the elections, returns, and qualifications of its
members." On the other hand, the courts are less reluctant to review the
actions of a municipal legislative body, in part because many municipal
actions are classified as quasi-judicial and hence are not protected by any
constitutional protection for legislative actions.

Statutes typically require a legislator with a conflict of interest at a
meeting of the body to:

• Disclose the interest and its general nature prior to any discussion of the matter.

• Not to participate in any discussion and debate on the matter.

• Not to vote on any question relating to the matter.

• Not to attempt to influence the votes of members before or during the meeting and not to attempt to persuade members to change their votes after a meeting.

Should the meeting be in camera, the legislator must leave the meeting or the part of the meeting during which the matter in which he has a pecuniary interest is under consideration. If the member was not present at the meeting when the matter was acted upon, the member typically is directed to disclose publicly any pecuniary interest in the matter at the next meeting and is forbidden to attempt to influence other members relative to the matter.

Any member of a legislative body may call for the enforcement of the conflict-of-interest statute if a member does not recuse himself/herself from participating in the decision-making process relative to a matter involving an alleged conflict of interest. In addition, a citizen may bring a court action against a legislator for failing to recuse himself/herself from participating in the decision-making process on the matter.

The disclosure requirement may create a problem for small municipal governing bodies as members recuse themselves from participating in action on certain matters. Conflict-of-interest laws typically contain a provision allowing a specified number of municipal council members smaller than a quorum to act upon the matter. The Ontario Municipal Conflict-of-Interest Act declares that a quorum exists provided two members remain to participate in a matter.[103] If only one member or no member is able to participate, the council may apply to a judge for authorization to consider and vote on the matter. Requirements of disclosure of interest are viewed by many legislators as an invasion of privacy, a subject discussed in greater detail in Chapter 4.

Ethical questions can be raised by the enactment of temporary laws if these laws should be permanent ones. It is a common practice for legislative bodies to enact temporary laws to cope with an emergency situation or to experiment with a new approach. If the latter is successful, the new approach is incorporated into the permanent laws.

If a temporary law is reenacted every two years, questions may be raised relative to a link between interest group campaign contributions and reenactment of the temporary laws. The New York State legislature in 1974 enacted a law providing for compulsory binding arbitration of impasses in collective bargaining negotiations between a police or firefighter union and a municipal employer.[104] The 1974 law was made valid for a period of two years as an experiment, but has been reenacted in identical form every two years subsequently. Similarly, a 1977 law provided for two years for agency shop dues; that is, the state or municipal employer must withhold from a nonemployee's salary agency shop dues equivalent to union dues and remit the proceeds to the concerned union.[105] A temporary identical law has been enacted every two years subsequently.

The ethics of deliberate gerrymandering of legislative districts is questionable. In certain instances, the deliberate gerrymander is the product of a court order or the threat of the U.S. attorney general not to approve a redistricting plan under provisions of the federal Voting Rights Act of 1965 unless districts are gerrymandered to promote the election of black or Hispanic candidates. In other instances, the gerrymander is simply the product of an attempt by the political party controlling a legislative house to ensure that the party retains control of the house after the election. Whereas it is possible to justify on ethical grounds the first type of gerrymander as a remedial action for past wrongs, there is no ethical justification for the second type of gerrymander.

Similar ethical questions may be raised with respect to political campaign advertisements which deliberately distort the facts or otherwise misrepresent the facts. During the 1990 gubernatorial campaign in Massachusetts a newspaper headline—"Questions Linger over Belloti's Corruption Record"—appears in a television campaign advertisement. The headline was deceptive as the article focused on the record of State Attorney General Belloti's record on fighting corruption and did not charge that Belloti was corrupt.[106] A similar incident occurred during the 1990 Texas gubernatorial campaign when Republican candidate Clayton Williams was subject to television advertisements showing a newspaper headline that "Lawsuits Allege Williams a 'Deadbeat,'" but failing to reveal that his opponent—Governor Ann Richards—made the allegation and not the newspaper or another party.[107]

PENALTIES FOR VIOLATIONS

Conflict-of-interest statutes stipulate that public officers and employees guilty of violations may receive a punishment ranging from a reprimand to fines to imprisonment. Reliance for advice upon an official counsel does not protect a public officer against prosecution for violation of a statute.[108]

As a general rule, willfulness is a requirement for a misdemeanor or a felony conviction under conflict-of-interest or official misconduct statutes.[109] In some instances, the courts have interpreted the statutes as requiring willfulness for a conviction. Unless the statute stipulates a willful violation as a ground for conviction, a public officer may be subject to prosecution if evidence is revealed that he/she has a personal interest in the matter even though he did not participate in the governmental transaction or lacked knowledge of the transaction. Hence, there has been a tendency to add the willful violation to the statutes to exempt from penalty officers who had a conflict of interest by inadvertence.

The fact that a public officer was unaware of the statutory prohibition of having a prohibited interest will not prevent a court from invalidating a contract, but may result in no punishment of the officer other than removal from office.[110] Furthermore, a profession of ignorance of the law will protect an officer against civil penalties, including punitive damages.[111] However, violations of the statutes that are nonintentional and/or nonmalicious still may lead to the removal of the violator from office.

The Ontario Municipal Conflict-of-Interest Act authorizes a municipal council to purchase insurance to protect members from the expenses of conflict-of-interest litigation or reimburse a member for costs incurred. Such reimbursement can be provided, however, only if the member was found not to have a conflict of interest.[112]

SUMMARY AND CONCLUSIONS

Statutes have failed to eliminate all conflicts of interest of public officers and employees as revealed by recent cases in the news media. Complex prohibitions of such conflicts are found in the common law, constitutions, statute law, and judicial decisions. The Daedalian nature of the prohibitions in a number of jurisdictions places an inordinate burden upon public servants who may have to conduct a thorough study to determine whether a particular course of action represents a conflict of interest.

There are two points of view relative to the scope of conflict-of-interest statutes. One viewpoint holds that the prohibition of conflicts must be a broad one in order to protect the public interest. The other viewpoint expresses concern that the broader the scope of the statutes, the more difficult it will be to recruit highly qualified individuals who may conclude that such statutes make the public service a financially burdensome service. Applying the statutes to uncompensated members of part-time boards and commissions makes recruitment of members exceedingly difficult.

General prohibitions of conflicts of interest have proven to be inadequate and remote interest statutes have been enacted to provide more specific guidance to public employees. These statutes, however, are not effective in dealing with the broad gray area between a clear conflict of interest and a totally ethical action. Codes of ethics, the subject of

Chapter 3, have been adopted to provide greater guidance to public officers and employees, and boards of ethics have been established to provide advice on ethical questions, upon request, to government officials and employees.

NOTES

1. An Act to Prevent Frauds upon the Treasury of the United States, 10 Stat. 170 (1853).

2. Constitution of the State of New York, art. XIII, § 2.

3. Ibid., § 3.

4. *Rapp v. Carey*, 44 N.Y.2d 157, 375 N.E.2d 745 (1978).

5. "Conflict of Interests: State Government Employees," *Virginia Law Review*, October 1961, p. 1039.

6. *State ex rel. Brown v. Blew*, 20 Wn.2d 47, 145 P.2d 554 (1944).

7. Milton Kaplan and Richard B. Lillich, "Municipal Conflicts-of-Interest: Inconsistencies and Patchwork Prohibitions," *Columbia Law Review*, vol. 58, 1958, p. 167.

8. Subcommittee on National Policy Machinery, United States Senate, *The Private Citizen and National Service* (Washington, D.C.: United States Government Printing Office, 1961), p. 3.

9. Tim Beidel, "Ex-Clerk Says Co-brokered Insurance No Secret Under GOP," *The Times Union* (Albany, New York), August 7, 1992, p. B-3.

10. California Government Code, §§ 1091(a) and 1091:1 (1980 and 1992 Supp.); and New York Public Officers Law § 74(3) (McKinney 1988).

11. *Model State Conflict-of-Interest and Financial Disclosure Law* (New York: National Municipal League, 1979), p. 3.

12. Ibid., p. 2.

13. Ibid., p. 3.

14. *People v. Elliot*, 115 Cal. App.2d 410 at 417, 252 P.2d 661 at 665 (2d Dist. 1953).

15. *People v. Deysher*, 2 Cal.2d 141 at 146, 25 P.2d 499 (1934).

16. *Downs v. City of South Amboy*, 116 N.J.L. 511, 185 Atl. 15 (Ct. Err. & App. 1936).

17. *Quackenbush v. City of Cheyenne*, 52 Wyo. 155, 70 P.2d 579 (1937).

18. California Government Code, § 1091(b)(1) (1990 and 1992 Supp.).

19. *Yonkers Bus, Incorporated v. Maltbie*, 23 N.Y.S.2d 87 (Sup. Ct.), affirmed, 260 App. Div. 893, 23 N.Y.S.2d 91 (3d Dept. 1940).

20. "Conflict-of-Interests: State Government Employees," p. 1056.

21. Circular No. 50/29 (Dublin: Department of Finance, 1929), p. 2. See also Arizona Statutes, § 38-503(B) (1992 Supp.).

22. *Model State Conflict-of-Interest and Financial Disclosure Law*, p. 3.

23. For an example, see Revised Code of Washington, § 42.23.040 (1991).

24. California Government Code, § 1091 (1980).

25. New York Public Officers Law, § 74(3)(j) (1988); Texas Revised Civil Statutes Annotated, art. 6252-9, § 3(b) (1970); and Washington Revised Code, § 42.22.050 (1991).

26. California Government Code, § 1091.5(a) (1980 and 1992 Supp.); and New York Public Officers Law, § 73(3) (1988 and 1992 Supp.).

27. Minnesota Statutes Annotated, § 471.88(1-13) (1992 Supp.).

28. Matthew 6:24; Luke 16:13.

29. Nizam Al-Mulk, *The Book of Government or Rules for Kings* (New Haven: Yale University Press, 1960), p. 164.

30. New York County Law, § 411 (McKinney 1990).

31. *Opinions of the Attorney General of Alabama, April 1990-March 1991* (Montgomery: 1991), opinion 90-00295.

32. *Opinions of the Attorney General for the Year Ending December 31, 1989* (Albany: New York State Department of Law, 1990), p. 153.

33. *People ex rel. Ryan v. Green*, 58 N.Y. 295 (1874).

34. *Kennett v. Levine*, 40 Wn.2d 212 at 216-17.

35. *Opinions of the Attorney General for the Year Ending December 31, 1989*, p. 94.

36. Ibid., pp. 102–3.

37. Ibid., pp. 130–31.

38. Revised Code of Washington, §§ 35.24.142 and 35A.12.020 (1990).

39. *Ferle v. City of Lansing*, 189 Mich. 501, 155 N.W. 591 (1915).

40. *Opinions of the Attorney General of Alabama, April 1990–March 1991*, opinion 90-00127.

41. Ibid., opinion 90-00245.

42. Massachusetts General Laws, chap. 268A, § 7(c) (1990).

43. Ibid., § 9.

44. "Conflicts-of-Interest of State Legislators," *Harvard Law Review*, vol. LXXVI, 1963, p. 1226.

45. Revised Code of Washington, § 42.23.030 (1991 Supp.).

46. *Northport v. Northport Townsite Company*, 27 Wash. 543 at 549 (1902).

47. *Capital Gas Company v. Young*, 109 Cal. 140, 41 Pac. 869 (1895).

48. *Crass v. Walls*, 36 Tenn App. 546 at 554, 249 S.W.2d 670 at 674 (1953).

49. Ibid.

50. New York Public Officers Law, § 73(4)(a) (1992 Supp.); and California Government Code, § 1102 (1980).

51. New York State Finance Law, § 174(1) (McKinney 1989).

52. *Report of Investigation Concerning Awarding of No-Bid Consulting Contracts and Related Contracting Matters, New York State Division of Substance Abuse Services* (Albany: New York State Office of Inspector General, 1992), p. 1.

53. *Gillen Company v. Milwaukee*, 174 Wis. 362 at 372, 183 N.W. 679 at 682 (1921). The Massachusetts law allows such an interest if it consists of ownership of less than one percent of the stock of the contracting corporation. See Massachusetts General Laws, chap. 268A, §§ 7 and 20(a) (1990 and 1992 Supp.).

54. New York Laws of 1989, chap. 242, § 1; and New York Public Officers Law, § 1(1)(i) (McKinney 1991 Supp.).

55. *Noble v. Davison*, 177 Ind. 19, 96 N.E. 325 (1911).

56. *Hefferen v. City of Green Bay*, 266 Wis. 534, 64 N.W.2d 216 (1954).

57. *Stone ex rel. Village of Manchester v. Osborn*, 24 Ohio App. 251, 157 N.E. 410 (1927).

58. *Collinsworth v. City of Catlettsburg*, 236 Ky. 194, 32 S.W.2d 982 (1930).

59. New York Public Officers Law, § 73(4) (McKinney 1992 Supp.); and Constitution of Oklahoma, art. V, § 23.

60. See, for example, Pennsylvania Statutes Annotated, tit. 71, § 776.3 (1990).

61. *James v. City of Hamburg*, 174 Iowa 301, 156 N.W. 394 (1916).

62. *City of Oakland v. California Construction Company*, 15 Cal.2d 473, 104 P.2d 30 (1940).

63. Massachusetts General Laws, chap. 268A, § 2(b) (1990). The Congress has enacted a similar ban on the solicitation or acceptance of gifts. Ethics Reform Act of 1989, 103 Stat. 1746, 5 U.S.C. § 7353 (1993 Supp.).

64. Ethics Reform Act of 1989, 103 Stat. 1745, 31 U.S.C. § 1352 (1993 Supp.).

65. Ibid., 103 Stat. 1745, 5 U.S.C. § 7351(2)(c) (1980 and 1993 Supp.). For commission authorized exceptions, see 5 C.F.R. § 2635.304.

66. See New York Laws of 1965, chap. 1030; and New York Penal Law, §§ 200.45 and 200.50 (1988).

67. *People v. Herskowitz*, 41 N.Y.2d 1096 (1977).

68. New York Laws of 1986, chap. 834; and New York Penal Law, § 200.5(2) (1988).

69. New York Laws of 1987, chap. 813, § 21; and New York General Municipal Law, § 805-a(1) (McKinney 1992 Supp.).

70. New York Laws of 1987, chap. 813, § 2; and New York Public Officers Law, § 73(5) (McKinney 1988).

71. *People v. Charles*, 61 N.Y.2d 321, 462 N.E.2d 118 (1984).

72. John Caher, "Zumbo Revealed Coyne Tie to Crozier," *The Times Union* (Albany, New York), August 7, 1992, pp. 1 and A-8.

73. Charter of the City of New York, chap. 68, § 2604(14) (1989).

74. *Private Interest Over Public Trust: An Investigation into Certain Improprieties by the Leadership at the Division of School Safety* (New York: City of New York Special Commissioner of Investigations for the New York City School District, 1992), pp. 40–68.

75. Ibid., p. 40.

76. New York Laws of 1965, chap. 1030; and New York Penal Law, § 200.30 (1988).

77. See 18 U.S.C. §§ 1904 and 1906-907.

78. New York Laws of 1987, chap. 813, § 21; and New York General Municipal Law, § 805-a(b) (McKinney 1992 Supp.).

79. New York Public Officers Law, § 74(3)(b) (1988). See also Arizona Statutes, § 38-504(B) (1985).

80. Farm Credit Act Amendments of 1986, 100 Stat. 1877, 12 U.S.C. § 2001 (1989).

81. *United States v. Quinn*, 141 F.Supp. 622 at 624 (S.D.N.Y. 1956).

82. Pennsylvania Statutes Annotated, tit. 71, § 776.7 (1990).

83. New York Laws of 1987, chap. 813, § 2; and New York Public Officers Law, § 73(2) (McKinney 1988).

84. New York City Charter, § 886(b) (1957).

85. New York City Charter, § 886 (1960).

86. *Guide to the Conflict-of-Interest Law* (Boston: Massachusetts State Ethics Commission, 1983), p. 7.

87. Massachusetts General Laws, chap. 268A, § 1(k) (1990).

88. *Model State Conflict-of-Interest and Financial Disclosure Law*, p. 29.

89. Civil Post-employment Act of 1872, 17 Stat. 202, 5 U.S.C. § 99.

90. New York Laws of 1987, chap. 813, § 2; and New York Public Officers Law, § 73(8) (McKinney 1988).

91. *Forti v. New York State Ethics Commission*, 75 N.Y.2d 596, 554 N.E.2d 876 (1990).

92. Massachusetts General Laws, chap. 268A, §§ 5(c) and 18 (1990).

93. Ibid., chap. 268A, §§ 5(a) and 18(a) (1990).

94. *Report of the Special Committee on Ethics* (Albany: The Legislature of the State of New York, 1964), p. 4.

95. New York Public Officers Law, § 73 (10) (McKinney 1988).

96. Patrick J. Dellay, "Curbing Influence Peddling in Albany: The 1987 Ethics in Government Act," *Brooklyn Law Review*, vol. 53, 1988, pp. 1065–66.

97. *Investigation of Senator Alan Cranston: Report of the Select Committee on Ethics* (Washington, D.C.: United States Senate, 1991), vol. I, p. 42.

98. Ibid.

99. For details, see Janet Hook, "Passion, Defiance, Tears: Jim Wright Bows Out," *Congressional Quarterly Weekly Report*, June 3, 1989, pp. 1289–94.

100. Ethics Reform Act of 1989, 103 Stat. 1760, 5 U.S.C. app. § 501 (1993).

101. Robert Pear, "Judge Lifts Honoraria Ban on Federal Workers," *The New York Times*, March 31, 1993, p. A19.

102. California Government Code, § 8920(b)(3) (West, 1992).

103. Ontario Municipal Conflict-of-Interest Act, 1983, § 7(1).

104. New York Laws of 1974, chap. 724-25; and New York Civil Service Law, § 209(4)(c-d) (McKinney 1983 and 1992 Supp.).

105. New York Laws of 1977, chap. 677-78; and New York Civil Service Law, § 208(3) (McKinney, 1983 and 1992 Supp.).

106. Tom Precious, "Democrats at Odds over Anti-Ferraro Ads," *The Times Union* (Albany, New York), September 10, 1992, p. 1.

107. Ibid.

108. *People v. Becker*, 112 Cal. App.2d 324, 245 P.2d 103 (2nd Dist. 1952).

109. Arizona Revised Statutes Annotated, § 38-443 (1985); California Government Code, § 1097 (1980); and Wisconsin Statutes Annotated, § 946 (1982 and 1992 Supp.).

110. *Ferle v. City of Lansing*, 189 Mich. 501, 155 N.W. 591 (1915).

111. California Public Contract Code, § 10280 (1985); and Mississippi Code Annotated, § 2302 (1973 and 1992 Supp.).

112. Ontario Municipal Conflict-of-Interest Act, 1983, § 14.

Chapter 3

Codes of Ethics

A degree of confusion exists in statutes containing conflicts-of-interest provisions and codes of ethics. As noted in Chapter 2, the common law and early statutes provided criminal penalties for violations of conflicts-of-interest provisions. These provisions, while helpful in serving preventive and remedial purposes, are incapable of dealing effectively with the increasing number of multifaceted and subtle ethical problems—involving borderline questions of propriety—encountered by public officers and employees in modern society. Recognition of the inadequacy of the conflicts-of-interest approach led legislative bodies to adopt codes of ethics containing a more detailed frame of reference, facilitating self-regulation of the conduct of officers and employees by establishing guidelines relative to acceptable and unacceptable behavior. These guidelines are subjective ones and hence an officer is not subject to criminal sanctions for their violation. The codes often established boards of ethics charged with the duty of providing advice on the ethics of an action contemplated by public officials.

The U.S. House of Representatives in 1958 adopted a resolution containing the following Code of Ethics for Government Service.

Any person in government service should:

1. Put loyalty to the highest moral principles and to country above loyalty to Government persons, party, or department.
2. Uphold the Constitution, laws, and legal regulations of the United States and of all governments therein and never be a party to their evasion.

3. Give a full day's labor for a full day's pay; giving to the performance of his duties his earnest effort and best thought.

4. Seek to find and employ more efficient and economical ways of getting tasks accomplished.

5. Never discriminate unfairly by the dispensing of special favors or privileges to anyone, whether for remuneration or not; and never accept for himself or his family, favors or benefits under circumstances which might be construed by reasonable persons as influencing the performance of his governmental duties.

6. Make no private promises of any kind binding upon the duties of office, since a Government employee has no private word which can be binding on public duty.

7. Engage in no business with the Government, either directly or indirectly, which is inconsistent with the conscientious performance of his governmental duties.

8. Never use any information coming to him confidentially in the performance of governmental duties as a means for making private profit.

9. Expose corruption wherever discovered.

10. Uphold these principles, ever conscious that public office is a public trust.[1]

Confusion results from enactment of "codes of ethics" containing sanctions for violations of their provisions. The New York State Code of Ethics, the first one enacted by a state legislature, provides that violators of code provisions "may be fined, suspended, or removed from office or employment in the manner provided by law."[2] Similarly, the Minnesota Code of Ethics, which contains guidelines on behavior, also lists specific actions deemed to be conflicts of interest subject to disciplinary action.[3] We, however, will use the term *code of ethics* to refer to statutorily established codes containing guidelines relative to acceptable and unacceptable conduct in the public service.

The International City Management Association maintained in 1962, "it is desirable . . . to include legal provisions in a code of ethics, without imputation of lack of integrity, in order to maintain common minimal standards. Practically all else in a code should be voluntary and directed at an ever-increasing refinement of ideals and conduct."[4]

ETHICS CODES

In a society that is becoming increasingly complex, outright dishonesty is only one facet of the problem of unethical conduct in government service. Recognizing that it is impossible to anticipate every conceivable ethical question that may arise in the future, many legislative bodies enacted codes of ethics containing standards and guidelines for dealing with actions by officials and employees in situations falling in the "gray" area between what is clearly proper behavior and improper behavior. Codes have three major objectives:

1. Maintaining high ethical standards in the public service.
2. Increasing citizen confidence in the integrity of government officers and employees.
3. Assisting officials and employees in determining the proper course of action when faced with uncertainty regarding the propriety of a contemplated action, thereby preventing them from unwittingly entangling public and private interests.

In drafting a code of ethics, the legislative body should seek input from public officers, public employees, and citizens. A code drafted with such input is apt to be respected more than a code imposed upon public officers and employees without consultation, and should reflect more fully the subtleties of the ethical problems encountered in the public service.

The rationale for adoption of a code of ethics was set forth clearly in the legislative declaration of purpose in the 1954 New York State law establishing the code of ethics:

Some conflicts of material interests which are improper for public officials may be prohibited by legislation. Others may arise in so many different forms and under such a variety of circumstances that it would be unwise and unjust to proscribe them by statute with inflexible and penal sanctions which would limit public service to the very wealthy or the very poor. For matters of such complexity and close distinctions, the Legislature finds that a code of ethics is desirable to set forth for the guidance of state officers and employees the general standards of conduct to be reasonably expected of them.[5]

Although codes of ethics typically are enacted by legislative bodies, California voters in 1990 adopted a code by ratifying Proposition 112 which was placed on the ballot by the state legislature.

Chief executives also may issue the equivalent of a code by executive order. President George Bush in 1989, for example, issued Executive Order 12674 containing principles of ethical conduct including, "employees shall protect and conserve federal property and shall not use it for other than authorized activities" and "employees shall disclose waste, fraud, abuse, and corruption to appropriate authorities." In 1990, President Bush issued Executive Order 12731 refining the principles contained in Executive Order 12674.

A 1985 editorial in *Georgia County Government* highlighted one of the values of a code:

> The most surprising thing is that until they consider adoption of a code, many government bodies admit they have never openly discussed the limitations their code addresses. They all seem to have an unspoken set of values, but nothing against which to measure them. Formal adoption of a code of ethics and/or conduct not only encourages discussion of conditions that might reflect negatively on the office holders, but should compel each person in government office to examine his or her situation. As many public careers have been ruined by the appearance of wrong as by actual wrong-doing.[6]

How detailed should a code of ethics be? A code should deal more specifically with certain matters than conflicts-of-interest laws. Nevertheless, a brief one is preferable to a highly detailed and rigid code. A specific standard cannot be written to cover every conceivable situation that might arise, especially a subtle one involving unethical conduct.

Codes stress that holding office is a public trust and that standards of political morality are higher than those of the marketplace. Section 1A of the code of the Village of Glen Ellyn, Illinois, emphatically stipulates that "what is acceptable in private business may not be proper conduct by elected and appointed officials." The Rockville, Maryland, Code of Ethics opens with a declaration of policy:

> That no man can fairly serve two masters whose interests are, or may be, in conflict is a principle of ancient and respective lineage. A particularly serious application of this principle occurs where one who is employed as a servant of the public has a financial or personal interest that in a particular situation conflicts or may conflict with the public interest.[7]

Specific Provisions

Typically, codes of ethics provide guidance relative to actions that might create public suspicion of violations of trusts, impairment of independence of judgment in performing official duties, disclosure of confidential information, acceptance of gifts, favoritism in official actions, seeking unwarranted privileges or exemptions by a public officer or employee, and relations with colleagues. With respect to the latter, an Australian Public Service Board circular contains guidelines relating to the Code of Conduct and stipulates that "an office-holder should be frank and honest in official dealings with colleagues."[8] The board also advises officials to avoid malice in their reports:

Situations in which a report could potentially be regarded as having been made with malice include:

- Where the report knowingly includes false allegations.

- Where the language of the report is deliberately unnecessarily strong, in a manner which might unreasonably harm the person being reported on.

- Where extraneous material is deliberately introduced so as to create a misleading impression.[9]

The United Kingdom Association of First Division Civil Servants drafted a code of ethics containing similar provisions which stipulate that civil servants should provide their minister with all pertinent information and ensure that they do "not suppress, delay, or misuse information or select it in a way which would advance particular social, economic, or political points of view. They should have regard to the guidelines which exist to prevent government statistics being used in a misleading manner."[10]

Unnecessary procrastination in decisionmaking and delivery of services is unethical. Similarly, failure of full-time government officials and employees to devote the required time to their official duties clearly is unethical. The Geneva, New York, Code of Ethics—art. XV, § 152—stipulates that "appointive officials and employees shall adhere to the rules of work and performance established as the standard for their positions by the appropriate authority." The New Orleans Code of Ethics—§ 5 A(1)—contains a similar provision. "Full-time employees shall perform a full day's work each and every working day," and also stipulates that "the members of all boards and commissions of the City shall be held to the standards of a prudent administrator" (§ 3F).

The Code of Ethics of Falls Township, Pennsylvania, stresses in section 1B the responsibility of appointed and elected officials and employees "for the proper, efficient, and economical management of all public funds, property, and other resources." The code (§ 1C) also forbids any official or employee to "discriminate against any person on the basis of age, race, creed, sex, national origin, or political belief."

To help promote equal treatment of all citizens, section 4(c) of the Code of Standards of Required Conduct of the City of Lynchburg, Virginia, provides that "no employee shall grant any special consideration, treatment, or advantage to any citizen beyond that which is available to every other citizen." Similarly, the Seattle, Washington, code stipulates that an official or employee "shall be deemed to be in conflict with the performance of" his official duties if he intentionally "requests or permits the use of City-owned vehicles, equipment, materials, or property for personal use or profit unless such use is available to the public generally, provided that this paragraph shall not apply to the use of City-owned vehicles, equipment, materials, or property provided to such officer or employee in accordance with municipal policy for the conduct of official City business."[11]

The use of government equipment for private purposes presents particularly difficult problems. The Newington, Connecticut, Code of Ordinances stresses that "no official or employee shall use or permit the use of town . . . equipment . . . except as provided by law or in accordance with administrative direction as ordained by established policy."[12] Amplifying this provision, the town manager, on September 15, 1975, issued Administrative Letter 9 authorizing the following classes of employees to take town vehicles assigned to them to their homes upon receiving special permission from the manager:

a. Employees (usually supervisory or administrative) who are subject to call-out in the event of a problem or emergency.

b. Employees who are required to work beyond normal working hours without extra compensation.

The letter defines "town business" to "include authorized attendance at professional and/or work related meetings, classes, seminars, conferences, testimonials, ceremonies, etc. in which the attendee has a legitimate involvement."

Administrative Letter 9 also provides:

A town vehicle may be used during the work day or while an employee is on duty to attend to the personal needs and errands of the employee to which a vehicle is assigned, provided local travel of this type is limited to the area of the Town or to areas of adjacent towns which are within three (3) miles of a Town of Newington boundary and provided that, where travel out-of-town on business is concerned, extra travel for such personal needs and errands shall be limited to a corridor along the most direct route of not more than ten (10) miles in width, and provided further that pursuit of any such personal needs and errands shall not involve violation of work rules, personnel regulations, directions of superiors, or the law.

Examples of permitted personal use of town vehicles include minor retail shopping; personal appointments with a dentist, a lawyer, or a physician; attendance at funerals, wakes, religious services, and community events; and lunch or a refreshment break during an authorized time.

Officials are cautioned "that all such uses should be tempered with discretion in terms of frequency, distance from normal travel routes, and the amount of time involved." Family members may ride in such vehicles only "in cases of bona-fide emergency, acts of mercy, infrequent situations of family necessity, or unless specifically allowed by the permission of the Town Manager."

Determining whether government information is confidential often is a difficult task. The Minnesota Code of Ethics for executive branch employees defines confidential information as "any information obtained under government authority which has not become part of the body of public information and which, if released prematurely or in nonsummary form, may provide unfair economic advantage or adversely affect the competitive position of an individual or a business."[13]

Codes of ethics also address the question of whether a public officer or employee should accept a favor by recognizing that the receipt of some types of gifts or favors will not produce a conflict of interest. The Minnesota Code of Ethics permits the acceptance of (1) gifts of nominal value, (2) plaques presented for service to a charitable cause, (3) reimbursement expenses for travel or meals which are not reimbursed by the state and "have been approved in advance by the appointing authority as part of the work assignment," (4) honoraria for papers and demonstrations made by employees without compensation on their own time, and (5) tips received by food service and room cleaning personnel in Itasca State Park.[14] Relative to gifts, the code does not define nominal value which has been interpreted as gifts with no market value.

The New York City charter's standard of conduct generally forbids a city officer or employee to give or receive from his/her superior or subordinate any gift of more than negligible monetary value.[15]

Individual government agencies often have codes of conduct with standards higher than the government-wide standards which are viewed as minimum standards. New York City agencies, for example, may set higher standards than the standards established by the City's conflicts-of-interest board. The Procurement Policy Board, for example, issued a Statement of Ethics Policy stipulating that contracting personnel should "accept no gifts, favors, or entertainment from contractors or prospective contractors."[16]

Should all provisions of a code of ethics apply to all public officers and employees or should specific provisions in the code apply only to named officers? An examination reveals that most codes do not include provisions applicable to specific officers other than members of the legislative body. It is apparent, however, that administrative officers and employees with inspection or regulatory responsibilities have a greater opportunity than others to engage in unethical activities. As a consequence, section 4 of the Smithtown, New York, code contains provisions relative to the town attorney, building inspector, assessor, town engineer, and director of planning. The building inspector, for example, is forbidden by section 4(b) to "engage in the real estate, insurance, building contracting business, or buildings materials business, directly or indirectly . . . during the course of his employment." Westchester County, New York, is careful to exclude volunteer firemen and volunteer civil defense workers, except a chief engineer or assistant chief engineer, from the definition of a "Municipal Officer or Employee."[17]

THE BOARD OF ETHICS

The effectiveness of a code of ethics is enhanced by a section creating a mechanism for the provision of advisory opinions to public officers and employees contemplating an action that raises in the minds of the concerned individuals the possibility of a conflict of interest. Advice on ethical issues can be provided by either a single officer or a board; the latter is most common. The ethics officer or board should be charged with responsibility for rendering advisory opinions on the propriety of proposed actions in uncharted areas, investigating charges of unethical behavior and reporting findings to appropriate officials, and recommending to the legislative body amendments to the code of ethics.

The federal Ethics in Government Act of 1978 established within the Office of Personnel Management an Office of Government Ethics headed by a director charged with fourteen specific responsibilities.[18] However, the Office of Government Ethics Reauthorization Act of 1988 converted the Office into an independent executive agency, effective October 1, 1989.[19] President George Bush in 1989 issued Executive Order 12674, amended by Executive Order 12731 in 1990, requiring the Office to issue and administer a uniform set of standards of conduct for executive branch employees. Although the U.S. General Accounting Office on two occasions recommended that the Office of Government Ethics issue regulations establishing a uniform system of confidential financial disclosure, the Office has not done so.[20] The Office reported, in 1992, that "agencies required regular employees who filed public reports to take a total of 1,452 remedial actions in 1990 and 18,854 in 1991.[21]

At the state government plane, commissions—such as the Alabama Ethics Commission and the Ohio Ethics Commission—perform duties similar to those performed by the federal Office of Government Ethics. In Kansas, the State Commission on Governmental Standards and Conduct also is responsible for registering lobbyists and administering laws regulating lobbyists.[22] Similarly, the Minnesota Ethical Practices Board administers lobbyist registration and regulation and also administers campaign finance disclosure, economic interest disclosure, representation disclosure, and public financing of campaign programs.[23] Responsibility for rendering opinions also may be assigned by state law to the attorney general.

The Rhode Island State Ethics Commission has a unique power. The Rhode Island Supreme Court in 1992 opined that a 1986 amendment to the state constitution grants the commission power to enact ethics laws separate from the ones enacted by the general assembly.[24]

The Model City Charter authorizes the city council to "establish an independent Board of Ethics to administer and enforce the conflict-of-interest and financial disclosure ordinances."[25] Members of the board may not hold any other city office.

The typical local government board of ethics consists of five members appointed for a three- or five-year term of office by the local government legislative body or the local chief executive officer with the approval of the legislative body. Some local boards have ex officio members such as the corporation counsel. The five members of the Board of Ethics in Windsor, Connecticut, are appointed by the town council for a five-year term and must be electors "known for their personal integrity."[26] The five members of the Board of Ethics of the Borough of Matanuska-Susitna, Alaska, are appointed by the borough executive with the approval of the borough assembly.[27] The Township of Piscataway, New Jersey, Board of Ethics consists of five members appointed by the mayor with the advice of two-thirds of the township council for a two-year term.[28]

The Buffalo, New York, Board of Ethics is composed of the mayor, comptroller, president of the council, and four electors appointed by the council for a four-year term.[29] The board is charged with the duties of rendering advisory opinions to city officials and employees pursuant to their written request, and publishing "its advisory opinions with such deletions as may be necessary to prevent disclosure of the identity of the officer or employee involved."[30] The Seattle, Washington, Board of Ethics also serves as the Fair Campaign Practices Commission.[31] And the three members of the Township of Falls, Pennsylvania, Board of Ethics are appointed by the township supervisors and must include one "professional or executive level employee. . . ."[32] Relative to the other two members, "the Supervisors shall take care to appoint persons unlikely to use the Board for partisan political ends."

Penalties for Violations

State legislatures in recent years have established boards or commissions on ethics authorized to impose penalties for violations of the code. In 1991, for example, the Rhode Island Ethics Commission fined former Governor Edward D. DiPrete $30,000 for ordering the award of a contract to an engineering firm headed by a major contributor to DiPrete's campaign fund, improperly influencing the award of a state contract to his campaign fund-raiser and business partner, and failing to file required conflict-of-interest statements relative to the two cases.[33]

Decisions of a commission finding that a public officer is guilty of a violation of the code of ethics can be appealed to the courts. A hearing officer for the Florida Commission on Ethics found a county commissioner guilty of using county employees to write an article used in her election campaign on the ground that a citizen could not have a similar article prepared by county employees. On appeal, the Florida District Court of Appeals in 1991 reversed the finding that there was no evidence that the appellant acted with wrongful intent since there was no provision in the state statutes that would have placed the appellant on notice that she was committing an unethical act.[34]

Advisory Opinions

The Minnesota Code of Ethics for executive branch employees advises an individual with a potential conflict of interest "to avoid the situation."[35] This guidance, however, does not help the employee to determine whether his/her contemplated action would constitute a conflict of interest. Hence, a code of ethics should require a local official or employee to notify his/her supervisor in writing whenever he/she suspects that a present or anticipated action may violate the code. Whether the potential violation is real or only apparent is of concern. Many potential conflicts are minor and inconsequential, and unavoidable in a complex modern society. All requests for advice should be considered confidential information.

The code should make the supervisor responsible, within a specified period of time, for making a written determination and notifying the person seeking the advice whether the action poses a threat to the public interest. The supervisor should be free to request the advice of the board of ethics if there is a board and any determination made by the supervisor should be appealable to the board. This procedure provides a relatively simple mechanism whereby a public official or employee could be protected against a possible violation of the code. The Code of Ethics of the Township of Teaneck, New Jersey, specifically authorizes the township manager to request from the board of ethics an advisory opinion relative to "whether certain proposed courses of conduct or activity of his appointees might be considered a violation of the Code."[36]

Should a supervisor fail to make a written determination within the specified time period, the matter automatically should be referred to the board of ethics for a determination. In the event the board fails to make a written determination within the required time period, the code should provide that failure of the board to act shall be deemed that an advisory opinion was issued and that the facts and circumstances of the particular case do not constitute a violation of the code. The rendered or deemed rendered opinion, unless amended or revoked, should be binding on the board of ethics in any subsequent charge concerning the official or employee who sought the opinion and acted on it in good faith, unless material facts were omitted or misstated by the official or employee in the request for the advisory opinion.

The principal function of a board of ethics is to issue advisory opinions in response to the requests of officials and employees. The Rhode Island Governor's Committee on Ethics in 1986 recommended that the State Ethics Commission also should be authorized to issue an advisory opinion if there is an appearance of unethical conduct, "even when no actual impropriety can be shown to have occurred, unless the official or employee involved has already publicly disclosed the relative facts."[37]

Published advisory opinions, with deletions preserving the anonymity of the official or employee involved, will guide all officials and employees who may encounter similar future situations involving ethical questions and serve as a common law of ethics. The deletion of names in a small local government, however, may not protect the privacy of an official or employee and the question must be raised whether all advisory opinions in such a government should be published?

What constitutes bona fide confidential information that may not be disclosed is a common question addressed in advisory opinions. A board, for example, might inform an inquiring official that he/she could disclose information classified by a superior as confidential since the classification is solely for partisan political reasons.

Whether a gift can be accepted by a public officer or employee frequently is the subject of a request for an advisory opinion. The New York State Ethics Commission points out that "gifts come in many forms and from many people: a key chain from the company that delivers overnight mail; tickets to the ball game from a vendor who deals with your agency; even flowers from a satisfied taxpayer. Some companies consider the distribution of such 'freebies' to be part of an effective marketing plan, while others consider it good public relations."[38]

The Code of Ethics, adopted in 1990 by the International City Management Association, stipulates that "members should not accept directly or indirectly a gift if (1) it could be reasonably inferred or expected that the gift was intended to influence them in the performance of their official duties, or (2) the gift was intended to serve as a reward for any official action on their part."[39] The code stresses that "it is important that the prohibition of unsolicited gifts be limited to circumstances related to improper influence. In such *de minimis* situations as cigars, meal checks, etc., some modest maximum dollar value should be determined by the member as a guideline."[40]

The code of ethics should prohibit acceptance of a gift of "economic value" by a public officer or employee if the acceptance directly or indirectly might convey the impression of compromising the impartiality of the public servant's position or impairing the independence of his/her judgment in the exercise of official duties. In a period of inflation, there is a greater need for developing standards of value. The board of ethics can generate a body of precedents dealing with the gift problem to guide public servants.

Adoption of city charter amendments in 1989 by New York City voters resulted in the replacement of the board of ethics by the conflicts-of-interest board. The former board of ethics had the greatest amount of experience in issuing advisory opinions and the following are illustrative of the types of questions raised by city officials and employees, and the replies of the board. An assessor attached to the tax commission inquired whether the code of ethics prohibits him from investing in private real estate transactions in an area of the city in "which he did not currently assess." The board advised that such an investment would constitute a code violation. "Although the writer may not be assigned to the area assessing the property in question, his interest in such property is in our opinion sufficient to create a conflict of interest because the property in question is part of the assessable area under the jurisdiction of the department in which he is employed and for the further reason that assessors are subject to reassignment and in addition all property assessments are the responsibility of the same department and the same class of employees with whom the City employee works side by side."[41]

May a county legislator and other candidates accept endorsements by unions representing municipal employees? The Westchester County, New York, Board of Ethics responded: "An endorsement is not unethical per se, but an elected official must conscientiously refrain from allowing such an endorsement to influence, in any way, judgments which he or she must make as a public official, which affect the interest of the endorser. It is also the consensus of the Board that no such official should on his or her initiative directly or indirectly seek such an endorsement."[42]

A Westchester County legislator inquired whether he could serve as an officer or member of a board of directors of a charitable or nonprofit organization which receives funding by or through the county. The board replied that "a county legislator should abstain from participating in or voting upon any matter affecting the organizations with which he is associated. Conversely, we believe a legislator should exercise the same restraint when acting on behalf of such associations; i.e., he should abstain from representing such associations in their dealings with the County."[43] The legislator also was advised to file a written disclosure statement with the clerk of the County Board of Legislators.

The Florida Commission on Ethics was asked in 1991 whether a mayor of a city must disclose as gifts items given to her by the sponsor of a golf tournament for her assistance in promoting and operating the tournament in the city when the total value of the items exceeds one hundred dollars. The commission, in opinion 91-45, held the items do not have to be disclosed, under provisions of Chapter 90-502 of the Laws of Florida, in circumstances where the mayor in her private capacity gives equal or greater consideration to the donor. The opinion also explained the mayor would not have to disclose as a gift reimbursement of travel expenses for attending a meeting of the directors of the Florida League of Cities.

The Rhode Island Ethics Commission in 1990 advised in opinion 90-20 that the State Code of Ethics will not permit a member of the East Providence City Council to discuss or vote on the transfer of a liquor license when the individual seeking the transfer is the plaintiff and the councilman is a defendant in a suit. In opinion 90-39, the commission held that there will be no code violation if a Pawtucket law enforcement officer in his capacity as owner of a firm accepts a contract to collect delinquent taxes for the city. The opinion was based upon the representations of the officer that no employees in his collection agency will represent themselves as members or representatives of the Pawtucket Police Department.

The Minnesota State Ethical Practices Board advised in 1991 that there is no conflict of interest if the potential conflict is too speculative and remote, and the decision regarding a disclosure of a potential conflict is the public officer's decision.[44]

Advisory opinions on ethical questions raised in the executive branch also can be issued by other public officers. The New York State attorney general, for example, issued an opinion in 1988 advising that opposition of a local planning board member to an earlier application did not establish a conflict of interest if the concerns expressed are addressed in the current application and membership of the board member in a neighborhood association expressing concern but not opposition to the application did not constitute a conflict of interest.[45]

Legislative Advisory Opinions. Members of legislative bodies and their staff encounter potential conflicts of interest similar to ones encountered by executive branch employees, but also encounter situations unique to a legislature. In consequence, many state legislatures and each house of the Congress established committees on ethics charged with, among other duties, rendering advisory opinions to members and staff employees.

The Committee on Standards of Official Conduct of the U.S. House of Representatives and the Select Committee on Ethics of the U.S. Senate have issued numerous advisory opinions in response to requests on a wide variety of issues, including campaign funds, divestiture of investments, dual employment, exertion of improper influence, franking privilege, gifts, interns, post-employment, and use of official facilities.

The House Committee determined that the following are not gifts subject to House Rule LXIII:

1. Bequests and other forms of inheritance;
2. Loans made in a commercially reasonable manner (including requirements that the loan be repaid and that a reasonable rate of interest be paid);
3. Political contributions as defined by the Federal Election Commission, and otherwise reported as required by law;
4. Food, lodging, transportation, and entertainment provided on an official basis by federal, state, and local governments, or political subdivisions thereof;
5. Food, lodging, transportation, and entertainment provided by a foreign government within a foreign country;
6. Communications to a Member's office in Washington and his district, including subscriptions to newspapers, magazines, and other materials;
7. *Bona fide* awards presented in recognition of public service and available to the general public;

8. Suitable mementos of a function honoring the Member, office, or employee;
9. Consumable products provided by home-state businesses to a Member's office that are primarily intended for consumption by persons other than the Member and his staff;
10. Food and beverages consumed at banquets, receptions, and similar events.[46]

House Rule XLVII, effective January 1, 1979, limits the honorarium received by a member for a speech or article to a maximum value of $750. The committee advised that the amount of a reported honorarium can be reduced by the amount of nonreimbursed travel expenses.[47] Rule XLVII subsequently was amended and currently forbids a member to accept any honorarium.

In response to another request, the commission opined that a member may communicate with an executive or independent agency to "request information or a status report; urge prompt consideration; arrange for interviews or appointments; express judgments; call for reconsideration of an administrative response which he believes is not supported by established law, federal regulation, or legislative intent; perform any other service of a similar nature in this area compatible with the criteria hereinafter expressed in this advisory opinion."[48] The committee added:

1. A Member's responsibility in this area is to all his constituents equally and should be pursued with diligence irrespective of political or other considerations.
2. Direct or implied suggestion of either favoritism or reprisal in advance of, or subsequent to, action taken by the agency contacted is unwarranted abuse of the representative role.
3. A Member should make every effort to assure that representations made in his name by any staff employee conform to his instruction.[49]

The U.S. Senate Select Committee on Ethics advised that a senator may include his position and committee memberships in the Senate on stationery utilized in an election campaign, but quoted section 713 of title 18 of the United States Code which prohibits use of "any printed or other likeness of the great seal of the United States . . . or any facsimile thereof, . . . on any stationery, for the purpose of conveying, or in a manner reasonably calculated to convey, a false impression of sponsorship or approval by the Government of the United States."[50]

A senator inquired whether he could frank a card to key officials of federal agencies providing services in his state to obtain information enabling his office to respond to "emergency or constituent's request for assistance on the weekend" and use the frank for the return of the information to his office? The committee quoted the regulations governing the use of the mailing frank—"The sending back to a Senator, or officer of the Senate, of a return-addressed and franked piece of mail by an addressee does not constitute a loan of the frank if the mail matter was frankable and if the return use of the frank remains under the Senator's or officer's control"—and opined the frank could be used for the purpose indicated.[51]

The Select Committee was asked in 1989 whether a senator may appoint as staff director of a committee an individual whose spouse is a professional staff member of the committee. The interpretative ruling noted that a question is raised under the antinepotism statute (5 U.S.C. § 3110) and held that the Senate employee could be appointed as the supervisor of a relative provided the person appointed as supervisor "recuses himself from any appointment, employment, promotion, or advancement decisions concerning that relative."[52]

In 1992, the Select Committee determined that a member of the staff of Senator Jesse Helms could participate in a program in Russia sponsored by the Legislative Study Institute and the Russian government for two months.[53]

Investigations

The board of ethics should be directed by the code of ethics to investigate possible code violations upon the written request of the chief executive or legislative body of the government. In all other cases, the board should not be allowed to conduct an investigation of possible code violations unless a charge(s) against an official or employee has been signed under oath or affirmation by the person making the charge(s) or the board by a majority vote adopts a formal resolution defining the nature and scope of the inquiry. The New Orleans Code of Ethics, for example, authorizes "any qualified elector to file written complaints in the form of an affidavit with the Civil Service Commission concerning violations. . . ."[54]

The Seattle, Washington, Code of Ethics specifies that "all officers, employees, departments, and agencies of the City shall make available to the Board of Ethics all books, papers, documents, information, and assistance requested by said Board. . . ."[55]

Investigations conducted by a board should be confidential and its findings of code violations should be reported to the concerned officers or employees and their supervisors. The Seattle ordinance stipulates that the appropriate city supervisor must file with the board, within fourteen calendar days of receiving the board's decision, a written report of the disciplinary action taken.[56]

A board of ethics should be authorized to issue subpoenas and have them served and enforced. Persons appearing before the board should be required to testify under oath or affirmation. An individual whose name is mentioned adversely during testimony before the board should be notified and allowed to appear before the board or file a sworn statement.

Upon deciding to investigate the conduct of a public officer or employee, the board of ethics should notify the alleged violator at least thirty days prior to a hearing and he/she should have the right to be present and represented by counsel at the hearing, examine and cross-examine witnesses, and call witnesses on his/her behalf. It is advisable for the board to arrange for the preparation of a stenographic record or tape recording of each hearing.

The Massachusetts State Ethics Commission includes in its annual report details of its investigations. A former town counsel of North Andover acknowledged that he violated state law and paid a civil penalty of $2,000 because he held a financial interest in town insurance contracts; a Boston school committee member violated the conflict-of-interest law by appointing her son to a clerk typist position on her staff and granting him a retroactive pay increase; the mayor of Newburyport admitted violating state law by appointing his son to the police department; a former Cambridge superintendent of schools admitted that he violated state law by borrowing money from two employees and subsequently recommending that the school committee grant one of the employees a sabbatical leave of absence; and the Ashland town assessor confessed to violating the state conflict-of-interest law by participating in decisions relative to the timing and manner of collecting his own delinquent real property taxes.[57]

The Philadelphia Board of Ethics conducted an investigation and ruled, in 1986, that Mayor W. Wilson Goode was guilty of an impropriety by failing to report that he had purchased fourteen suits of clothing at discount prices, and ordered him to submit a formal report that he obtained the suits through an official of the Amalgamated Clothing and Textile Workers Union.[58]

Charges by the media that raise ethical questions about the actions of public officers often lead to an investigation being launched by the board of ethics. An official subject to media charges can call upon the board to investigate the charges. In 1967, Manhattan Borough President Percy E. Sutton requested the New York City Board of Ethics "to evaluate the propriety of my conduct as a public official with regard to the stories that have appeared in the *New York Post* alluding to improper conduct by me as a public official." The *Post* articles could have led readers to infer that Mr. Sutton had an interest in two multiple dwellings charged with many violations by the city's Department of Buildings. After an extensive investigation, the board concluded that "Mr. Percy E. Sutton did not have any interest, direct or indirect, in the ownership of 505 West 142nd Street to 502 West 141st Street properties," and that "there has been no violation of the Code of Ethics and Related Laws and that there has been no impropriety in his conduct during the period of his public service with respect to the properties in question."[59]

Investigations obviously can be conducted by organizations in addition to the board of ethics. The prosecuting attorney may launch an investigation, the concerned legislative body possesses the authority to establish a select investigating commission, and the chief executive officer by executive order can create an investigating commission. Governor Mario M. Cuomo of New York, for example, issued an executive order establishing the Office of State Inspector General with full authority "to examine and investigate the management and affairs of the covered agencies . . . ," a subject examined in greater detail in Chapter 7.[60]

The apparent widespread existence of corruption in the government of New York City prompted Governor Cuomo and New York City Mayor Edward I. Koch, in 1986, to appoint a State-City Commission on Integrity in Government. Although thorough studies were conducted by the commission and its reports contained detailed recommendations, the latter were ignored by the New York State legislature.[61]

The judicial system in each state has a code of judicial conduct and a separate mechanism for investigating complaints against judicial personnel and for issuing advisory opinions. In 1991, the Board of Commissioners on Grievances and Discipline of the Ohio Supreme Court issued twenty-nine advisory opinions on ethical questions arising under the State Code of Professional Responsibility, Code of Judicial Conduct, Rules for the Government of the Bar, Rules for the Government of the Judiciary, and the Ohio Ethics Law.[62] Canon 5C of the Ohio Code of Judicial Conduct, for example, stipulates "a judge should refrain from financial and business dealings that tend to reflect adversely on his impartiality, interfere with the proper performance of his judicial duties, exploit his judicial position, or involve him in frequent transactions with lawyers or persons likely to come before the court on which he serves."

Distribution of Advisory Opinions

It is essential that opinions of the boards of ethics legislative ethics committees, and other public officials be readily available to public officers, public employees, and citizens. The federal Office of Government Ethics in 1981 established a system for issuance of formal advisory opinions interpreting the conflict-of-interest statutes. Requests for such opinions must be submitted in writing and contain specified information. Interested parties are afforded the opportunity to submit written comments on questions that will be the subject of a formal opinion. Government employees relying upon a formal opinion in good faith are not subject to prosecution for actions taken. The Office issued two opinions as of June 1988—the first in February 1982 and the second in January 1983.[63] As of the same date, the Office had issued 205 informal opinions in the form of letters and memoranda, and placed 65 informal opinions in its library. Although the Office sends a digest of certain informal opinions to each agency annually, interviewed agency ethics officials reported they desire more access to the Office's information opinions.[64]

If public officers and employees are simply handed copies of advisory opinions and the code of ethics, it is probably that a significant number will not read the opinions and/or the code, and relatively few of those who read the opinions and the code will acquire a complete and proper understanding. Hence, a provision should be included in a code to ensure that it and important advisory opinions are always understood fully by all public officers and employees. The code should require that it and important advisory opinions be read and explained carefully to new officers and employees. A perfunctory reading of the code obviously would be a waste of everyone's time. The explanation might be incorporated into an orientation program for all new officers and employees. The code might contain a requirement that every new public officer and employee must sign a statement that he/she has read the code.

Consideration also should be given to including a requirement that the code be read and explained carefully to all public officers and employees at least once a year. Their knowledge and understanding of the code in most instances will be dimmed by time unless refreshed by a new reading and explanation which emphasizes code amendments and advisory opinions issued by the board of ethics. Such a requirement would impress further upon officers and employees the determination of the government to stamp out unethical conduct.

SUMMARY

Codes of ethics have been developed to supplement the common law and statutory conflict-of-interest provisions by addressing ethical questions that fall between actions that clearly are unethical and actions that clearly are ethical. The code guidelines assist public officers and employees in determining whether contemplated actions are unethical.

A code by itself is inadequate in guiding public officers and employees and there is a need for a board or commission to interpret code guidelines in response to requests for opinions based upon specific facts. The principal function of the typical board is to provide advice when requested, but it is not uncommon for a board to be authorized to conduct investigations upon receipt of complaints that a public officer or employee has been involved in an unethical action. A board also should be directed to conduct a continuing educational program to ensure that all public servants are aware of their ethical obligations.

As noted, boards of ethics issue advisory opinions on a wide variety of subjects, including required disclosure of financial information by public officers and employees. Chapter 4 examines legal requirements for the disclosure of financial information by candidates for public elected office, lobbyists, public officers, and public employees.

NOTES

1. *Ethics Manual for Members, Officers, and Employees of the United States House of Representatives* (Washington, D.C.: United States Government Printing Office, 1987), p. 9.

2. New York Laws of 1954, chap. 696 and *New York Public Officers Law*, § 74(4) (McKinney 1988).

3. Minnesota Statutes Annotated, § 43.A.38(5) (1988).

4. *A Suggested Code of Ethics for Municipal Officials and Employees* (Chicago: International City Management Association, 1962), p. 6.

5. New York Laws of 1954, chap. 696, § 1.

6. *Georgia County Government*, September 1985, p. 76.

7. Rockville, Maryland, Ordinance 6-74, § 15-1.01.

8. *Circular No. 1980/6* (Canberra: Office of the Australian Public Service, 1980), p. 2.

9. Public Service Board, *Guidelines on Official Conduct of Commonwealth Public Servants* (Canberra: Australian Government Printing Office, 1979), p. 4.78.

10. Treasury and Civil Service Committee, *Civil Servants and Ministers: Duties and Responsibilities* (London: Her Majesty's Stationery Office, 1986), vol. II, p. 65.

11. Seattle, Washington, Ordinance No. 100435, § 7(8).

12. Town of Newington, Connecticut, Code of Ordinances, § 2-53.

13. Minnesota Statutes Annotated, § 43A.38(1)(b) (1988).

14. Ibid., § 43A.38(2)(a-e) (1988).

15. New York City Charter, chap. 68 (1989).

16. "What You Should Know. . . ." (New York: City of New York Procurement Policy Board, n.d.), p. 4.

17. Westchester County, New York, Local Law No. 12-1970, § 1(a).

18. Ethics in Government Act of 1978, 92 Stat. 1964, 5 U.S.C. § 5316 (1979 Supp.).

19. Office of Government Ethics: Reauthorization Act of 1988, 102 Stat. 3031.

20. Bernard L. Ungar, *Office of Government Ethics: Need for Additional Regulation Development and Oversight* (Washington, D.C.: United States General Accounting Office, 1992), pp. 4–5.

21. *Second Biennial Report to Congress* (Washington, D.C.: United States Office of Government Ethics, 1992), p. 53.

22. Kansas Statutes Annotated, §§ 46-268 to 46-275 (1986).

23. Minnesota Statutes Annotated, §§ 10A.01 *et seq.* (1988 and 1992 Supp.).

24. *In re Advisory Opinion to the Governor (Ethics Commission)*, 612 A2d 1 (R.I. 1992).

25. *Model City Charter*, 7th ed. (Denver: National Civil League, 1989), art. VII, § 7.01(b).

26. Town of Windsor, Connecticut, Ordinance No. 70-5, § 10.

27. Borough of Matanuska-Susitna, Alaska, Code of Ethics, § 2.52.510.

28. Township of Piscataway (New Jersey) Code of Ethics, § 4-15.5(a).

29. Buffalo (New York) Code, chap. VIII, § 90.

30. Ibid., § 91.

31. Seattle (Washington) Ordinance No. 100435, § 3.

32. Township of Falls (Pennsylvania) Code of Ethics, § IIIA.

33. "Rhode Island Panel Fines Ex-Governor," *The Times Union* (Albany, New York), December 21, 1991, p. A-10.

34. *Blackmun v. State Commission on Ethics*, 16 FLW D2605 (Fla. 1st DCA, 1991).

35. Minnesota Statutes Annotated, § 43A.38(6) (1988).

36. Township of Teaneck (New Jersey) Ordinance No. 1662, § 9.1.

37. *Strengthening Ethical Standards in Rhode Island Government* (Providence: Governor's Committee on Ethics in Government, 1986), p. 12.

38. *New York Ethics: A Guide to the Ethics Law* (Albany: New York State Ethics Commission, n.d.), p. 9.

39. City Management Code of Ethics (Washington, D.C.: International City Management Association, 1972), p. 16.

40. Ibid.

41. *Opinion No. 2—Propriety of Endorsement for Public Office* (White Plains: Westchester County Board of Ethics, October 16, 1975), p. 1.

42. *Opinions Nos. 51 to 100* (New York: New York City Board of Ethics, n.d.), opinion no. 53.

43. *Opinion No. 3* (White Plains, New York: Westchester County Board of Ethics, December 11, 1975), p. 1.

44. *Annual Report* (St. Paul: Minnesota Ethical Practices Board, 1991), p. 1.

45. *Opinions of the Attorney General for the Year Ending December 31, 1988* (Albany: New York State Department of Law, 1989), pp. 117–20.

46. Staff of The Committee on Standards of Official Conduct, *Ethics Manual for Members, Officers, and Employees of the United States House of Representatives* (Washington, D.C.: United States Government Printing Office, 1987), pp. 29–30.

47. Ibid., p. 75.

48. Ibid., p. 176.

49. Ibid.

50. United States Senate Select Committee on Ethics, *Interpretative Rulings of the Select Committee on Ethics* (Washington, D.C.: United States Government Printing Office, 1989), p. 130.

51. Ibid., pp. 138–39.

52. United States Senate Select Committee on Ethics, *Interpretative Ruling Number 441*, April 4, 1989 (mimeographed).

53. Notice of Determination by the Select Committee on Ethics Under Rule 35, Paragraph 4, Permitting Acceptance of a Gift of Educational Travel from a Foreign Organization," *Congressional Record*, September 23, 1992, p. S14833.

54. New Orleans Code of Ethics, § 6.

55. Seattle (Washington) Ordinance No. 100435, § 4.

56. Ibid., § 6.

57. *Annual Report: Fiscal Year 1985* (Boston: Massachusetts State Ethics Commission, 1985), pp. 7–8.

58. "Ethics Board Criticizes Philadelphia's Mayor," *The New York Times*, February 26, 1986, p. A18.

59. *Opinions Nos. 101 to 150* (New York: New York City Board of Ethics, n.d.), opinion no. 120.

60. Executive Order No. 79 (Albany, New York: Executive Chamber, January 29, 1986).

61. *News Release* (Albany, New York: Executive Chamber, March 11, 1986).

62. Information supplied to author by Secretary Jonathan W. Marshall of the Board of Commissioners on Grievances and Discipline of the Supreme Court of Ohio in a letter dated January 6, 1992.

63. *Ethics: Office of Government Ethics' Policy Development Role* (Washington, D.C.: United States General Accounting Office, 1988), p. 5.

64. Ibid., pp. 5–6.

Chapter 4

Mandatory Information Disclosure

The protection of the public interest against conflicts of interest and other unethical acts is dependent upon the ability of governments to detect such conduct and prosecute offenders. To assist in the process of detection, governments have enacted statutes requiring candidates for elective office, lobbyists, and public officers and employees to file financial reports.

It is not surprising in a nation based upon democratic principles that governments would initiate action to ensure that elections are conducted fairly. The early laws—termed corrupt practices acts—prohibit bribery, personation, treating, betting on elections, and payment of one voter's poll tax by another person.[1] These acts were supplemented in the late nineteenth century by civil service constitutional and statutory provisions curtailing patronage and prohibiting assessment of officeholders as a means of raising party campaign funds. More recent statutes regulate the amounts that may be contributed to candidates and the amounts they may spend in primary and general election campaigns. Corporations and labor unions currently are forbidden to contribute to election campaigns in sixteen and eight states, respectively. In addition, Montana forbids regulated corporations to contribute to campaigns.

To protect citizens against the possible evil influence exercised by interest groups on the lawmaking process, the Congress and all state legislatures have enacted laws regulating lobbying. These statutes require lobbyists to register and report their finances, and also prohibit the offering of bribes.

Statutes also have been enacted requiring all or some public officers and employees to make an annual public disclosure of their finances on the theory that such disclosure will make it more difficult for the public servants to engage in certain types of unethical behavior, and facilitate enforcement of the conflict-of-interest and other ethics laws. Furthermore, the disclosure requirements encourage public officers and employees periodically to reassess the relationship between their interests and the government's interest.

These mandatory disclosure laws are types of "sunshine" acts which—in conjunction with freedom of information laws and open meeting laws examined in Chapters 5 and 6, respectively—are premised upon the belief that public knowledge of a potential conflict of interest will reduce the opportunity and temptation for unethical behavior in the public service.

CORRUPT PRACTICES ACTS

The major purpose of corrupt practices acts is to curb the corruption that may be associated with the excessive use of money in election campaigns. Citizens want an energetic campaign during which candidates clearly state their views, but such campaigns on a national or a state basis are expensive in an age of television.

The acts establish maximum permissible amounts of campaign contributions and expenditures, and require filing of reports by candidates, their election committees, and political action groups. The statutes are based upon the fear that unregulated election finance might lead to candidates becoming indebted to large contributors and result in favoritism toward the contributors if the candidates win election to public office. The acts rely heavily upon publicity to ensure campaign receipt and expenditure limits are not violated.

In 1986, the State-City Commission on Integrity in Government in New York reported:

candidates . . . frequently collect and spend grossly excessive amounts on campaigns. Contemporary campaign finance resembles a veritable gold rush. The huge sums involved create vast opportunities for influence peddling and other abuses. And they give rise to a substantial appearance of impropriety, a belief that large contributors receive a *quid pro quo* from those they support, that office-seekers are for sale.[2]

Campaign finance reports reveal that major contributors, including political action committees (PACs), donate substantially more funds to incumbents than to challengers, thereby accounting in part for the high rate of reelection of incumbents in important offices. The reason for this finding is simple: incumbents are in a position to help the special interests. Contributors, however, often maintain that they are not seeking to influence incumbents, but are only rewarding them for their excellent performance. The result is an uneven playing field for candidates in elections, particularly if the offices are statewide ones necessitating expensive media promotion.

The decline of political parties as financing vehicles for candidates and their replacement by PACs have changed the nature of campaign finance in recent years. Incumbents generally have a significant advantage over nonincumbents in raising campaign funds, particularly from PACs.

The federal and state corrupt practices acts limiting contributions to campaigns must conform with the 1976 decision of the U.S. Supreme Court in *Buckley v. Valeo*, a decision involving the Federal Election Campaign Act of 1971 and its 1974 amendments.[3] The Court ruled constitutional the contribution limits placed on individuals, the disclosure and reporting requirements, and public financing provisions. However, the Court opined "that the limitations on campaign expenditures, on independent expenditures by individuals and groups, and on expenditures by a candidate from his personal funds are constitutionally infirm."[4]

The expenditure ceilings were held to impose "direct and substantial restraints on the quality of political speech."[5] Most importantly, the Court ruled that the limit on personal expenditure by a candidate "imposes a substantial restraint on the ability of persons to engage in protected First Amendment expression."[6] The Court added that "it is of particular importance that candidates have the unfettered opportunity to make their views known so that the electorate may intelligently evaluate the candidates' personal qualities and their positions on vital public issues before choosing among them on election day."[7]

This decision is of great importance since it allows wealthy individuals to spend as much of their own funds on their election campaigns as they choose. The fear is that only wealthy individuals can be elected to major offices, such as seats in the U.S. Senate and the governorship in major states.

A second U.S. Supreme Court decision of considerable importance is the 1978 one invalidating a Massachusetts law restricting corporate contributions to issue campaigns "that materially affect its business, property, or assets" on First Amendment grounds.[8] As a result of this decision, corporations are free to spend unlimited funds in referendum campaigns if the proposals affect the corporations' business interests.

Reports filed by tobacco companies on September 4, 1992, with the Massachusetts Office of Campaign and Political Finance reveal approximately $4.5 million were contributed to the Committee Against Unfair Taxes and other organizations opposed to an initiative proposition placed on the November 3, 1992 ballot that would increase the cigarette tax by twenty-five cents per pack. The amount exceeds the $3.3 million spent by Governor William Weld in his 1990 election campaign.[9] Opponents of a second initiative proposition on the same ballot—establishing environmental standards on packaging—contributed more than twenty-eight times as much money as supporters with the bulk of the opposition funds contributed by large corporations.[10]

The Regulatory Body

Since corrupt practices acts were enacted prior to the creation of state ethics commissions, the regulation of campaign finances continues to be the responsibility of other bodies or offices in several states. In Alabama, the corrupt practices act is administered by the attorney general. Nevertheless, candidates for statewide offices in Alabama are required to file a statement of economic interests with the State Ethics Commission within ten days of announcing their candidacies. Failure to file the statement will result in the commission removing candidates from the ballot.

The Georgia Ethics in Government Act of 1986 requires candidates to file public reports on contributions and expenditures with the State Ethics Commission and also requires each candidate to file a financial disclosure statement for the twelve-month period prior to qualifying for office, and annually file a financial disclosure statement for each preceding calendar year. The commission is authorized to levy a fine of up to $1,000 for failure to file the campaign disclosure or personal financial disclosure statement. Interestingly, the Georgia act and the New Jersey act place no limits on the amount of money a candidate or his campaign committee may receive or spend in an election and only require filing of reports on campaign finance.

Minnesota law requires the treasurer of a political committee to register with the State Ethical Practices Board within fourteen days of receiving contributions or making expenditures exceeding $100.[11] All accounts must be kept by the treasurer for four years to facilitate a possible examination or audit. The treasurer must forward any anonymous contributions to the board.

The Model State Campaign Finance Law provides for a State Campaign Finance Commission responsible for administering the Law.[12] The seven members would be appointed by the Governor with the approval of the Senate for seven-year terms and no more than four members may belong to the same political party. The commentary on this section of the Model Act points out that this provision parallels the requirements of the U.S. Constitution, as interpreted by the U.S. Supreme Court in *Buckley v. Valeo*, that there must be a separation of powers for appointments since the national commission appointees have regulatory and enforcement powers.

The State Campaign Finance Commission is required by the Model Law to investigate the sworn complaint of a citizen.[13] Individuals affected by a final decision of the commission, except a decision to refer a violation to the attorney general or local prosecutor, may seek judicial review of the decision.[14]

The commission is authorized by the Model Law to issue advisory opinions on its own volition or at the request of any person relative to his/her duties "in a given factual situation."[15] If the person requesting advice on a contemplated action submits accurate information and follows the advisory opinion, the person will be protected against civil and/or criminal penalties in the event he is charged with a violation. In effect, the commission will establish a common law relative to campaign finance that will provide guidance to all persons involved in election campaigns. The Minnesota Ethical Practices Board, in 1990, for example, advised that a campaign committee's payment for defective campaign materials that were not used may be deemed a "noncampaign disbursement."[16]

The Federal Election Commission was created by the Election Campaign Act Amendments of 1974 and is composed of eight members, including two ex officio members—secretary of the U.S. Senate and clerk of the U.S. House of Representatives—who are represented at the commission by two special deputies.[17] The commission has broad regulatory powers, administers the public financing program for presidential elections, and issues advisory opinions. Kenneth A. Gross, a former associate general counsel for the commission, wrote in 1991 that the Congress should amend the act because "of the critical inadequacies of the current enforcement scheme."[18]

Regulatory Provisions

The corrupt practices act must define the term *contribution* carefully. The Model State Campaign Finance Law defines a contribution as "a gift, subscription, advance, deposit of money or anything of value, a payment, a forgiveness of a loan and a payment of a third party, made for the purpose of influencing the result of an election. A 'contribution' includes that portion of a gift, etc., which exceeds the fair market value of anything received in return."[19]

The Model Law also includes within the definition of contribution tickets purchased for fund-raising events, discounts or rebates not extended to the general public, and the money or property of the candidate used in the campaign.[20] The act excludes voluntary services provided by others in the campaign.

A campaign committee or political party or committee may not accept contributions or expend funds under the Model Law until a statement of organization, including detailed information on its officers and purposes, is filed with the commission. The statement must include the name and party affiliation of candidate(s), name of referendum issue the party or committee is opposing or supporting, a list of bank safety deposit boxes and other depositories used with names and numbers of all accounts and numbers of safety deposit boxes, and other information requested by the commission.[21] The purpose of the requirement is to prevent the concealment of illegal contributions prior to the official constituting of the committee.

The information filed offers protection to the general public and to contributors. The latter can check to ensure that contributions publicly are accounted for. Furthermore, the information is essential if the Commission is to determine the total contributions spent to assist a candidate through a variety of campaign committees. The requirement also offers the committees protection against the unauthorized solicitation of campaign funds and allows the commission to order the halt of solicitation if the statement of organization has not been filed.

The Model Law required the report of campaign contributions to include:

a. A list of every person, committee, or organization who has made contributions with an aggregate value exceeding one hundred dollars ($100), showing, for each contributor, name, home address, occupation, business name and address, and the amount or fair market value of each contribution;

b. A list of all loans extended to the party or committee, the name and address of the lender and, if secured or co-signed by a person other than the candidate, the name and address of that person;

c. If any pledges have been used to obtain a loan or other goods and services, a list of the pledges and the amount of each pledge and the name, home address, occupation and business name and address of the pledger.

d. The total amount of all other contributions not listed in any other category, and the total proceeds from the sales of such items as campaign pins, buttons, badges, flags, emblems, hats, banners, literature, and similar material; and

e. The total amount of proceeds of ticket sales to every dinner, luncheon, cocktail party, rally, and other fund raising event so long as the contribution per ticket after expenses are deducted does not exceed one hundred dollars ($100). Where the contribution exceeds one hundred dollars ($100), contributors shall be listed separately in accordance with subdivision (a) of this section. For each fund raising event listed under this subdivision, a report shall have been filed in accordance with Section 13.[22]

The reporting requirements of the Model Law are considerably more detailed than earlier requirements because of frequent evasions of the less detailed laws. Among other things, the required disclosure of loans is important, since loans become contributions if they are not repaid by election day.

The Model Law also contains detailed reporting requirements for all fund-raising events. These requirements are designed to prevent candidates from making excessive profits by charging excessive rates for goods and services consumed in the event. The Law also makes illegal the expenditure of campaign contributions for purposes not related to the purposes of the political party or committee and requires a campaign committee to terminate its activity after the election and pay all its debts and liabilities.[23]

The Model Law establishes limitations on campaign contributions by individuals which differ according to whether the campaign is a local or a statewide one, and makes it illegal for a person to make a contribution in a name other than his/her own.[24] Individuals independently expending funds exceeding $100 on behalf of a candidate or referendum issue are required to register with the commission and file expenditure reports.[25] Whereas many state corrupt practices acts make it illegal for a candidate or committee to accept anonymous contributions, the Model Law permits such contributions up to a maximum of twenty-five dollars per year.[26]

Minnesota, for example, limits contributions to elected officers by individuals, political committees, and political parties, according to the office involved. An individual or political committee may not contribute more than $20,000 in an election year or $3,000 in a nonelection year to candidates for governor and lieutenant governor, but a political party may contribute $100,000 in an election year and $15,000 in a nonelection year. For a state representative, the limits are $750 by an individual or political committee in an election year and $250 in a nonelection year. A political party may contribute $3,750 in an election year and $1,250 in a nonelection year. Interestingly, there are no limits for candidates for elective judgeships.

Minnesota also established campaign limits indexed to the consumer price index. In 1990, the limits were $1,626,691 for governor/lieutenant governor; $271,116 for attorney general; $135,559 for secretary of state, state auditor, and state treasurer; $40,669 for each state senator; and $20,335 for each state representative.[27]

In New York State, there are no limits on contributions given to political party campaign committees. The New York State Commission on Government Integrity reported:

The only existent applicable limits are the aggregate annual limits on the total amounts which can be given by any one contributor to all recipients: for individual contributors, $150,000 per year; for corporations, $5,000 per year per corporate entity; but in the case of PACs, an unlimited amount. As a result, party committees attract substantial amounts of interest group (particularly PAC) contributions.[28]

The corrupt practices acts in several states prohibit state legislators from accepting campaign contributions during certain parts of a legislative session, and other laws make it a crime to solicit campaign funds from employees of the state while they are working. Arizona law forbids contributions to the governor's campaign fund during the bill-signing period.

Campaign contributions by business corporations or labor unions are forbidden by the Model Law except for referendum issues, which are allowed by the U.S. Supreme Court's 1978 decision in *First National Bank of Boston v. Bellotti*.[29] However, these entities are allowed to organize and operate political action committees which may make contributions.

Contributions by firms which do business with a government and by unions representing government employees, if allowed, suggest the possibility of a quid pro quo arrangement. Congress enacted a law making it illegal for an individual "knowingly to solicit" a campaign contribution from a government contractor and a second law prohibiting a government contractor from contributing to political campaigns.[30] Governor Daniel A. Walker of Illinois in 1973 issued Executive Order Number 5 requiring suppliers to the state and business firms regulated by the state to file an annual statement of political contributions. The order was attacked as violating the First Amendment to the U.S. Constitution. The court rejected this argument, but invalidated the order on the ground the constitution of the state did not grant the governor authority to issue such an order.[31]

The individual who pays for printed materials, including billboards and posters, must have his name and address on the materials and the individual paying for a radio or television advertisement similarly must have his/her name included in the advertisement under provisions of the Model Law. New York State, for example, lacks such a requirement.

Influential state legislators often are able to raise large sums for campaign purposes and use the surplus funds for their personal benefit and/or to gain political influence over other legislators by giving some of the funds to other candidates. Kansas prohibits such transfers, and Maryland limits the amount that may be transferred during a legislator's four-year term.[32] In Arizona, surplus campaign funds may not be expended for personal benefit.

Regulating independent expenditures on behalf of specific candidates is a difficult task. Most states require the reporting of such expenditures, and Florida specifically requires the person making such an expenditure to notify all candidates affected within twenty-four hours of the expenditure and to indicate the candidate supported or opposed by the expenditure.[33] A second difficult regulatory area is the use of surplus campaign funds. Most states forbid the personal use of such funds, and Delaware law identifies volunteer fire departments as eligible recipients of such funds.[34]

The Model Law provides criminal penalties for violations of certain sections of the law and civil penalties for violating any reporting requirement.[35]

Enforcement and Effectiveness of the Laws

The enforcement of corrupt practices laws leaves much to be desired. Although complete reports of campaign funds raised and expended may be required, reports often are filed late and fail to contain all required information. During election campaigns candidates may denounce the financial reports of their rivals in order to impress the voters. After the elections, however, these records usually are of little interest to anyone and are not audited for accuracy and completeness. The New York State Commission on Government Integrity reported:

Current State Board of Elections recordkeeping practices have enormously impeded our efforts to evaluate fully the funding practices in legislative races and underscore the need for a new Campaign Finance Enforcement Agency. Our analysis has been hampered to a large extent by often illegible, fragmented, incomplete, erroneous, and sometimes duplicative filings. On a number of occasions candidates have filed a number of "supplemental" or periodic statements, and then in other statements have repeated all the same information, without indicating that one or the other is the definitive filing. The format followed by filers is often inconsistent, even within a single filing, and often differs from candidate to candidate. Both legislative party campaign committees and individual candidates make filings through multiple committees; not all committees file statements for all periods. The Board of Elections . . . does not ensure that all existing committees file statements for all reporting periods.[36]

Although the reports of receipts and disbursements typically are incomplete and difficult to understand, candidates and members of party committees rarely are prosecuted, and the penalty of loss of office seldom is applied. To help solve the historical enforcement problem, Common Cause includes within its Model Conflict-of-Interest Act authorization for any citizen to file a sworn complaint with the ethics commission and a grant of citizen standing to sue if the responsible officials refuse to enforce the act.[37]

The contribution formulas in corrupt practices acts often give the appearance of a rational scheme, but in fact confuse the voters because of the complexity of the formulas. The New York State Election Law currently limits only campaign contributions. Relative to a candidate for a statewide office in a primary or general election, an individual is limited to a maximum of $0.005 times the number of voters, and the maximum family contribution is limited to $0.025 times the number of voters.[38] The state's election law was amended in 1976 to permit (for the first time) corporations to contribute up to $5,000 to any election campaign.[39] One product of the change in the Law was the obscuring of the identity of the individual contributor, since numerous contributions now are made in the name of a business corporation.

It is difficult for the public to determine with ease the amount of money contributed to a candidate for a major office if a series of committees "Concerned Citizens for Smith," "Smith for Governor," "Citizens for Smith," etc.) have been created. Each may be required to file a campaign report, but generally no effort is made by the enforcement commission to consolidate all reports filed on behalf of a given candidate.

Another enforcement problem involves loans made to a candidate or a candidate's campaign committee during the election campaign. The New York State Commission on Integrity in Government reported that Andrew Stein's committee promoting his election as New York City council president borrowed approximately $1.2 million. Of this sum, approximately $300,000 was borrowed directly from twelve individuals or entities. An additional $900,000 was borrowed from commercial banks and guaranteed by twenty-three Stein supporters. . . . three years later, much of that debt remains outstanding. Although over $800,000 . . . borrowed from commercial banks has been repaid, more than half . . . was repaid to the banks by the individual guarantors, many of whom, like real estate developers Donald Trump and William Zeckendorf, do business with New York City.[40]

Loans often are forgiven after an election. If a candidate who borrowed money is elected to office, the forgiving of a loan can be viewed as an attempt to purchase future favors. If a loan is not forgiven, the elected officer may owe large sums to individuals and/or firms that are regulated by or do business with the government.

One possible approach to solving this problem was outlined by the State-City Commission on Integrity in Government which recommended that all loans to a candidate or campaign committee be treated "as a contribution from the maker or the guarantor of the loan, subject to the $1,000 contribution limitation."[41] Loans made by a bank on the same terms as are available to the general public would be exempt under the commission's proposal.

The Federal Election Commission examines closely contributions to candidates for Congress and president. In 1993, ten contributors to congressional elections agreed to pay penalties of $64,000 assessed by the Federal Election Commission for violations of the legal limit on campaign contributions.[42] In contrast, most state campaign finance commissions lack adequate resources to enforce the corrupt practices acts and the problem is becoming more acute with the sharp increase in the number of political action committees which file required reports. In general, these reports are unaudited because the commission lacks staff and in some instances computers. The New Jersey commission has only two auditors and one field investigator, and the Connecticut commission has no computers.[43]

State legislatures have not been keen on appropriating adequate funds for agencies that monitor members' election campaigns, particularly in an era when campaign costs are rising sharply. In 1988, campaign costs for a seat in the New Jersey state legislature exceeded $100,000 in several districts and the cost was $3,000,000 in a few districts in California.[44]

A detailed report by a New York State investigating commission in 1987 concluded:

To the extent that New York's laws and procedures require campaign financing disclosure at all, they require too little and too late, and they permit some filings to be made in locations too remote from the particular campaign for easy scrutiny of the local citizenry and press. Current New York law permits disclosure of individual contributors without disclosure of their employers or business affiliations. Disclosure of corporate contributors can be made without disclosure of affiliated or subsidiary corporations. Moreover, . . . recipients of many campaign expenditures are never disclosed.[45]

Penalties for violating a corrupt practices act tend to be small. Assemblyman Anthony Seminerio of New York ignored fourteen report filing deadlines between 1990 and 1993 and he "received at least $5,450 from mob-linked sources in 1992 and 1993, according to disclosure forms filed by various unions and trade industry groups."[46] The penalty for not filing a required form is only $100. The commission's report also disclosed that enforcement agencies lack adequate resources and serve chiefly as depositories for the required disclosure form.[47]

Interest groups may not exceed the limit on campaign contributions directly, but may find other ways to help public officers financially. For example, the New York Life Insurance Company, United Brotherhood of Teamsters, and other organizations purchased large numbers of copies of a book—*Reflections of a Public Man*—written by Speaker Jim Wright of the U.S. House of Representatives, which paid the author an unusually high royalty of 55 percent.[48] In writing the book, the Speaker was assisted by a House staff member, which is a second unethical act as public resources may not be used to promote the economic interests of a public officer. Corporations also evade campaign expenditures prohibitions or limitations by soliciting officers of the corporations to make individual contributions to a candidate's campaign committee. This technique is known as bundling.

Conflicts of interest occasionally arise in fund-raising activities. In 1987, for example, two members of the state board regulating dentists in Massachusetts wrote a letter to all dentists in the Commonwealth urging that they contribute to Governor Michael Dukakis' election campaign.[49]

Several types of fund-raising activities—solicitation of small contributions from individuals and sale of campaign materials—are legal and ethical, although Oklahoma prohibits cash contributions, and Arkansas and Kansas attribute contributions by minors to their parents. Other fund-raising activities, while legal, raise ethical questions. Testimonial dinners often are abused as pressure is exerted on organizations regulated by the governor or the recipients of government contracts to purchase blocks of tickets. In New Hampshire, all state contracts are subject to approval by the elected executive council. A newspaper editor commented:

The invitation list for tonight's fund-raiser is peppered with representatives of non-profit organizations and business that rely on Council approval for their survival. The implicit message of holding an all-Council fund-raiser is this: Pay us the tribute, or your contracts may have trouble getting past us. It seems like something more out of an Iranian bazaar than what we expect in the New Hampshire State house.[50]

A related problem involves "laundering" of campaign funds by the use of "straws," that is, a contributor persuades another person to use the contributor's money to make a donation to a candidate in order to hide the origin of the money or because the contributor already has contributed the maximum amount allowed by law. Contributors of $1,000 to a 1981 party planned for the wife of Mayor Kevin White of Boston included city hall secretaries, each paid an annual salary of $14,000, who informed investigators that the money had been won "at the racetrack or (they) just had it lying around."[51] Effective use of "laundering" renders the disclosure requirements of little value in protecting the public.

A fine line divides the use of newsletters by elected officials to keep their constituents informed and electioneering. Recognizing the unfairness of allowing incumbents to distribute newsletters at public expense during an election campaign, state legislatures have enacted laws prohibiting the distribution of such newsletters during a stipulated period of time preceding an election. The time period frequently is short and is only thirty days in New York State. Incumbents in a number of state legislatures have found other ways of using public funds to promote their election prospects. The New York State Senate has a fully equipped television station which produces films for members to distribute to their local public access television stations and the assembly has a paid staff with television cameras and microphones which interviews members as they leave the chamber and provides the tapes to television stations in the members' home districts.[52] And the New York State Senate minority leader had the audacity to place election campaign workers on the Senate payroll.

Joshua Goldstein defined "soft money" in congressional election campaigns as "any political contribution not regulated by federal law" and identifies the largest sources as "contributions made to the national parties for use in state and local elections, and those made directly to state and local party organizations."[53] The largest sources of the funds are contributions by corporations, labor unions, and individuals who have reached the maximum limit allowed by federal law. The contributions often are solicited by the national party organizations which indicate the funds will be targeted to specific party candidates in the donors' state.

Many types of campaign expenditures are legitimate and include the maintenance of party and campaign headquarters; salaries of campaign workers; and the cost of printing, stationery, postage, and advertising in newspapers, periodicals, radio, and television; telephone bills; transportation of candidates and speakers; rental of meeting halls; campaign buttons and ribbons; and payment of watchers at the polls.

Other types of campaign expenditures clearly are unethical and often illegal. Bribery, treating, loans, and gifts in exchange for an individual's vote or support are abuses and are prohibited in most places by law. It is, of course, impossible to determine the extent of illegitimate expenditures, but it is reasonable to conclude that it is considerable. Treating voters to cigarettes and cigars, clothing, drinks, liquor, and entertainment is done covertly or openly in an effort to win votes. Candidates occasionally contribute to fraternal, religious, eleemosynary institutions or buy tickets to various public affairs—such as dances, fairs, and theatrical programs—in order to win or avoid losing voters. The support of newspapers and periodicals may be purchased through paid political advertising which masquerades as news.

Each house of the Congress of a state legislature possesses authority to investigate the activities of one or more of its members. On rare occasions, a legislative committee will conduct an investigation to determine whether a member had a conflict of interest and violated the corrupt practices act. In 1967, following a committee report, the U.S. Senate censured Senator Thomas Dodd for personal use of campaign funds even though such use did not violate an existing law or Senate rule.[54]

More recently, a U.S. Senate Select Committee in 1991 released a report of an investigation of allegations that five senators held meetings with the Federal Home Loan Bank Board relative to the Lincoln Savings & Loan Association whose owner, Charles H. Keating, Jr., had arranged for large sums to be contributed to the campaign committees of organizations affiliated with the senators.[55] The committee concluded that the "evidence demonstrates that Senator Cranston engaged in a pattern and practice of mixing fund raising and substantive legislative or regulatory issues."[56]

Public Financing of Elections

Incumbents often lack challengers in primary elections because potential challengers are unable to raise sufficient funds. In New York State, for example, 147 of 190 members of the state legislature seeking reelection had no primary election opponent in 1992.[57] Campaign expenditures data for the 1992 U.S. House of Representatives election reveal the great advantage incumbents have in soliciting campaign funds. Each incumbent member spent an average of $582,330 compared to an average of $154,607 spent by the challenger.[58]

Various reform organizations examined the problems associated with campaign finance and concluded that the only way to ensure that nonincumbents have an opportunity to compete on a level playing field in terms of campaign finance is partial public funding of such campaigns. Several states, including Michigan, Minnesota, New Jersey, and Wisconsin, and several local governments, including New York City, Sacramento County, Seattle, and Tucson have public funding for elections.

Public financing of election campaigns encourages individuals with limited fund-raising ability to seek election, reduces the influence of contributions by individuals, and permits candidates to spend most of their time campaigning instead of fund-raising. One purpose of public funding is to establish expenditure ceilings. To qualify for public funding, a candidate must agree to limit total campaign spending.

The Florida law establishing the election campaign financing trust fund requires a candidate for governor to raise $150,000 in order to be eligible for public funding, and the candidate may not expend more than five million dollars in the campaign.[59]

The Minnesota Ethical Practices Board administers the public funding of campaign programs which is financed by state income tax checkoffs. In 1990, 452 candidates (92.8% of all candidates) signed agreements with the board to abide by campaign expenditure limits in order to qualify for payments from the State Elections Campaign Fund.[60] Minnesota and Wisconsin are the only states providing significant public financing of state legislative election campaigns. No state provides funding for primary election campaigns.

The New York State Commission on Government Integrity recommended:

public funding of all statewide elections with funds raised by a check-off on state income tax set between two and four dollars per return. In the primary, there should be a system of matching small contributions. In the general election, a grant should be given to each major party candidate (with proportionate amounts based upon voter registration to any minor party fielding statewide candidates and whose candidate received more than 50,000 votes in the last election).[61]

In 1988, the New York City Council enacted local law 8 providing for partial funding of campaigns and reducing the amount an individual can contribute to a candidate for a citywide office accepting public funding from $100,000 to $6,000 and requiring contributors to disclose their home and business addresses, occupation, employer, and business address of any person who solicited the contribution.[62]

The Presidential Election Campaign Fund Act of 1966 authorizes the Federal Election Commission to distribute matching funds to presidential candidates in primary and general elections provided the candidates agree to limits on expenditures.[63] Each candidate, however, may spend a maximum of $50,000 of his/her own money on the campaign.

The nominees of the Democratic and Republican parties are each entitled to receive twenty million dollars in public funds for their election campaign adjusted for the increase in the cost of living. Since the cost-of-living index was 2.762 in 1991, each of the candidates of the two major parties in 1992 received $55.4 million.[64] In addition, $34.1 million was certified in 1992 by the Federal Election Commission for distribution to ten primary candidates and $11.048 million to each of the two major parties for their nominating conventions.[65]

REGULATION OF LOBBYISTS

The Congress and all states regulate in some manner the activities of interest or pressure groups and their representatives. Massachusetts, in 1890, was the first state to enact a law requiring lobbyists to register, and its example has been followed by thirty-two states. Lobbyists are regulated because they may engage in unethical activities to influence the actions and decisions of government officers. Although the term *lobbyist* suggests an individual who attempts to influence the policy decisions of a legislative body, state lobbyist laws often include within the definition of the term lobbying attempts to influence the decision to adopt or reject a proposed administrative rule or regulation and decision of a rate-making body of the state.[66]

Popular distrust of lobbyists has been fostered by the secret and dishonest activities of a number of lobbyists, including bribery and rewards, over the years and their exposure by the media or legislative investigating committees. Lobbyists can be ethical and can play an important role in the governance system. Legislators are faced today with highly technical issues and often lack competent staff to provide advice. An important source of such information for legislatures is the lobbyist who is aware that provision of inaccurate information and data to a legislator or a legislative committee will destroy his/her credibility.

It is difficult to draw a precise dividing line between proper and improper lobbying activities. Bills in legislatures affect the property and rights of citizens and business firms, and they clearly have the legitimate right to make their views known on specific bills to legislators. The best protection for the public is a system of regulation of paid lobbyists which ensures that their activities are exposed in broad daylight. Chapter 10 examines "revolving door" restrictions upon lobbying of agencies by their former officials.

Lobbyists not only seek to defeat or have specific bills enacted into law. In some instances, lobbyists attempt to influence the election of legislative leaders and appointment of chairs of bill reference committees. Interest groups also seek to strengthen their influence by a media campaign extending over a period of years to build public support for their positions on issues by supplying favorable information to newspaper, radio, and television editors. Public utilities in particular cultivate citizen support because their rates are regulated by a state commission.

Registration and Disclosure

The registration laws require lobbyists to identify their employers and to reveal the amount of their compensation and their expenditures. The lobbyists also may be required to file a list of the groups they represent. Regulatory laws typically prohibit the payment of a fee on a contingent basis for the enactment or defeat of a bill.[67]

Congressional lobbyists are required to register and file quarterly reports with the clerk of the House of Representatives and the clerk of the Senate.[68] Each report has an identification number and must contain (1) the name, address, and nature of business of the individual or organization; (2) the length of time the legislative interests are expected to continue; (3) the general legislative interests of the person filing the report including short titles of statutes and bills, bill numbers, citations for statutes, and position for or against each statute and bill; and (4) relative to publications issued in connection with legislative interests, a description of the publications, quantity distributed, date of distribution, name of the printer if the publications were paid for by the filer or the name of the donor if the publications were received as a gift.[69]

Lobbyists in Alabama must register with the State Ethics Commission and submit monthly reports of their activities during the period the state legislature is in session.[70] The reports must identify the bills the lobbyists are interested in, any direct business relationship that a lobbyist may have with a legislator, any loans made to a legislator or a legislative staff member by a lobbyist, and the amount expended during the previous month on lobbying activities.

In Minnesota, lobbyists must register and file reports on their principals and the amount of compensation received with the State Ethical Practices Board in order to allow officers and the public to know what interests are being represented by whom and how much money is spent to influence governmental policies.[71] A candidate for a constitutional or a legislative office or a candidate's campaign committee is forbidden by Minnesota law to solicit or accept a contribution from a registered lobbyist or a political committee other than a political party during a regular session of the state legislature. For the year ending June 30, 1991, 1,260 registered lobbyists filed 2,385 reports on behalf of 1,050 clients on each reporting date for a total of 7,150 filings for the year.[72]

The Minnesota Ethical Practices Board issues advisory opinions to lobbyists and advised one, in 1990, that payment of a bonus by a company to an employee who is a lobbyist is not "compensation which is dependent upon the result or outcome of any legislative . . . action" under Minnesota statutes, provided the payment was not discussed with the lobbyist prior to his efforts to influence legislative decisions.[73] The board also advised that the governing body of a metropolitan government unit has authority to determine what is a "major decision" for purposes of the lobbyist disclosure provisions of state law.[74]

The regulation of lobbying laws typically exempt certain individuals from the registration requirements. The New York law, for example, exempts state officials acting in their official capacity; newspapers, other periodicals, radio and television stations; and "any person who merely appears before an open meeting or public hearing of a standing committee or select committee of the Legislature, or a state agency or agencies."[75] The law also forbids an employee of the state legislature to "promote or oppose the passage of bills or resolutions by either house" outside "the scope of his legislative employment."[76]

Not surprisingly, the constitutionality of the laws requiring lobbyists to register and report information on their employers and compensation has been challenged. The Washington State Supreme Court in 1974 opined:

Informed as to the identity of the principal or a lobbyist, the members of the Legislature, other public officials, and the public may more accurately evaluate the pressures to which public officials are subjected. Forewarned of the principals behind proposed legislation, the legislator and others may appropriately evaluate the "sales pitch" of some lobbyists who claim to espouse the public weal, but, in reality, represent purely private or special interests.[77]

An appeal of the decision of the Washington State Supreme Court was dismissed by the U.S. Supreme Court.[78]

The number of lobbyists and the amount spent on lobbying has increased significantly in recent years. The New York Temporary State Commission on Lobbying, for example, reported that the number of lobbyists increased from 941 representing 569 clients in 1978 to 1,978 lobbyists representing 1,017 clients in 1991.[79] Spending on lobbying in 1991 totaled $30.3 million.

Enforcement

The lobbying registration and disclosure laws generally are enforced inadequately, and the filed reports seldom are scrutinized for their accuracy. The regulatory agency may serve primarily as a records depository because it lacks sufficient enforcement powers. It is not surprising that the regulatory body may possess little enforcement power, since the regulated lobbyists typically have great influence in a state legislature. The rationale supporting required reports is that an informed public will be able to counter the influence of lobbyists. It is obvious that the reports of lobbyists must be examined and analyzed carefully if they are to serve a useful purpose. Furthermore, it is essential that the reports be publicized widely in the media.

The New York State definition of lobbying is restrictive and prevents the Temporary State Commission on Lobbying from obtaining information on the influence exerted by lobbyists on the adoption of legislative resolutions and the decisions of administrative agencies not related directly to the adoption of rules and regulations. The New York State Commission recommends that the state legislature redefine the term lobbying to mean "communicating directly or soliciting others to communicate with any official, or staff person of any official, in the legislative or executive branch of government for the purpose of influencing any legislative, administrative, or official action to be taken by that official or staff person."[80]

State officials often are not required to register as lobbyists even though they engage in lobbying activities. The New York State Commission recommends that the lobbying act "should be amended to require state agency officials who lobby to register and report as legislative representatives, and the agencies themselves should be required to report as clients."[81]

FINANCIAL INTEREST DISCLOSURE

The intertwining of personal interests with the public interest is a perennial problem that can be detected in many instances by requiring public officers to file financial disclosure statements. Such requirements can be established by constitutions, statutes, initiative and referendum, municipal ordinances, and executive orders. The requirements are related closely to codes of ethics and often are included in such codes. Although the disclosures may have primarily symbolic value, they also help to sensitize public officers with respect to potential conflicts by necessitating that each officer review situations where a conflict between his/her personal interest and the public interest may develop. Furthermore, a filed financial interest disclosure statement can be used as supportive evidence if a complaint is filed against an officer.

Washington State voters approved initiative 276 in 1972 requiring disclosure of the financial interests of elected officers and lobbyists. The Washington Supreme Court, in 1974, rejected challenges to the initiative maintaining it infringed upon privacy, was impermissively too broad, and impinged on the right of a citizen to seek and hold office and the right of the electorate to choose candidates of their choice.[82]

The Illinois Supreme Court in 1974 upheld Executive Order Number 4 requiring economic disclosures by state officers and employees.[83] The New York Supreme Court, a general trial court, in 1977 invalidated executive orders issued by Governor Hugh L. Carey requiring officers earning more than $30,000 a year in exempt, noncompetitive, or unclassified positions in departments with heads appointed by the governor on the ground the orders were an unwarranted exercise of legislative power and violated the intent of the state legislature which had enacted a conflict-of-interest law.[84]

Required Disclosure

The British Local Government Act of 1972 and the standing orders of the Merseyside County Council require a member of the council, when a matter in which he has a pecuniary interest is discussed, to disclose his interest and withdraw from the meeting unless the council invited the member to remain.[85]

A different approach is taken by the Keene, New Hampshire, city charter which directs a member of the city council with a possible conflict of interest to transmit a detailed statement to the city clerk and stipulates that the council by a majority vote will determine whether there is a conflict.[86] Because a member of the council owned property the city wished to acquire and the concerned councilor discussed the matter with other councilors in private, the city charter was amended in 1981 to provide: "Even if permitted to participate in the discussion on the City Council floor, no Councilor having a conflict-of-interest may discuss the issue in which he/she has a conflict with any other Councilor in any other place or any other time."[87]

The Federal Ethics in Government Act of 1978, as amended by the Ethics Reform Act of 1989, requires specified officers and employees to file annually, by May 15th, a detailed financial report.[88] Except as noted below, reports are filed by covered officers and employees with a designated agency official. The president, vice president, governors of the board of governors of the U.S. Postal Service, designated agency officials, candidates for president and vice president, and officers whose positions require senate confirmation file their reports with the director of the Office of Government Ethics. Members of the uniformed services file their reports with the concerned secretary.

Each agency is required within thirty days of receiving a financial disclosure report to permit inspection of the report or to furnish a copy of the report. The act specifically makes it illegal for any individual to obtain or use a report:

a. for any unlawful purpose;

b. for any commercial purpose, other than news and communications media for dissemination to the general public;

c. for determining or establishing the credit rating of any individual;

d. for use, directly or indirectly, in the solicitation of money for any political, charitable, or other purpose.[89]

The Florida Constitution was amended in 1976 to require a "full and public disclosure" of financial interest of constitutional officers and candidates for such offices.[90] Full disclosure is defined as filing annually with the secretary of state a sworn statement of net worth and identifying each asset and liability in excess of $1,000 and its value, plus a copy of the individual's most recent federal income tax return or a sworn statement of each source and the amount of income from each source exceeding $1,000.

The Minnesota Code of Ethics requires a public officer to disclose publicly a pending official action or decision presenting a potential conflict of interest because the action or decision will affect the financial interests of the officer or the interests of a business firm with which he/she is associated.[91] The potential conflict-of-interest notice must be filed with the officer's immediate superior who must assign the matter to another officer not having a potential conflict of interest. If the officer has no immediate superior, the officer must assign the matter to a subordinate or request the appointing authority to designate another officer to determine the matter. If the officer with a potential conflict is a legislator, he/she may request the legislative body to excuse the legislator from participating in the action or decision. Minnesota also requires a public office to file a representation disclosure statement with the State Ethical Practices Board (within fourteen days of a hearing) if the officer represented a client for a fee at a hearing conducted by a state board, agency, or commission, in order to establish a public record of such representation.[92]

Minnesota also requires reporting of all compensation in excess of fifty dollars a month as an officer, director, owner, member, partner, employee, employer, trustee, or beneficiary of a trust, but does not require reporting of alimony, child support payments, social security payments, unemployment compensation, or workers' compensation.[93] The code also excludes reporting of savings accounts, money market certificates, treasury bills, bonds, notes, dividends, or shares in a pension fund.

In drafting a financial interest disclosure law, consideration should be given to the question of whether the requirement should mandate the listing in detail of all the assets of the covered officials and employees. The requirements in Rockville, Maryland, answer this question by providing that "a savings account in a bank or other savings institution, or an insurance policy, are not considered to be a financial interest in the bank, institution, or insurance company and should not be reported."[94] In addition, "ownership of tangible personal property should not be reported unless it is used for income producing purposes."

A mandated disclosure requirement preferably should be restricted to a listing of sources of income and should not include the amounts, other than possibly indicating whether they exceed a specified sum, received from each source. The New York State Board of Public Disclosure in 1976 exempted members of the Board of the State Municipal Assistance Corporation, who are part-time officers, from the state requirement that the officers disclose the value of their assets.[95] Nevertheless, the officers must identify their assets without disclosing their value.

The Common Cause Model Conflict-of-Interest Act requires public officers to identify the following interests involving themselves, their spouses and their dependent children if they held a 10 percent or greater equity interest in any business firm during the preceding year:

1. The name, address, nature of association, and amount of interest in any business with which he was associated and in any entity in which a position as trustee was held; and, if the business or entity has done business or been regulated by the state or any political subdivision thereof, the date and nature of such business or regulation;

2. The name, address, and nature of business of any person from whom income in the value of $1,000 or more was received, the nature of services rendered, the amount, and, if the person has done business with or been regulated by the state or any political subdivision thereof, the date and nature of such business or regulation; provided that the source of any income received for mental health services need not be included;

3. Legal description of all real property in the state, the fair market value of which exceeds $2,500, in which a direct or indirect financial interest was held, and, if the property was transferred during the preceding calendar year, a statement of the amount and nature of the consideration received or paid in exchange for such interest, and the name and address of the person furnishing or receiving such consideration;

4. The name and address of each creditor to whom the value of $1,000 or more was owed and the original amount, the amount outstanding, the terms of repayment, and the security given for each such debt; provided that debts arising out of retail installment transactions need not be included;

5. The nature and amount of any interest of $1,000 or more in a time or demand deposit in a financial institution or in an insurance or endowment policy or annuity contract;

6. The name and address of any person from whom a gift or gifts valued in the aggregate of $25 or more were received, and the value and the circumstances of each gift; and

7. Such other information as the person required to file the statement or the commission deems necessary to carry out the purposes of this act.

Thomas S. Belford and Bruce Adams of Common Cause maintain the resignation of certain public officers may promote the public interest. They wrote, "certain self-serving realtors, lawyers, and developers who sit on planning boards, for example, might resign rather than disclose and be replaced by people committed to sound planning rather than high profits."[96]

The Model State Conflict-of-Interest and Financial Disclosure Law requires state officials and candidates and members of their households to disclose their economic interest in terms of four categories: "Category I, less than $5,000; Category II, $5,000-$24,999; Category III, $25,000-$99,999; and Category IV, $100,000 or more."[97] This type of requirement alerts the commission and citizens to identify possible major or potential conflicts of interest, including the use of confidential information.

The Model Law also requires the reporting of the names of household members and the "names under which any of them do business," a listing of direct and indirect interests in real property, a listing of securities, the names and addresses of creditors if covered individuals have a debt exceeding $1,000 during the previous year (except a credit card or retail installment contract), names and addresses of individuals or businesses making payments exceeding $1,000, names and addresses of businesses or governmental clients if the officer or a household member is an officer, director, partner, or has an equity interest exceeding a specified percent, and a listing of all gifts exceeding a specified dollar value from individuals "other than relatives or a person to whom the state official or candidate is engaged or intends to marry."[98]

According recognition to the fact that a blanket prohibition of ownership of stock in a corporation doing business with the town would be unfair, the Bel Air, Maryland, Code of Ethics stipulates in section 22-4(b)(4) that the Board of Ethics,

with the unanimous approval of the Commissioners of Bel Air, may specifically authorize any town official or employee to own stock in any corporation or to maintain a business in connection with an entity participating in any transaction of the town if, upon full disclosure of all pertinent facts by such official or employee to the Board and the Commissioners, both the Board and the Commissioners determine unanimously that such stock ownership does not violate the public interest.

Drafters of local government financial disclosure requirements should consider exempting certain officers and employees from the requirement because it not only would be an unnecessary invasion of privacy in certain cases, but also could result in a significant number of officers and employees resigning their positions. Many individuals may refuse to accept an appointive position because they consider disclosure to be an inordinate burden. Local government in small communities is to a large extent part-time citizen government, relying upon volunteers serving without compensation or receiving only minor stipends. Who would be willing to serve on a village planning board if members must make a complete disclosure of their personal and family finances? Service on a nonpaid board or commission represents a sacrifice of time and money. A disclosure requirement might make the sacrifice too great for many competent individuals. The code of ethics might include a provision similar to Rule 151 of the British House of Commons: "A member may not vote on any question in which he has a direct financial interest. If he votes on such question, his vote may, on motion, be disallowed."

The Greenbelt, Maryland City Code—Art. VI, § 2-38—requires only members and candidates for the city council and the city manager to file annually a statement of financial interest. The Arlington County, Virginia, Board adopted an ordinance requiring board members and the county manager to file annually with the clerk of the board a report of financial interests. The manager is directed to issue an executive order requiring "heads of County Departments, and such other employees as he deems advisable" to file a similar report.

A state government financial disclosure requirement also may make the recruitment of high-level officials difficult. Governor Hugh L. Carey of New York issued Executive Order Number 10 in 1975, requiring an annual public disclosure of finances of all employees in exempt, noncompetitive, or unclassified positions in the executive branch earning in excess of $30,000 annually and heads of state departments and agencies appointed by the governor. In addition, the approximately 2,000 covered officers were forbidden to hold a second position with a government or a private firm. In 1976, the governor expanded the coverage of the disclosure requirement by issuing Executive Order Number 10.1, covering more than 10,000 employees in "managerial or confidential positions" earning more than $30,000 annually.

Many highly qualified businessmen and professionals, earning a substantial salary in private employment, concluded that the governor was asking them to make too big a sacrifice by requiring a public disclosure of their personal finances should they accept a lower-paying state position. Because of recruitment problems, the governor persuaded several legislators of his political party to resign from the state legislature to become eligible for positions in the executive branch.

In recent years, there has been a tendency for candidates for major offices to disclose their finances voluntarily to ensure voters that the candidates do not have conflicts of interest or arrange to have their finances handled by a blind trust for the period they hold office. In 1984, Democratic vice-presidential candidate Geraldine A. Ferraro, for example, released detailed records of her and her husband's finances.[99]

Enforcement

A financial disclosure law will be most effective if it is drafted carefully, is enforced by an independent commission, citizens are granted standing to sue in the event the commission fails to enforce the law, and civil and criminal penalties are authorized as punishment for violations of the law.

Any citizen should be authorized to file a sworn complaint with the commission which must investigate the complaint. If the commission finds there has been a violation of the law, the commission should be authorized to order the violator(s) to cease and desist the violation and to bring a criminal prosecution if the facts warrant prosecution.

The effectiveness of the mandatory financial disclosure requirements will be enhanced if an independent and permanent board or commission is responsible for administering the disclosure law. Members of the board, five or seven, should be forbidden to hold any other public office or be employed by a government to ensure their independence. At the state level, the governor should appoint the members with the advice and consent of the Senate, and no more than a simple majority of the members should be members of the same political party. Members should be subject to removal only for cause and after a public hearing. Adequate staff for processing the filed reports, auditing the reports, and conducting field investigations is essential.

As noted in Chapter 3, the administering board can be the board of ethics. In common with the usual function of a board of ethics, the administering board should be authorized to issue advisory opinions on its own initiative and in response to requests. The Minnesota Ethical Practices Board, for example, is responsible for administering the corrupt practices act and the law requiring public officers and employees to file financial disclosure statements and lobbyists to register and disclose information relative to their principals. The six-member board is appointed by the governor with confirmation by a three-fifths vote of each house of the state legislature. No more than three members may belong to the same political party and there must be one former legislator representing each major political party and two individuals who have not been a public officer or political party officer for at least three years prior to appointment to the board. The board's jurisdiction extends to all state and local government employees and officers.

The State-City Commission on Integrity in Government in New York recommended that its proposed Commission on Ethics should be responsible also for administering the campaign finance reports "because campaign contributions may conveniently take the place of otherwise illegal gifts."[100] The State-City Commission suggested that the Commission on Ethics also should be responsible for administration of state regulation of lobbying.

If more than one board or commission is responsible for administering the campaign finance, lobbying, and financial disclosure requirements, it is essential that provisions be made in law for coordination of the boards' activities and the exchange of information.

Members of Congress and state legislators who violate financial disclosure laws are subject to disciplinary proceedings by their respective houses. In 1984, the U.S. House of Representatives voted to reprimand Representative George Hansen of Idaho for withholding information on his wife's financial transactions which were undertaken to assist the Hansens to solve their debt problems.[101] Earlier, a jury convicted the representative on four felony charges relating to the matter.

In the same year, the House Ethics Committee found Representative Geraldine Ferraro of New York, the 1984 Democratic vice-presidential candidate, guilty of violating the Ethics in Government Act a minimum of ten times, but did not recommend formal House action against her because she was retiring from the House.[102]

SUMMARY AND CONCLUSIONS

Constitutional, statutory, and executive order provisions requiring the reporting and public disclosure of campaign finance, lobbying expenditures, and personal finances of government officials and employees are premised upon the belief that an informed public can play a major role in ensuring that governmental policy-making and administration are conducted in an ethical manner that protects the interests of the citizenry. While the mandatory information disclosure requirements have been helpful, their effectiveness has been limited in many jurisdictions by loose requirements, little or no efforts to determine the accuracy of the filed information, limited enforcement action, and often inadequate publicity in the media.

This chapter has identified the weaknesses in the reporting requirements and presented recommendations to improve the governance system by ensuring that all actions are in accordance with high ethical standards. Chapter 5 examines freedom of information laws which supplement the mandatory information disclosure requirements by making government information and data, with limited exceptions, available to the public.

NOTES

1. The requirement in many states that an individual must pay a poll tax in order to vote in elections was nullified by the twenty-fourth amendment to the U.S. Constitution.

2. *The Quest for an Ethical Environment* (New York: State-City Commission on Integrity in Government, 1986), p. 5.

3. *Buckley v. Valeo*, 424 U.S. 1 (1976). See also Marlene A. Nicholson, "Basic Principles or Theoretical Tangles: Analyzing the Constitutionality of Government Regulation of Campaign Finance," *Case Western Law Review*, vol. XXXVIII, no. 4, 1987-88, pp. 589–607.

4. *Buckley v. Valeo*, 424 U.S. 1 at 143.

5. Ibid. at 39.

6. Ibid. at 52.

7. Ibid. at 52–53.

8. *First National Bank of Boston, et al. v. Bellotti*, 435 U.S. 765 (1978).

9. Toni Locy, "Tobacco Firms Pay $4.5m to Fight Tax," *The Boston Globe*, September 5, 1992, pp. 1 and 24.

10. Ibid., p. 24.

11. Minnesota Statutes Annotated, § 10A.02(8) (1988 and 1993 Supp.).

12. Model State Campaign Finance Law (New York: National Municipal League, 1979), pp. 3–4.

13. Ibid., p. 12.

14. Ibid., p. 14.

15 Ibid., p. 15.

16. *Annual Report* (St. Paul: Minnesota Ethical Practices Board, 1991), p. 11.

17. Election Campaign Act Amendments of 1974, 88 Stat. 1263, 18 U.S.C. § 608 (1975 Supp.).

18. Kenneth A. Gross, "The Enforcement of Campaign Finance Rules: A System in Search of Reform," *Yale Law & Policy Review*, vol. IX, no. 2, 1991, p. 279.

19. Model State Campaign Finance Law, pp. 3–4.

20. Ibid., p. 4.

21. Ibid., p. 17.

22. Ibid., p. 21.

23. Ibid., pp. 27–28.

24. Ibid., p. 30.

25. Ibid., p. 38.

26. Ibid., p. 31.

27. *Annual Report* (Minnesota), p. 6.

28. *The Albany Money Machine: Campaign Financing for New York State Legislative Races* (New York: New York State Commission on Integrity in Government, 1988), p. 15.

29. Ibid., p. 39; and *First National Bank of Boston v. Bellotti*, 435 U.S. 765 (1978).

30. Federal Election Campaign Act of 1974, 88 Stat. 1263, 2 U.S.C. §§ 441(1) and 441(a)(2) (1985).

31. *Buettell et al. v. Walker*, 319 N.E.2d 502 (1974).

32. Richard G. Smolka, "Election Legislation, 1990-91," *The Book of the States 1992-93* (Lexington, Ky: The Council of State Governments, 1992), p. 263.

33. Ibid.

34. Ibid.

35. Model State Campaign Finance Law, pp. 40–43.

36. *The Albany Money Machine*, pp. 25–26.

37. Common Cause Model Conflict-of-Interest Act, §§ 10(a) and 11(c). The act is contained in the *Municipal Year Book 1975* (Washington, D.C.: International City Management Association, 1975), pp. 176–79.

38. *New York Election Law*, § 14-114(1)(a) (1978).

39. Ibid., § 14-116(2) (1978 and 1992 Supp.).

40. *Unfinished Business: Campaign Finance Reform in New York City* (New York: New York State Commission on Government Integrity, 1988), pp. 15–16.

41. *Report on a Bill on Campaign Financing and Public Funding of Election Campaigns* (New York: State-City Commission on Integrity in Government, 1986), p. 6.

42. "FEC Imposes Civil Penalties for Violations of the $25,000 Annual Limit," *Record* (Federal Election Commission), April 1993, pp. 1 and 3.

43. Peter Kerr, "Campaign Donations Overwhelm Monitoring Agencies in the States," *The New York Times*, December 27, 1988, pp. 1 and B2.

44. Ibid., p. 1.

45. *Campaign Financing: Preliminary Report* (New York: New York State Commission on Government Integrity, 1987), pp. 2–3.

46. Harvey Lipman, "Campaign Ignores Filing Deadlines," *Times Union* (Albany, New York), November 8, 1993, p. A-5.

47. Ibid., p. 3.

48. John Herbers, "Demand for Ethics in Government Has Outstripped Supply," *The New York Times*, June 19, 1988, p. E4.

49. John A. Farrell, "Campaign Says Dentist Solicitation Improper," *The Boston Globe*, October 28, 1987, p. 9.

50. "Shameful Shakedown," *The Keene Sentinel*, September 15, 1987, p. 4.

51. Paul Taylor, "Boston Mayor Off the Cakewalk," *Newsday*, January 10, 1983, p. 7.

52. Kevin Sack, "The Great Incumbency Machine," *The New York Times Magazine*, September 27, 1992, pp. 47–49, 52, 54, and 62.

53. Joshua Goldstein, *The $43 Million Loophole: Soft Money in the 1990 Congressional Elections* (Washington, D.C.: Center for Responsive Politics, 1991), pp. 10–11.

54. *United States Senate Report Number 193*, 90th Congress, 1st. Session (Washington, D.C.: United States Government Printing Office, 1967), p. 27.

55. *Investigation of Senator Alan Cranston* (Washington, D.C.: United States Senate Select Committee on Ethics, 1991), vols. I-II.

56. Ibid., vol. I, p. 57.

57. Sam H. Verhovek, "Incumbent Legislators Face Few Primary Challenges," *The New York Times*, September 15, 1992, p. B6.

58. "The Ethics Window," *The New York Times*, March 21, 1993, p. 16E.

59. Florida Laws of 1991, chap. 91-107; and Florida Statutes Annotated, § 106.32 (1992).

60. *Annual Report* (Minnesota), p. 6.

61. *Campaign Financing: Preliminary Report*, pp. 39–40.

62. New York City Local Law 8 of 1988 and New York City Administrative Code, §§ 3-701 to 3-714.

63. Presidential Election Campaign Fund Act of 1966, 85 Stat. 563, 26 U.S.C. §§ 6096 and 9001 (1991).

64. Federal Election Commission Record, September 1992, p. 4.

65. Ibid.

66. For an example, see New York Legislative Law, § 3(c) note (McKinney 1991).

67. New York Legislative Law, § 11 note (McKinney 1991).

68. Regulation of Lobbying Act of 1946, 60 Stat. 839, 2 U.S.C. §§ 261 and 288d (1985 and 1992 Supp.).

69. For detailed information on reports filed, see the *Congressional Record*, September 9, 1992, pp. HL 201-HL 292.

70. Alabama Act No. 1056 of 1973; and Code of Alabama, § 36-25-18 (1991).

71. Minnesota Statutes Annotated, chap. 10A (1988 and 1993 Supp.).

72. *Annual Report* (Minnesota), p. 8.

73. Ibid., p. 11.

74. Ibid., p. 12.

75. New York Legislative Law, § 3(c)(1-5) note (McKinney 1991).

76. Ibid., § 66-a (1991).

77. *Fritz v. Gorton*, 411 P2d 911 at 931 (1974).

78. *Fritz v. Gorton*, 417 U.S. 902 (1974).

79. *Annual Report* (Albany: New York Temporary State Commission on Lobbying, 1991), p. 4.

80. Ibid., p. 8.

81. Ibid., p. 9.

82. *Fritz v. Gorton*, 411 P2d 911 (1974).

83. *Illinois State Employees Association v. Walker*, 57 Ill.2d 512, 315 N.E.2d 9 (1974).

84. *Rapp v. Carey*, 390 N.Y.S.2d 573 (1977).

85. United Kingdom Local Government Act, 1972, par. 94; and Merseyside County Council Standing Orders, par. 37.

86. Keene (New Hampshire) City Charter, § 26.

87. Ibid.

88. Ethics in Government Act of 1978, 92 Stat. 1880, 5 U.S.C. § 5332 (1985); and Ethics Reform Act of 1989, 103 Stat 1716, 5 U.S.C. app. § 101 note (1993 Supp.).

89. Ethics Reform Act of 1989, 103 Stat. 1738, 5 U.S.C. app. § 105 (1993 Supp.).

90. Constitution of Florida, art. II, § 8(a).

91. Minnesota Statutes Annotated, § 10A.02(8) (1988 and 1993 Supp.).

92. Ibid.

93. Ibid.

94. Information/Instruction Sheet, City of Rockville (Maryland) Statement of Employment and Financial Interest.

95. Ronald Smothers, "M.A.C. Employees Exempt on Assets," *The New York Times*, June 18, 1976, p. D12.

96. Thomas S. Belford and Bruce Adams, "Conflict-of-Interest Legislation and the Common Cause Model Act," *The Municipal Year Book 1975* (Washington, D.C.: International City Management Association, 1975), p. 172.

97. *Model State Conflict-of-Interest and Financial Disclosure Law* (New York: National Municipal League, 1979), p. 17.

98. Ibid., pp. 18–24.

99. Jeff Gerth, "Ferraro Opens Her Tax Figures and Husband's," *The New York Times*, August 21, 1984, pp. 1 and B8.

100. *Report and Recommendations on Conflict-of-Interest and Financial Disclosure Requirements* (New York: State-City Commission on Integrity in Government, 1986), p. 8.

101. Steven V. Roberts, "House Reprimands Idaho Republican in Financial Disclosure Case," *The New York Times*, August 1, 1984, p. A14.

102. Jane Perlex, "House Panel Reports Ferraro Violated Ethics Law," *The New York Times*, December 5, 1984, pp. 1 and A20.

Chapter 5

Freedom of Information

Democratic government is premised upon informed and widespread citizen participation. The purposeful withholding of information by governments on their activities, with the exceptions of certain sensitive matters, frustrates the operation of a democratic system and raises important ethical questions. A governmental policy of nondisclosure of information on important policy issues and bureaucratic operations denies the interested citizen the knowledge needed to form and express intelligent opinions designed to influence the decision-making process and may facilitate, as well as hide, unethical behavior by elected officers and bureaucrats. Furthermore, as Francis E. Rourke pointed out, classifying information as confidential may promote "bureaucratic power interests if it helps create a mystique of expertise—a reputation that would be seriously damaged by public discovery of the fact that a good deal of information locked away in an agency's vaults is purely routine or even inaccurate data."[1]

All governments have a legitimate need to keep a small number of types of information confidential. No one denies the fact that national security dictates the classification of certain information, yet questions can be raised as to whether there is a genuine national security reason for the withholding of information on specific activities by military authorities. There also is general agreement that law enforcement bodies need to keep certain information confidential and that disciplinary investigations of civil servants should be conducted in closed sessions. Plans for government purchases of large tracts of land and construction of major public works have to be kept secret initially to prevent land speculators from profiting from knowledge of planned governmental actions.

The New Zealand Freedom of Information Act identifies each of the following as a "good reason" for withholding official information if disclosed "would be likely":

a. To prejudice the security or defence of New Zealand or the international relations of the Government of New Zealand; or
b. To prejudice the entrusting of information to the Government of New Zealand on a basis of confidence by—
   i. The government of any other country or any agency of such a government; or
   ii. Any international organization; or
c. To prejudice the maintenance of the law, including the prevention, investigation, and detection of offences and the right to a fair trial; or
d. To damage seriously the economy of New Zealand by disclosing prematurely Government economic or financial policies, such as those relating to—
   i. Exchange rates or the control of overseas exchange transactions;
   ii. The regulation of banking or credit;
   iii. Taxation;
   iv. The stability, control, and adjustment of prices of goods and services, rents, and other costs, and rates of wages, salaries, and other incomes;
   v. The borrowing of money by the Government of New Zealand; or
   vi. The entering into of overseas trade agreements.[2]

Sweden has four constitutional documents. The Freedom of the Press Act stresses the encouragement of the free interchange of opinion and provides that access to official documents may be restricted only relative to:

1. The security of the Realm or its relations with a foreign state of an international organisation;
2. The central finance policy, monetary policy, or foreign exchange policy of the Realm;
3. The inspection, control, or other supervisory activities of a public authority;
4. The interest of preventing or prosecuting crime;
5. The public economic interest;
6. The protection of the personal integrity or economic conditions of private subjects;
7. The preservation of animal or plant species.[3]

Governmental secrecy may be justified by the need to protect the privacy of citizens and the trade secrets of business firms. In a democratic society, the citizen should be guaranteed protection against invasion of personal privacy. A government clearly has a legitimate need for information of a personal nature on citizens, but must initiate action to ensure such information will not be disclosed in a manner constituting invasion of personal privacy. Similarly, public disclosure of all government information on private commercial and industrial firms could harm seriously the profitability of many firms.

Determining the extent of the most desirable degree of citizen access to official information is a difficult task. An Irish Department of Public Service circular cautions public officers and employees that "particular care should be taken to avoid releasing official information in the course of informal or unguarded conversations."[4] Standing orders of the Merseyside County Council in England provide that "no member shall disclose to any person the whole or part of the contents of any agenda, report, or other document which is marked 'Private and Confidential' unless the document has been made available to the public or the press by or on behalf of the Council or committee." In Greece, the public officer or employee "is expected to preserve the confidentiality of events or information made known to him in the course of carrying out his duties."[5]

The Campaign for Freedom of Information submitted a memorandum to a parliamentary committee in the United Kingdom advancing three major arguments in support of a freedom of information statute:

First, simply because Britain has become excessively secretive to the point where it is (a) difficult for the public to appreciate where power and influence lies, (b) possible for public servants not to be properly accountable, (c) impossible for the public to participate effectively, (d) possible for justice not to be seen to be done, and (e) possible for error and inefficiency to increase and remain undetected.

Second, the quality of policy making would be improved if all of the information developed for the formulation of policy were open to wider analysis, correction, or criticism.

Third, the more it can be possible for the public to understand what is being done and why, the more likely it will be that a national consensus can be developed on major issues.[6]

In 1986, the government of the United Kingdom rejected a proposal for granting citizens "new statutory rights of access to government information" and was not convinced that the release of additional information "would make for more effective government."[7]

Purposeful delay in providing information in response to requests by citizens is unethical. There is no ready solution to this problem. In 1980, Prime Minister George Rallis of Greece stated that the refusal of government employees to provide information over the telephone was a remnant of the mentality of the "employee-satrap."[8] He added that the provision of information via the telephone facilitates and expedites communications between the government and the citizenry, and every public employee has the obligation to provide information willingly and politely. Should his/her department not be the appropriate one, the employee must inform the citizen of the proper department to contact and, if possible, its telephone number.

So-called "sunshine" laws are designed not only to open records and official meetings to the public, but also seek to ensure that high ethical standards are maintained by public officers and employees by making most of their activities visible to the citizenry. These laws are traceable in origin to corrupt practices acts, examined in Chapter 4, regulating campaign finance and requiring public disclosure by candidates for elective office and campaign committee of detailed information on contributions and expenditures. In general, the corrupt practices acts have not been enforced vigorously and penalties seldom have been imposed for failure to disclose all information or file reports on time. "Sunshine" provisions can be included in a code of ethics since their inclusion may reduce the opportunity for unethical actions by officers and employees, and build public confidence in their integrity.

In addition to examining a freedom of information statute for provisions authorizing the withholding of certain types of information, it is essential to examine other statutes authorizing the withholding of information. The U.S. Internal Revenue Code's Confidentiality and Disclosure of Returns and Return Information Act permits the withholding of information.[9] Whereas the Florida Public Records Law contains only a few general exemptions, other statutes make specific records confidential.[10]

Citizen ease of obtaining information on public activities varies from government to government with U.S. government information, with specified exceptions, generally accessible readily. A similar situation prevails in most states and many local governments in the United States. The most hidden world is the world of public authorities. Donald Axelrod wrote (1992) that "these independent bodies have become the backdoor government, the invisible government, the shadow government."[11]

FREEDOM OF INFORMATION STATUTES

The U.S. Congress and state legislatures have enacted freedom of information statutes. The coverage of the statutes, bureaucratic cooperation or obstructionism, and the degree of conflict of these statutes with privacy statutes vary considerably.

The National Statute

Citizen participation in government obviously is promoted if information is freely available in a readily accessible form. The national government collected a relatively small amount of information, other than decennial census data, until the 1930s. The volume of government information increased sharply as New Deal programs were initiated in the 1930s. Noting the great increase in executive orders and administrative rules and regulations, Erwin N. Griswold in 1934 issued a plea for better publication of such legislation.[12] The Congress responded with the Federal Register Act of 1935 and the Code of Federal Regulations Amendments of 1937, with the Federal Register providing notice of proposed and promulgated rules and regulations, and the Code of Federal Regulations containing the codified rules and regulations.[13]

The great growth of the national government during the New Deal and World War II included a proliferation of agencies which issue administrative rules and regulations. To systematize the system, the Congress enacted the Administrative Procedure Act of 1946 which established uniform standards for administrative actions affecting the public, provided for public participation in rule-making activities, and required "agencies to keep the public currently informed of their organization, procedures, and rules."[14]

With the development of the cold war and the fear of communism, there was a startling increase in information withheld from the public. Section 3 of the Administrative Procedure Act was titled "Public Information," yet the section "has been used as an authority for withholding, rather than disclosing information. Such a 180-degree turn was easy to accomplish given the broad language of 5 U.S.C. § 1002."[15] The act contained no provision authorizing citizens to force government officials to disclose information.

The House of Representatives' Committee on Government Operations in 1966 reported:

The statutory requirements that information about routine administrative actions need be given only to "persons properly and directly concerned" has been relied upon almost daily to withhold Government information from the public. A most striking example is the almost automatic refusal to disclose the names and salaries of Federal employees. . . .

If none of the other restrictive phrases of 5 U.S.C. § 1002 applies to the official Government record which an agency wishes to keep confidential, it can be hidden behind the "good cause found" shield. Historically, Government agencies whose mistakes cannot bear public scrutiny have found "good cause" for secrecy. A recurring example is the refusal by regulatory boards and commissions which are composed of more than one member to make public their votes on issues or to publicize the views of dissenting members.[16]

Congress enacted the Freedom of Information Act (FOIA) in 1966 to ensure broad citizen access to records of executive department and agencies.[17] The act does not apply to the president, vice president, members of Congress, and the judiciary. The good cause withholding authorization of the Administrative Procedures Act was repealed and information that must be made available to citizens was expanded to include agency policy statements, interpretations, staff manuals, and instructions that affect any citizen.

To facilitate citizen location of information, each agency must maintain an index of all documents required to be made available to the public. A person making a request for information must provide a reasonable description of the requested information, but this FOIA requirement cannot be used as a reason for withholding information. Each agency is directed to adopt a reasonable access rule which lists the place and time where records are available and fees for a records search or copying.

The national government does not maintain a central index of records on individual citizens. If an individual wishes to examine government records concerning him/her, the citizen must identify the department or agency with such records. A veteran of the armed forces, for example, would be aware that the Department of Veteran Affairs or the Department of Defense would have such records. In other instances, it may be difficult for a citizen to determine the departments and agencies which hold such records.

FOIA recognizes the importance of keeping certain types of information confidential and stipulates that the act "does not apply to matters that are"

1. (a) Specifically authorized under criteria established by an Executive Order to be kept secret in the interest of national defense or foreign policy and (b) are in fact properly classified pursuant to such Executive Order;

2. Related solely to the internal personnel rules and practices of an agency;

3. Specifically exempted from disclosure by statute (other than section 552b of this title), provided that such statute (a) requires that the matters be withheld from the public in such a manner as to leave no discretion on the issue, or (b) establishes particular criteria for withholding or refers to particular types of matters to be withheld;

4. Trade secrets and commercial or financial information obtained from a person and privileged or confidential;

5. Inter-agency or intra-agency memorandums or letters which would not be available by law to a party other than an agency in litigation with the agency;

6. Personnel and medical files and similar files the disclosure of which would constitute a clearly unwarranted invasion of personal privacy;

7. Records or information compiled for law enforcement purposes, but only to the extent that the production of such law enforcement records or information (a) could reasonably be expected to interfere with enforcement proceedings, (b) would deprive a person of a right to a fair trial or an impartial adjudication, (c) could reasonably be expected to constitute an unwarranted invasion of personal privacy, (d) could reasonably be expected to disclose the identity of a confidential source, including a State, local, or foreign agency or authority or any private institution which furnished information on a confidential basis, and, in the case of a record or information compiled by criminal law enforcement authority in the course of a criminal investigation or by an agency conducting a lawful national security intelligence investigation, information furnished by a confidential source, (e) would disclose techniques and procedures for law enforcement investigations or prosecutions, or would disclose guidelines for law enforcement investigations or prosecutions if such disclosure could reasonably be expected to risk circumvention of the law, or (f) could reasonably be expected to endanger the life or physical safety of any individual;

8. Contained in or related to examination, operating, or condition reports prepared by, on behalf of, or for the use of an agency responsible for the regulation or supervision of financial institutions; or

9. Geological and geophysical information and data, including maps, concerning wells.[18]

Relative to the above exceptions, "any reasonably segregable portion of a record shall be provided to any person requesting such record after deletion of the portions which are exempt under this subsection."[19] The statute emphasizes that the section on exemptions "is not authority to withhold information from Congress."[20]

Voluminous national security information has been classified and handled by executive order since 1938 and currently is governed by

Executive Order 12356 issued by President Ronald Reagan on April 6, 1982. The Archivist of the United States is directed to review for declassification historically significant documents. The Information Security Oversight Office (ISOO) of the General Services Administration monitors the national security information program and issued Directive No. 1 stipulating that systematic reviews generally would commence thirty years after documents were generated.

Executive Order 11652, issued by President Richard M. Nixon on March 8, 1972, provided for lowering the classification of national security information automatically as follows: ten years for top secret, eight years for secret, and six years for confidential information. ISOO discovered that automatic declassification did not function as intended, and Executive Order 12356 replaced the system by providing that such materials will remain classified "as long as required by national security considerations," but the initial classification, to the extent possible, must set a specific date for declassification.

A 1993 report by the U.S. General Accounting Office revealed:

Of the more than 1.9 million pages examined under mandatory reviews from 1984 through 1992, 53 percent were declassified in full and 39 percent were declassified in part. Furthermore, another 93 percent of 260,000 pages reviewed again pursuant to appeal were declassified in full or in part during this period. This high percentage indicates that long retention periods prior to declassification may not be warranted.[21]

In 1987, President Ronald Reagan issued Executive Order No. 12600—containing "Predisclosure Notification Procedures for Confidential Commercial Information"—which direct heads of agencies to establish procedures to notify submitters of confidential commercial information that a Freedom of Information Act request has been made for the information. Section 2(b) authorizes the heads of agencies to allow submitters of such information to designate at the time of submittal "or a reasonable time thereafter," information which would cause "substantial competitive harm" if disclosed. In addition, the procedures can allow the submitter a reasonable period of time to object to the disclosure of submitted information. In the event a requester brings a suit to force disclosure of confidential commercial information, the concerned agency must notify promptly the submitter.

The investigatory file exemption in the 1966 Act could be used to hide unethical and unlawful activities by law enforcement agencies. The exemption was interpreted broadly by the U.S. Court of Appeals for the

District of Columbia Circuit in several decisions in 1973 and 1974. A citizen sought Federal Bureau of Investigation (FBI) records relative to the spectrographic analysis of the bullet that killed President John F. Kennedy. The court opined that the documents were not accessible because they were compiled by the FBI for law enforcement purposes.[22] Similarly, the same court held that the Department of Defense did not have to release records relative to the My Lai massacre.[23] In addition, the same court ruled that letters exchanged by the National Highway Traffic Safety Administration and motor vehicle manufacturers relative to potential vehicle safety defects were protected by exemption 7.[24]

The Congress was disturbed by the court's decisions and amended the act in 1974 to specify that exemption 7 applies only to records compiled for law enforcement in specific instances where release of the document would cause harm.[25]

FOIA also is designed to ensure agency compliance with request for information by (1) granting standing to any person to file a complaint in the U.S. District Court "in the district in which the complainant resides, or has his principal place of business, or in which the agency records are situated, or in the District of Columbia. . . ," (2) requiring the concerned agency to respond to the complaint within thirty days, and (3) assigning docketing priority to the case.[26]

FOIA places the burden of proof on the agency withholding the information.[27] Nevertheless, the agency has the advantage of knowing the precise contents of information withheld in contrast to the plaintiff who may have to speculate about the content. Don Lively noted that "worse yet, when faced with a conclusory and generalized exemption claim, a plaintiff is further handicapped in attempting to secure a meaningful basis for testing or rebutting the agency assertion. Similarly, without more, a court can not meaningfully review the basis for nondisclosure."[28]

Bureaucratic Opposition. Freedom of information statutes encounter strong opposition from a number of bureaucrats who prefer operating in camera. Such opposition raises serious ethical questions. Samuel J. Archibald, staff director of the House Special Subcommittee on Government Information from 1955 to 1966, reported in 1979 that bureaucrats:

developed secrecy by delay, taking many weeks to answer an initial request for access to a public record. They developed secrecy by dollars, charging far in excess of costs for copying public records. They used the investigatory files exemption as a major shield for secrecy. The original FOI Act included nine categories of public records which might be exempt from public disclosure. One category was investigatory files compiled for law enforcement purposes. Federal agencies often claimed their public records were investigatory files even though the investigation had been completed long ago. When all else failed, federal agencies forced insistent applicants for public records to go to court.[29]

To overcome delays in providing requested information, the 1974 amendments to the act established strict time limits that agencies have met readily. Archibald concluded his article with the statement that "somewhere, deep within the memory bank of each federal agency, is some sort of mechanism that tells the bureaucrats how to keep ahead of the lawmaker."[30]

Statutes historically contained penalties for disclosure of confidential information, but no penalty for withholding information. Hence, bureaucrats had an incentive to withhold information in order to avoid a possible penalty and for other reasons, including the hiding of incompetence or wrongdoing. FOIA authorizes the District Court to assess attorney fees and other costs against the United States and if the court "issues a written finding that the circumstances surrounding the withholding raise questions whether agency personnel acted arbitrarily or capriciously with respect to the withholding, the Civil Service Commission shall promptly initiate a proceeding to determine whether disciplinary action is warranted against the officer or employee who was primarily responsible for the withholding."[31] The commission is directed to submit its findings and recommendations to the "administrative authority of the agency concerned" who is directed to "take the corrective action that the Commission recommends."[32]

In addition to promulgating rules and regulations in conformance with FOIA, federal agencies have developed informal procedures for responding to requests under FOIA. In 1992, the Subcommittee on Investigations and Oversight of the U.S. House Committee on Science, Space, and Technology uncovered a U.S. Department of Energy document providing advice to officials with respect to responding to requests for information under FOIA. Suggestions included:

At the conclusion of meetings or at the end of the day review your notes and consider whether you really need to retain them. If you do, take time to rewrite them in such a way as to minimize any adverse impact should they be publicly disclosed. Then destroy your old notes. Avoid retaining drafts of documents. Each draft constitutes a separate document potentially subject to disclosure.

Use yellow stick-ons or other similar attachable tabs to annotate personal copies of documents you wish to retain. Annotations on a document make the annotated copy a separate document potentially subject to disclosure.

If retained, yellow stick-ons would also be subject to FOIA disclosure. However, since there is no obligation under FOIA to provide documents in any particular order or relationship to each other, furnishing out of context copies of stick-ons can render any information released significantly less meaningful. In this regard, printing rather than writing in script also generally makes it harder to assign authorship (and context) to a particular note or document.[33]

Robert G. Vaughn in 1984 reported the results of his study of the effectiveness of the act and concluded:

Confronted with delay in agency response, the costs of seeking judicial review, and the courts' treatment of agency delay, requesters are left to bargain with agencies over release of the requested information. While requesters believe that agencies will eventually release all or a substantial part of the information, little is gained by seeking judicial review, and agencies have no incentive to invest methods for more rapid compliance.[34]

Recognizing that citizens would experience difficulties in understanding the complexities of the Freedom of Information Act and in determining which departments and agencies hold records on individuals, the Committee on Government Operations of the U.S. House of Representatives prepared a citizen's guide on using the act.[35]

State and Provincial Statutes

State and provincial freedom of information statutes seek to make most government information readily available to requesters, but the approach taken varies considerably. Connecticut, for example, established a Freedom of Information Commission in 1975 which enforces the freedom of information and open meeting laws.[36] The commission has broad powers to conduct investigations, adjudicate disputes relative to the release of government information, and enforce the statutes. The commission also is authorized to comment on regulations adopted by departments and agencies to implement the freedom of information law.

In common with the federal law, the burden of proof to justify the withholding of information is placed upon the agency. Robert G. Vaughn concluded that the Connecticut approach is "an administrative alternative to the federal Act that deals effectively with agency delay."[37]

The 1974 New York State Freedom of Information Law applies to all local governments as well as state agencies.[38] Each agency and each local government must publish rules making all public records available for public inspection and copying, including the times and places the records are available, fees for copies, and required procedures. In addition, each state or local government agency is required to maintain and make available to the public a detailed list by subject matter of all public records and a record of final votes by each member of every agency.

The law defines the term *record* broadly as "any information kept, held, filed, produced or reproduced by, with or for an agency or the state legislature, in any physical form whatsoever including, but not limited to, reports, statements, examinations, memoranda, opinions, folders, files, books, manuals, pamphlets, forms, papers, designs, drawings, maps, photos, letters, microfilms, computer tapes or discs, rules, regulations, or codes."[39] The New York law contrasts sharply with the federal law which applies only to executive agencies. In 1992, President George Bush transmitted to the Congress the Accountability in Government Act of 1992 which, among other things, would extend the Freedom of Information Act to the Congress and the White House.[40] The Congress took no action on the proposed law.

Critics of the New York law, however, point out that it limits the records of the state legislature subject to disclosure and records pertaining to administrative matters can be kept confidential. The Committee on Open Government, which administers the law, wrote in 1991:

we believe that statutory guarantees of access would increase public confidence in the State Legislature as an institution. Over the course of years, the disclosure of records concerning the administrative and operational functions of state and local government agencies has not infringed upon the capacity of those agencies to carry out their duties effectively.[41]

The courts have interpreted the New York law broadly. In 1978, notes made by the secretary of the New York State Board of Regents during a meeting were held to be public records subject to disclosure.[42] And in 1984, the New York Court of Appeals, the highest state court, opined that minutes of meetings of an insurance company given to the Insurance Department for examination were records within meaning of the law and subject to disclosure.[43]

Clearly, no precise dividing line can be drawn between confidential and public information, and citizens can not play a full role in the governance system if important information is withheld from them. Since confidentiality can be employed as a shield to hide unethical actions from the public, a mechanism is needed to resolve disputes regarding the disclosure of official information marked confidential in lieu of a court suit. The New

York State legislature in 1977 created the Committee on Open Government charged with developing guidelines for the release of official information by state and local government agencies, and providing advice to citizens in the event of a dispute between citizens and a government agency.[44] The committee also provides advice relative to the open meeting law.

To prevent undue encroachment on personal privacy, the Committee on Open Government may promulgate guidelines for the deletion of identifying details for specific records that are to be made available.[45] When no such guidelines have been issued, the law allows an agency or a municipality to delete identifying details when making records available. Examples of invasion of personal privacy include disclosure of medical or credit histories, personal references of applicants for employment containing information confidentially disclosed to an agency or a municipality, and parts of investigatory files compiled for law enforcement purposes.

Laws in several states contain a provision similar to the one in the New York State General Municipal Law which forbids a municipal officer to disclose confidential information acquired in the course of his/her official duties.[46] One of the functions of the Committee on Open Government is to provide advice relative to what constitutes genuine confidential information. An inquiring officer may be informed by the committee that he could disclose information that his superiors had classified as confidential solely for partisan political purposes. The committee prepared 536 opinions under the Freedom of Information Law during the period from November 12, 1990, through November 4, 1991.[47]

In common with advisory opinions issued by boards of ethics, the published opinions of the committee, with deletions to preserve the anonymity of the officer or citizen involved, provide guidance for all officers and citizens encountering similar problems in the future. Committee precedents in effect become a common law on confidential information. The committee also plays an important role by advising the state legislature and the governor of needed changes in statutes and administrative rules and regulations.

After reviewing the Connecticut and New York approaches to facilitating the release of governmental information, Robert Vaughn recommended that the Congress create an agency similar to the New York State Committee on Open Government because such an agency "would prudently begin the development of the administrative alternatives necessary to preserve the concept of freedom of information."[48]

Although freedom of information statutes were designed to open government records with specified exceptions to citizens, the statutes have been used for unintended purposes. The New York State Committee on Open Government reported in 1991 "that the Freedom of Information Law is increasingly used as a preliminary or substitute for discovery in anticipation of or during litigation."[49] Furthermore, the committee reported that state regulatory departments "are inundated with requests, largely from 'professional' users of the Law; i.e., attorneys, banks, associations, and regulated entities."[50]

The Province of Manitoba Freedom of Information Act contains several interesting provisions. The application form contains a notice that the applicant is authorized to file a complaint with the ombudsman (see Chapter 7) should the concerned department not respond to the application within thirty days.[51] If an applicant discovers that a record contains information about himself or herself, the applicant may submit to the department:

a. A written objection respecting any error or omission of fact which the applicant alleges is contained in the record, and

b. A written objection to, or explanation or interpretation of, any opinion which has been expressed by a third party about the applicant and which is contained in the record.[52]

The written objection becomes part of the official record and may not be altered or removed from the record.

If a department receives an application for a record not under the department's custody, the head of the department is directed to determine whether the record is in the custody of another department and if another department has the record to send a written notice that the request has been forwarded to the other department.[53]

Conflicts with Privacy

Protection of personal privacy against disclosure of information by governments is an essential right of citizens. This right is particularly important if the governments obtained the information illegally. Furthermore, the guarantee of privacy encourages citizens to provide accurate and complete information to governmental agencies that otherwise would not be provided.

The widespread use of computers by governments to store and process vast amounts of data on individuals and business firms presents the possibility of the invasion of personal privacy and use of confidential business information by competing firms if the computer systems are not secure. According recognition to this possibility, the Congress enacted the Computer Security Act of 1987 mandating that each national department and agency within one year establish a plan for the privacy and security of each computer.[54]

Responding to a request of Senator John Glenn, the U.S. General Accounting Office undertook in 1992 a study of security and privacy issues relating to the Internal Revenue Service's tax system modernization program. The Office identified the following concerns:

• The architecture does not describe specifics of how user identification codes and profiles will be managed to appropriate control access to taxpayer information in the system.

• Contrary to standard practice, organizational units involved in administering, developing, and testing the software that controls system security are not independent of each other.

• There is no one person or organization accountable for incorporating privacy protection features into the architecture.[55]

The Internal Revenue Code's Confidentiality and Disclosure of Returns and Return Information Act is designed to protect the private interests of filers of income tax returns.[56] The act authorizes the disclosure of returns and return information to the filer provided the secretary of the treasury determines that the disclosure does not "seriously impair" tax administration.[57] This act can conflict with the Freedom of Information Act and it is unclear whether the former act is subject to a Freedom of Information Act analysis.

"Sunshine" acts may invade personal privacy and produce a conflict between two statutes. The federal Privacy Act of 1974 forbids any department or agency to disclose any personal record in its record system to another department or agency or to another individual without consent of the subject individual with specified exceptions.[58] A subject individual may review and copy his/her records, and the act stipulates a department or agency may collect and store only information relevant and essential to accomplishing a government objective, and directs the department or agency to notify the public of the existence and character of its personal information systems. The Freedom of Information Act, on the other hand, requires departments and agencies to make executive branch records available for inspection or copying except "to the extent required to present a clearly unwarranted invasion of personal privacy. . . ."[59]

David M. O'Brien wrote in 1979 that "the Freedom of Information Act encourages agencies to err on the side of disclosure by not forbidding disclosures and by neglecting to provide incentives to safeguard personal privacy; while the Privacy Act does not supersede the Freedom of Information Act, it permits disclosures only when required."[60] He also noted that "disclosure under the Freedom of Information Act might violate the Privacy Act."

Citizens are required by law to provide sensitive personal information to various national departments and agencies, yet they have little control over the uses of such information. The Privacy Act authorizes the disclosure of certain information, but requires each department or agency to maintain a record of such disclosures. Gloria Cox concluded:

Not only can information be moved about within the federal government, but state and local as well as private organizations may also be able to obtain it. Moreover, computer matching exposes to scrutiny the records of millions of individuals about whom there is no suspicion of wrongdoing. When the probability of inaccurate information appearing in files is added, the possibility of harm is evident.[61]

The right of privacy against disclosure, including confidentiality of personal information supplied to a government, has been recognized by the U.S. Supreme Court, yet the Court has not defined fully its nature and extent.[62] In 1987, the Court reversed a decision of the Supreme Court of Pennsylvania, based upon a criminal defendant's sixth and fourteenth amendments rights under the U.S. Constitution, by opining that a defendant—charged with incest and involuntary sexual intercourse—did not have the right to search unsupervised through the Commonwealth's files for exculpatory evidence.[63]

In 1993, the U.S. District Court opined the National Highway Traffic Safety Administration could not be forced to disclose, in response to a freedom of information request from a consumer organization, the names and addresses of individuals who filed complaints relative to motor vehicle safety because the highway safety concerns were outweighed by the privacy interests of the complainants.[64]

Voters in the State of Washington in 1972 approved Initiative 276—the Public Disclosure Act—containing provisions relative to campaign finance, regulation of lobbyists, financial disclosure by public officers, and public records.[65] The freedom of information provision prohibits the disclosure of information constituting an "unreasonable" invasion of the privacy of an individual. Until 1986, the provision had been interpreted by the State Supreme Court to prohibit disclosure only of information that "was highly offensive to a reasonable person" and hence was a broad disclosure requirement.[66] In 1986, the court broadened the privacy interpretation to include information identifying "particular, identifiable individuals as somehow unique from most of society."[67] Matthew Edwards is highly critical of the court's decision because the criteria employed by the court "are ambiguous, and potentially subject to an overly broad interpretation."[68]

In 1983, the New York State legislature enacted the Personal Privacy Protection Law placing detailed requirements upon departments and agencies, mandating that the Committee on Open Government prepare and publish a directory of each record system maintained by a department or agency, and authorizing the committee to issue advisory opinions and an individual to file a request with an agency to make personal information about the individual available to the requester.[69] The committee is directed to promulgate rules for the preparation of privacy impact statements by departments and agencies which must include:

a. The name of the agency and the subdivision within the agency that will maintain the system of records, and the name or title of the system of records in which such information will be maintained;

b. The title and business address of the official within the agency responsible for the system of records;

c. Where applicable, the procedures by which a data subject [requester] may gain access to personal information pertaining to such data subject in the system of records and the procedures by which a data subject may seek to amend or correct its contents;

d. The categories and the approximate number of persons on whom records will be maintained in the system of records;

e. The categories of information which will be collected and maintained in the system of records;

f. The purposes for which each category of information within the system of records will be collected and maintained;

g. The disclsoures of personal information within the system of records that the agency will regularly make for each category of information, and the authority for such disclosures;

h. The general or specific statutory authority for the collection, maintenance, and disclosure of each category of information within the system of records;

i. Policies governing retention and timely disposal of information within the system of records in accordance with law;

j. Each and every source for each category of information within the system of records;

k. A statement indicating whether the system of records will be maintained manually, by automated data system, or both.[70]

In addition, each department and agency must establish procedures to facilitate a requester to learn whether a records system contains information pertaining to him or her and "keep an accurate accounting of the date, nature, and purpose of each disclosure of a record or personal information, and the name and address of the person or governmental unit to whom the disclosure is made."[71]

The Appellate Division of the New York State Supreme Court in 1988 opined that information in a campaign financing investigation file of the State Election Board, containing references to a political candidate that was manually compiled and not indexed electronically to permit retrieval under the candidate's name, was not personal information.[72] In the same year, the Supreme Court [a general trial court] ruled that the Building a Better New York Committee lacked statutory standing to object to the release of the State Election Board's investigatory files containing information about the committee.[73]

The New York statute reflects the concern of several states over the collection of personal information by departments and agencies and their storage, use, and dissemination of such information. These statutes are called "fair information practices" laws and require each agency to describe publicly its data-keeping systems and policies, disclose to an individual who so requests information contained in his/her personal file in the agency's records, and ensure the accuracy and completeness of personal information. These laws provide for keeping confidential certain information such as data collected by an agency as part of its active civil or criminal investigation activities.

Public concern is growing in the thirty-four states that place few or no restrictions on access to information maintained by departments of motor vehicles on owners of motor vehicles. Representative James P. Moran of Virginia reported in 1993 that there are approximately 127,815 requests annually for personal information contained in the files of the Virginia Department of Motor Vehicles and licensees are not notified that their personal information has been released.[74] In many instances, the information is sold to direct marketers, but in other instances has been used by criminals.

Similarly, technological developments in the area of telecommunications have increased the opportunities for invasion of personal privacy. Thirty-five states have enacted laws or promulgated regulations allowing telephone users to block their number from being disclosed to others by means of per call or per line blocking or both.[75] Per line blocking refers to dialing 67 every time a call is made to block the number from being transmitted to others in contrast to per line blocking which automatically prevents the number from being transmitted. A related problem involves 800 and 900 numbers as list of calls to these numbers are now generated and sold to merchandisers without the callers being notified.

SUMMARY

Freedom of information laws are essential in an age where governments collect massive amounts of data and information. Only by having access to such information can the citizens gain the necessary information to form intelligent opinions on certain issues and to exercise oversight relative to the activities of public officers and employees.

Although these laws lower the barriers to government data and information, the exceptions allowed by the laws may permit bureaucrats to frustrate the goal of full disclosure of nonconfidential data and information. Citizens have standing to seek judicial relief if their requests for information are denied, yet the time delays and the costs associated with such relief often frustrate the citizens' attempts to obtain information.

Freedom of information statutes also may result in an invasion of personal privacy if certain types of data and information are released to the general public. Most governmental jurisdictions operate under a freedom of information act and a privacy act, and public officers have the difficult task of balancing the mandate to open government records to the public and the mandate to protect the privacy of citizens. One approach to solving this dilemma is the creation of a committee on open government, similar to the one in New York State, to provide advice on freedom of information and personal privacy.

Another type of "sunshine" statute is designed to ensure that meetings of public bodies, with specified exceptions, are open to the public and that decisions are not made in camera. Chapter 6 examines open meeting laws and problems associated with their implementation.

NOTES

1. Francis E. Rourke, "Bureaucratic Secrecy and Its Constituents," *The Bureaucrat*, Summer 1972, p. 117.
2. Official Information Act of 1982, Act number 156, Part I, § 6.
3. The Freedom of the Press Act, art. 2 (Sweden, 1989).

4. "Official Secrecy and Integrity," Circular 15/79 issued by the Irish Department of Public Service, p. 1.

5. E. Zacharioudakis, *Greek Public Administration* (Athens: National Printing Office, 1980), p. 42.

6. Treasury and Civil Service Committee, *Civil Servants and Ministers: Duties and Responsibilities* (London: Her Majesty's Stationery Office, 1986), Vol. II, p. 88.

7. *Civil Servants and Ministers: Duties and Responsibilities. Government Response to the Seventh Report from the Treasury and Civil Service Committee* (London: Her Majesty's Stationery Office, 1986), p. 11.

8. "Premier Orders Radical Reform of Public Service Behavior," *Athens News Daily Bulletin*, October 6, 1980, p. 1.

9. Internal Revenue Code, § 6103(c) (1982).

10. Florida Statutes Annotated, §§ 119.01 and 943.045 (1982 and 1993 Supp.).

11. Donald Axelrod, *Shadow Government: The Hidden World of Public Authorities and How They Control Over $1 Trillion of Your Money* (New York: John Wiley & Sons, 1992), p. 310.

12. Erwin N. Griswold, "Government in Ignorance of the Law—A Plea for Better Publication of Executive Legislation," *Harvard Law Review*, November 1934, pp. 198–215.

13. Federal Register Act of 1935, 49 Stat. 500, 44 U.S.C. § 1501 (1982); and Code of Federal Regulations Amendments of 1937, 50 Stat. 304.

14. Administrative Procedure Act of 1946, 60 Stat. 237, 5 U.S.C. § 551 (1982).

15. Committee on Government Operations, *Clarifying and Protecting the Right of the Public to Information, Report to Accompany S. 1160*, United States House of Representatives, Report No. 1497, 1966, p. 4.

16. Ibid., p. 6.

17. Freedom of Information Act of 1966, 80 Stat. 250 and 5 U.S.C. § 552 (1967 Supp.).

18. Ibid., 80 Stat. 250, 5 U.S.C. § 552(b)(1-9).

19. Ibid., 80 Stat. 250, 5 U.S.C. § 552(b).

20. Ibid., 80 Stat. 250, 5 U.S.C. § 552(d).

21. *Classified Information: Volume Could be Reduced by Changing Retention Policy* (Washington, D.C.: United States General Accounting Office, 1993), p. 21.

22. *Weisburg v. Department of Justice*, 489 F.2d 1195 (D.C. Cir. 1973), cert. denied, 416 U.S. 993 (1974).

23. *Aspin v. Department of Defense*, 491 F.2d 24 (D.C. Cir. 1973).

24. *Ditlow v. Brinegar*, 494 F.2d 1073 (D.C. Cir), cert. denied, 419 U.S. 984 (1974).

25. Freedom of Information Act of 1974, 88 Stat. 1561, 5 U.S.C. § 552(b)(7) (1977).

26. Ibid., 88 Stat. 1561, 5 U.S.C. § 552(a)(4)(B-D).

27. Ibid., 88 Stat. 1561, 5 U.S.C. § 552(a)(4)(B).

28. Don Lively, "Catch 7(A): The Plaintiff's Burden Under the Freedom of Information Act," *Villanova Law Review*, vol. 28, 1982–83, p. 77.

29. Samuel J. Archibald, "The Freedom of Information Act Revisited," *Public Administration Review*, July-August 1979, p. 316.

30. Ibid., p. 317.

31. Freedom of Information Act of 1974, 88 Stat. 1897, 5 U.S.C. § 552(a)(4)(F) (1977 and 1993 Supp.).

32. Ibid.

33. "Suggestions for Anticipating Requests Under Freedom of Information Act." Copy attached to a letter to Secretary of Energy James D. Watkins dated February 26, 1992, from Chairman Howard Wolpe, Subcommittee on Investigations and Oversight, United States House of Representatives.

34. Robert G. Vaughn, "Administrative Alternatives and the Federal Freedom of Information Act," *Ohio State Law Journal*, vol. 45, no. 1, 1984, p. 189.

35. Committee on Government Operations, United States House of Representatives, *A Citizen's Guide on Using the Freedom of Information Act and the Privacy Act of 1974 to Request Government Records* (Washington, D.C.: United States Government Printing Office, 1991).

36. Connecticut General Statutes Annotated, § 1-21j (1988 and 1992 Supp.).

37. Vaughn, "Administrative Alternatives and the Federal Freedom of Information Act," p. 199.

38. New York Public Officers Law, §§ 84-89 (McKinney 1988 and 1993 Supp.).

39. Ibid., § 86 (McKinney 1988).

40. The Accountability in Government Act of 1992 (Washington, D.C.: Office of the Press Secretary, The White House, April 9, 1992).

41. *1991 Report to the Governor and the Legislature* (Albany: New York State Committee on Open Government, 1991), p. 25.

42. *Warder v. Board of Regents of the University of the State of New York*, 97 Misc.2d 86 (1978).

43. *Washington Post Company v. New York State Insurance Department*, 61 N.Y.2d 557 (1984).

44. New York Public Officers Law, § 89(1)(a) (McKinney 1988).

45. Ibid., § 89(2)(a).

46. New York General Municipal Law, § 805-a(1)(b) (McKinney 1993 Supp.).

47. *1991 Report to the Governor and the Legislature*, p. 49.

48. Vaughn, "Administrative Alternatives and the Federal Freedom of Information Act," p. 214.

49. *1991 Report to the Governor and the Legislature*, p. 3.

50. Ibid., p. 4.

51. Freedom of Information Act, Statutes of Manitoba, 1985–86, chap. 6, § 5.

52. Ibid., § 13(1)(a-b).

53. Ibid., § 9(1)(a-b).

54. Computer Security Act of 1987, 101 Stat. 1729, 40 U.S.C. § 759(b) note (1992 Supp.).

55. *Tax Systems Modernization: Concerns Over Security and Privacy Elements of the Systems Architecture* (Washington, D.C.: United States General Accounting Office, 1992), p. 1.

56. Internal Revenue Code, § 6103 (1982).

57. Ibid., § 6103(c) (1982).

58. Privacy Act of 1974, 88 Stat. 1896, 5 U.S.C. § 552a (1982).

59. Freedom of Information Act of 1966, 88 Stat. 383, 5 U.S.C. § 552(6)(b) (1977).

60. David M. O'Brien, "Freedom of Information, Privacy, and Information Control: A Contemporary Administrative Dilemma," *Public Administration Review*, July-August 1979, p. 325.

61. Gloria Cox, "Implementation of the Routine Use Clause of the Privacy Act," *Policy Studies Review*, Winter 1991/92, p. 48.

62. See *Whalen v. Roe*, 429 U.S. 589 (1977); and *Nixon v. Administrator of General Services*, 433 U.S. 425 (1977).

63. *Pennsylvania v. Ritchie*, 107 S.Ct. 989 at 1003 (1987).

64. *Center for Auto Safety v. National Highway Traffic Safety Administration*, 809 F.Supp. 148 (D.D.C. 1993).

65. Washington Revised Code, §§ 42.17.080-.945 (1991 and 1993 Supp.).

66. Matthew Edwards, "Are Privacy and Public Disclosure Compatible? The Privacy Exemption to Washington's Freedom of Information Act," *Washington Law Review*, vol. 62, 1987, p. 257. See *Hearst Corporation v. Hoppe*, 90 Wn2d 123 at 135-36 (1978).

67. *In re Rosier*, 105 Wn2d 606 at 612 (1986).

68. Edwards, "Are Privacy and Public Disclosure Compatible?," p. 265.

69. New York Public Officers Law, §§ 91-99 (McKinney 1988 and 1993 Supp.).

70. Ibid., § 93(4)(a-k).

71. Ibid., § 94(2)(a) and (3)(a).

72. *Spargo v. New York State Commission on Government Integrity*, 140 A.D.2d 26 (1988).

73. *Building a Better New York Committee v. New York State Committee on Government Integrity*, 138 Misc.2d 829, 525 N.Y.S.2d 488 (1988).

74. James P. Moran, "Legislation to Protect Privacy and Safety of Licensed Drivers," *Congressional Record*, November 3, 1993, pp. E-2747-748.

75. Edward J. Markey, "Telephone Consumer Privacy Protection Act of 1993," *Congressional Record*, November 3, 1993, pp. E-2745–746.

Chapter 6

Open Meetings

Opening the decision-making process of governments to the public is essential if citizens are to be kept informed of policy proposals and the arguments for and against each proposal. Nevertheless, neither the common law nor the U.S. Constitution grants to citizens the right to attend meetings of governmental bodies, and the Congress and state legislatures did not grant citizens the right to attend meetings for decades. Utah in 1898 became the first state to require open meetings of municipal governing bodies and New York in 1976 became the fiftieth state to enact an open meetings law.

The national Government in the Sunshine Act of 1976 declares, "the public is entitled to the fullest practicable information regarding the decision making processes of the Federal Government" and the New York Open Meeting Law asserts, "the people must be able to remain informed if they are to retain control over those who are their public servants."[1]

Open meeting laws have five major advantages. First, the laws have the potential for reducing the opportunities for interest groups to bring undue pressure upon decision makers and inhibiting unethical conduct by the latter. Second, these laws should increase the responsiveness of a government to the citizens since the latter are afforded the opportunity to attend meetings and to express their views and concerns. Third, citizen input may improve the proposed law or board action. Fourth, meeting attendance may improve and agenda items may receive more thorough examination. Fifth, voters will be better able to judge the performance of elected officers on election day.

In common with freedom of information laws, open meeting laws must be drafted and enacted with phraseology guaranteeing the public will be provided with adequate information while simultaneously protecting the rights of each individual and not interfering with the ability of a government to execute its responsibilities. In consequence, the national law and the law in each state contain specified exceptions allowing collegial bodies to hold close sessions. In addition, the rules of the U.S. House of Representatives and the Senate authorize the holding of executive or secret sessions relative to specified matters.[2]

Various types of boards and commissions, including governing bodies, in small local governments on occasion hold telephone meetings which preclude citizens from participating in the meetings. State law should forbid the holding of telephone meetings unless there is a bona fide emergency necessitating such a meeting.

Courts have developed the appearance of fairness doctrine relative to the conduct of certain public hearings. When a government body, planning commission, civil service commission, or similar body is required by law to hold public hearings that affect individual or property rights, these quasi-judicial proceedings are governed by the strict fairness rules applicable to court cases. The doctrine holds that hearings must be fair and must not give even the appearance of being unfair. Among other things, a member of a decision-making body may not engage in ex parte communications with persons with an interest in a matter pending before the body.

THE NATIONAL LAW

The origin of the Government in the Sunshine Act is traceable to a bill—S. 3881—introduced by Senator Lawton Chiles in the Senate on August 9, 1972. The following year, Senator Chiles introduced a new comprehensive and more developed bill—S. 260—that had seventeen bipartisan cosponsors. In 1973, the Subcommittee on Reorganization, Research, and International Organizations sought the views of experts on the proposed law and in 1974 the subcommittee held hearings on the bill.[3]

Senator Chiles in 1974 reintroduced the bill—S.5—and an amended version was approved by a vote of 94 to 0 on November 6, 1975. Representative Don Fuqua introduced a companion bill—H.R. 466—in the House in 1975. This bill and a second one—H.R. 9868—were referred to the Subcommittee on Government Information and Rights of the House Committee on Government Operations. The latter offered a revised version—H.R. 11656—which was amended on July 28, 1976, and approved by a vote of 390 to 5. The House subsequently vacated passage of the bill and substituted S.5 after amending it to include language contained in the House bill.

A conference committee dealt with the different definitions of the term "meeting." It was defined in the Senate bill as "the deliberations of at least the number of individual agency members required to take action on behalf of the agency where such deliberations concern the joint disposition of official agency business." The House bill defined a meeting as "a gathering to jointly conduct or dispose of agency business by two or more but at least the number of individual agency members required to take action on behalf of the agency."

The Congress accepted the Conference Committee's definition of a meeting as "the deliberations of at least the number of individual agency members required to take action on behalf of the agency where such deliberations determine or result in the joint conduct or disposition of official agency business, but does not include deliberations required or permitted by subsection (d) or (e). . . ."[4] President Gerald R. Ford signed the bill into law on September 13, 1976.

Major Provisions

The open meeting law applies to any agency headed by a collegial body with two or more members with a majority appointed by the president with the advice and consent of the Senate. The collegial body may meet in camera only after a majority of the entire membership votes to close a meeting which will generate information that will:

1. Disclose matters that are (a) specifically authorized under criteria established by an Executive Order to be kept secret in the interests of national defense or foreign policy and (b) in fact properly classified pursuant to such Executive Order;
2. Relate solely to the internal personnel rules and practices of an agency;
3. Disclose matters specifically exempted from disclosure by statute (other than section 552 of this title), provided that such statute (a) requires that the matters be withheld from the public in such a manner as to leave no discretion on the issue, or (b) establishes particular criteria for withholding or refers to particular types of matters to be withheld;
4. Disclose trade secrets and commercial or financial information obtained from a person and privileged or confidential;
5. Involve accusing any person of a crime, or formally censuring any person;
6. Disclose information of a personal nature where disclosure would constitute a clearly unwarranted invasion of personal privacy;

7. Disclose investigatory records compiled for law enforcement purposes, or information which if written would be contained in such records, but only to the extent that the production of such records or information would (a) interfere with enforcement proceedings, (b) deprive a person of a right to a fair trial or an impartial adjudication, (c) constitute an unwarranted invasion of personal privacy, (d) disclose the identity of a confidential source and, in the case of a record compiled by a criminal law enforcement authority in the course of a criminal investigation, or by an agency conducting a lawful national security intelligence investigation, confidential information furnished only by a confidential source, (e) disclose investigative techniques and procedures, or (f) endanger the life or physical safety of law enforcement personnel;

8. Disclose information contained in or related to examination, operating, or condition reports prepared by, on behalf of, or for the use of an agency responsible for the regulation or supervision of financial institutions;

9. Disclose information the premature disclosure of which would:
    a. in the case of an agency which regulates currencies, securities, commodities, or financial institutions, be likely to (i) lead to significant financial speculation in currencies, securities, or commodities, or (ii) significantly endanger the stability of any financial institution; or
    b. in the case of any agency, be likely to significantly frustrate implementation of a proposed agency action, except that subparagraph (b) shall not apply in any instance where the agency has already disclosed to the public the content or nature of its proposed action, or where the agency is required by law to make such disclosure on its own initiative prior to taking final agency action on such proposal; or

10. Specifically concern the agency's issuance of a subpoena, or the agency's participation in a civil action or proceeding, an action in a foreign court or international tribunal, or an arbitration, or the initiation, conduct, or disposition by the agency of a particular case of formal agency adjudication pursuant to the procedures in section 554 of this title or otherwise involving a determination on the record after opportunity for hearing.[5]

To close a meeting or a portion of a meeting, a separate vote of the entire membership of an agency is required relative to each meeting or portion(s) of a meeting proposed to be closed to the public. Within one day, the agency must make public a copy of each such vote revealing the vote of each member with no proxy votes allowed. The agency must notify the public at least seven days in advance of a meeting which will be closed in toto or in part to the public. The announcement must provide the public with the name and telephone number of an agency official responsible for responding to requests for information about the meeting.

Relative to closed meetings, the general counsel of the agency must certify that the meeting may be closed to the public before an executive session may be held.

The act requires the electronic recording or transcription of every open and every closed meeting of the members of each collegial agency.[6] Theodore J. Jacobs, director of the Project for Open Government, reported in 1980 that a tape recording of a meeting of the board of directors of the Export-Import Bank assisted a congressional investigation of the circumstances involved in the bank's loan to Rupert Murdoch's company and the endorsement of President James E. Carter for reelection by Murdoch's *New York Post*.[7] Jacobs added that "without the requirements of the Sunshine Act, this meeting never would have been taped. The tape proved to be an immense aid in the Banking Committee's investigation. In the absence of a tape or transcript, it would be one person's recollection against another's."[8]

Each agency was required to publish within 180 days of the enactment of the act, in the *Federal Register*, a notice of regulations to implement the requirements of the act. The U.S. District Court is granted jurisdiction to enforce the provisions of the act and standing is granted to any citizen to bring an enforcement action.[9] An annual report must be submitted to the Congress containing data on the number of meetings, number of meetings closed to the public, reasons for closed meetings, and a description of any suit brought against the agency. The act specifically stipulates that the prohibition of ex parte communications "does not constitute authority to withhold information from Congress."[10]

Court Decisions

The U.S. Supreme Court has issued only one opinion interpreting the Government in the Sunshine Act. In *Federal Communications Commission v. ITT World Communications, Incorporated*, the Court reversed the decisions of the district court and the court of appeals for the District of Columbia which ruled that members of the commission were engaged in a meeting covered by the act.[11] The issue involved a narrow or a broad interpretation of the term *meeting*.

An agency's decision-making process involves collective inquiry, analysis and deliberation, and decision. The broad view holds that all three stages of the process should be open to the public. The narrow view holds that opening the first two stages to the public will inhibit collegial exchanges and possibly adversely affect the decision made by the body.

The district court and the court of appeals held that the meeting of three Federal Communications Commission members with their Canadian and European counterparts to plan telecommunications facilities was covered by the act. Although only three of the seven commission members participated in the meeting, they constituted a quorum of the commission's Telecommunications Committee and the courts ruled that the act covers meetings of committees.[12]

In a unanimous opinion, the Supreme Court reversed the lower courts' decision by holding that the open meetings law "does not extend to deliberations of a quorum of a subdivision upon matters not within the subdivision's formally delegated authority."[13] The Court added the meeting was not subject to the act because it had not been convened by the commission and also opined the act does not apply to "informal background discussions (that) clarify issues and expose varying views."[14]

Commenting on this decision, David A. Barrett in 1988 wrote:

First, the definition of meeting extends only to the deliberative and decision stages of the decision-making process. Second, the decision-making process is fluid, and the line between the collective inquiry and deliberative stages is often vague. Thus, in many collective inquiries, some incidental decision-oriented discussions are bound to occur. Third, the only way to guarantee public access to all decision-oriented deliberation, including merely incidental decision-oriented deliberation contained in the overlap between the stages, is to open the collective inquiry stage.[15]

A 1986 decision of the U.S. Court of Appeals for the District of Columbia Circuit addressed the issue of the release of transcripts of closed meetings when an exemption ceases to apply.[16] The Federal Energy Regulatory Commission in 1980 issued a decision holding that preference accorded to a municipality in hydroelectric licensing proceedings under the Federal Power Act applies to relicensing decisions.[17] Private utility companies challenged the ruling, but it was upheld by the U.S. Court of Appeals in 1982.[18] The utilities sought a review of the decision by the U.S. Supreme Court and on April 25, 1983, the commission held an executive session to consider responses to the petition for issuance of a writ of certiorari. The Clark-Cowlitz Joint Operating Committee, a Washington State municipal corporation, requested a copy of the transcript of the closed meeting and the request was denied by the commission upon the basis of Exemption 10 in the Sunshine Act. The committee maintained the meeting dealt with legal points and broad policy questions applicable to other proceedings pending before the commission and the basis for withholding the transcript terminated when the underlying civil action (*City of Bountiful*) had terminated.

The district court ruled that the commission's discussions were exempt from disclosure. A panel of the U.S. Court of Appeals for the District of Columbia Circuit in 1985 reversed the lower court's decision and the commission petitioned the Court for a rehearing *en banc* and the petition was granted. The full court reversed the panel's decision by noting it "did not believe Congress would have written an express temporal limitation into Exemption 9 and yet have intended a similar (unwritten) limitation to apply to Exemption 10."[19]

The Committee on Governmental Affairs of the U.S. Senate in 1989 wrote:

The District Court decision effectively cut the heart out of Sunshine, for agencies could assert in virtually all cases that the opening of discussions or release of transcripts to public view could have a chilling effect on future agency discussions. (If read broadly, the decision could mean that any discussion which arises in the context of litigation strategy is exempt from disclosure.) Thus, under the District Court's reasoning, exemptions from disclosure could become the rule rather than the exception, which clearly was not the intent of the Sunshine Act.[20]

The definition of an agency also has been subject to litigation. In *Hunt v. Nuclear Regulatory Commission*, the U.S. District Court in 1979 upheld the decision of the commission to close meetings of its Atomic Safety and Licensing Boards on the ground the open meeting requirement did not apply to adjudicatory hearings held by a licensing board.[21] This ruling was affirmed by the U.S. Court of Appeals.[22]

In *Symons v. Chrysler Corporation Loan Guarantee Board*, the district court for the District of Columbia opined in 1980 the board was subject to the open meeting requirement by rejecting the argument that the board was exempt from the act since its members were not appointed by the president with the advice and consent of the Senate, but served ex officio.[23] The Court of Appeals for the District of Columbia Circuit, however, reversed the district court's decision and opined that the Congress intended a narrower definition of the term *agency*, since it did not specify the board was subject to the act but had specified that the Depository Institutions Deregulation Committee, established in the same year, was subject to the act.[24]

In 1978, the issue of notation voting by members of the Federal Communications Commission was the subject of an important decision by the U.S. Court of Appeals. Instead of voting on motions at meetings, the commission circulated written materials to members who voted in writing on the proposals. Opponents of this practice alleged notation voting subverts the Sunshine Act since an agency could conduct business by notation voting instead of by meetings. The court rejected this interpretation of the act.

If all agency actions required meetings, then the entire administration process would be slowed—perhaps to a standstill. Certainly requiring an agency to meet and discuss every trivial item on its agenda would delay consideration of the more serious issues that require joint face-to-face deliberation. Clearly Congress did not intend such a result.[25]

The court, however, did not address the question of whether notation voting was restricted to voting on trivial items only.

As noted, the open meeting law contains exemptions from its requirements. The Nuclear Regulatory Commission divided its budget deliberations into two parts—preliminary staff briefings and markup/reclaim sessions. The first part was open to the public and the second section was closed on the basis of Exemptions 2, 6, and 9(b). Common Cause filed suit against the commission and the U.S. District Court for the District of Columbia ruled in favor of Common Cause, but the U.S. Court of Appeals for the District of Columbia reversed the lower court's injunction permanently enjoining the commission from holding in camera meetings of this type on the ground the injunction violated the specificity requirements of the Federal Rules of Civil Procedure.[26] The court of appeals, however, rejected the commission's contention that the act authorized the commission to hold closed meetings of this type:

If Congress had wished to exempt these deliberations from the Sunshine Act—to preserve the prior practice of budget confidentiality, to reduce the opportunities for lobbying before the President submits his budget to Congress, or for other reasons—it would have expressly so indicated.[27]

Time, Incorporated challenged the U.S. Postal Service's decision to close portions of the meetings of its board of governors which would consider the recommendations of the Postal Rate Commission and cited Exemption 10 as the basis for the closing. The board explained it was closing the meetings because postal rate increases might result in a civil action against the Postal Service.

Focusing upon Exemption 10, the Court of Appeals for the Second Circuit ruled in favor of the commission by holding that the act's provision—"otherwise involving a determination on the record after an opportunity for a hearing"—applied to rule-making proceedings "involving a determination on the record after an opportunity for a hearing (formal rule making)."[28] The Postal Rate Commission is required by law to hold a public hearing prior to making recommendations.

Agency compliance with Sunshine Act procedural requirements has been the subject of court decisions. The board of governors of the Federal Reserve System held two executive meetings under Exemption 4 which protects commercial and financial information, but did not provide a notice of the meetings until three hours after they were terminated. Although the District Court for the District of Columbia found that the board properly had closed the meetings, the court opined that a post-meeting notice did not satisfy the requirement that the meetings be announced "at the earliest practicable time."[29] The court stressed that closing a meeting without notice must be supported by "specific affidavits describing with sufficient justification the basis for such a claim, and not rest on conclusory hypotheses."[30]

Can a court invalidate decisions made in an illegal closed meeting? The answer is yes, but courts are reluctant to take such action. The U.S. Court of Appeals for the District of Columbia Circuit in 1982 ruled that the Civil Aeronautics Board had no grounds for closing its May 14, 1982, meeting to the public and opined the board had come "perilously close" to persuading the court to invalidate the board's decision.[31] The court decided to order the board to release the transcripts of the meeting.

Agency Compliance

The U.S. General Accounting Office in 1988 released a report on compliance by twelve agencies with the Sunshine Act and reported "a high degree of agency compliance with the selected provisions of the law we reviewed."[32] The surveyed agencies held 704 meetings of which 445 were closed and 32 were closed partly. Proper announcements were made of forty-three of the forty-seven closed meetings reviewed and "agency meeting records showed that meeting discussions fit cited exemptions in twenty-one of twenty-four meetings and twenty-one of the twenty-four meetings were held in accordance with the announced subject."[33]

A Congressional Research Service report reveals that 11,378 meetings were held in the period from 1979 to 1984; and 4,594 meetings (40%) were open, 4,879 (43%) were closed, and 1,905 (17%) were closed partly.[34]

Fifty-three of the fifty-nine agencies closed at least one of their meetings and 26,019 exemptions were used as the basis to close 4,879 meetings completely and to close 1,905 meetings partly.[35] The report indicates that "at least thirty-six agencies use notation voting; fifteen agencies do not use the procedure; and eight did not indicate in their annual reports whether they used the procedure."[36]

STATE SUNSHINE ACTS

All states have enacted open meetings laws containing provisions generally similar to the ones in the national act. New York in 1976 was the fiftieth state to enact such a law and it declares "every meeting of a public body shall be open to the general public."[37] A meeting is defined as "the official convening of a public body for the purpose of conducting public business" and the Appellate Division of the Supreme Court (a general trial court) has ruled that a meeting encompasses a "gathering of a public body for the purpose of transacting public business, whenever a quorum is present, whether or not a vote of the members of the public body is given."[38] A public body must publish notice of a meeting and take minutes.

The New York statute authorized a majority of the total membership of a public body to vote in open meeting to conduct an executive session relative to one of the following:

a. Matters which will imperil the public safety if disclosed;

b. Any matter which may disclose the identity of a law enforcement agent or informer;

c. Information relating to current or future investigation or prosecution of a criminal offense which would imperil effective law enforcement if disclosed;

d. Discussions regarding proposed, pending, or current litigation;

e. Collective negotiations pursuant to article fourteen of the Civil Service law;

f. The medical, financial, credit, or employment history of a particular person or corporation, or matters leading to the appointment, employment, promotion, demotion, discipline, suspension, dismissal, or removal of a particular person or corporation;

g. The preparation, grading, or administration of examinations; and

h. The proposed acquisition, sale, or lease of real property or the proposed acquisition of securities, or sale or exchange of securities held by such public body, but only when publicity would substantially affect the value thereof.[39]

The vote to conduct an executive session must identify the general area or the subjects to be considered and no funds may be appropriated during such a session. Minutes must be taken of any matter determined "by formal vote which shall consist of a record or summary of the final determination of such action, and the date and vote thereon. . . ."[40] The minutes must be made available to the public within one week of the meeting.

The New York law exempts the following from its requirements:

1. Judicial or quasi-judicial proceedings, except proceedings of the Public Service Commission and zoning boards of appeals;
2. a. Deliberations of political committees, conferences, and caucuses;
   b. for purposes of this section, the deliberations of political committees, conferences, and caucuses means a private meeting of the Senate or Assembly of the State of New York, or of the legislative body of a county, city, town, or village, who are members or adherents of the same political party, without regard to (i) the subject matter under discussion, including discussions of public business, (ii) the majority or minority status of such political committees, conferences, and causes, or (iii) whether such political committees, conferences, and caucuses invite staff or guests to participate in their deliberations; and
3. Any matter made confidential by federal or state law.[41]

No public notice of such meetings is required and no minutes must be taken since the meetings are exempt from the requirements of the law.

The Committee on Open Government, created by the Freedom of Information Law which is examined in Chapter 5, is directed to issue advisory opinions to inform citizens and public bodies of its interpretations of the open meeting law.[42] The Open Meetings Law grants standing to any citizen to enforce its provisions.[43]

The Mississippi Open Meetings Act covers all state and local government administrative policy-making bodies and other governmental bodies if they receive public funds and were created by statute or executive order.[44] The act exempts from its coverage the judiciary, hospital staffs, law enforcement officials, the National Guard, state Probation and Parole Board, and workmen's compensation committees.[45]

The act defines a meeting as "an assemblage of members of a public body at which official acts may be taken upon a matter over which the public body has supervision, control, jurisdiction, or advisory power" and hence covers lunches and other informal meetings.[46] If a meeting is entirely a social gathering, the meeting is exempt from the act. In common with the New York statute, the Mississippi act permits executive sessions of a body relative to eleven specified matters.[47] To hold an executive session, three-fifths of the members must vote in public to hold such a session and the vote must be recorded in the minutes of the meeting. Minutes must be available within thirty days of a meeting. The act stipulates that a public body may promulgate reasonable rules and regulations relative to participation by citizens in a meeting which, among other things, would allow citizens to raise questions throughout a meeting or at the conclusion of a meeting.

All state open meetings laws recognize the sensitivity of certain matters and stipulate that a public body may vote to hold an executive session to consider and act upon these matters. These exemptions open the door to possible abuses. To guard against such abuses, the New Hampshire statute prohibits a body to receive information, evidence, or testimony or to take a final action in executive session with the following exceptions:

a. The dismissal, promotion, or compensation of any public employee or the disciplining of such employee, or the investigation of any charges against him, unless the employee affected (1) has a right to a meeting, and (2) requests that the meeting be open, in which case the request shall be granted.
b. The hiring of any person as a public employee.
c. Matters which likely would affect the reputation of any person adversely, if discussed publicly, except members of the body or agency itself. However, if the person involved requests an open meeting, an executive session may not be held.
d. Consideration of the acquisition, sale, or lease of property which, if discussed in public, would likely benefit a party or parties whose interests are adverse to those of the general community.
e. Matters discussed by a legislative committee sitting in executive session which should not be made public as determined by a three-fifths roll call or recorded vote of the members present and voting at such meeting.
f. Collecting bargaining sessions conducted by a school district. . . .
g. Receipt of legal advice on legal matters only. . . .[48]

Court and Attorney General Decisions

Courts in each state have been called upon to interpret their respective open meetings law relative to what constitutes a meeting, whether an executive session may be held on a particular matter, the procedure for an agency or legislative body to enter into an executive session, adequacy of the notice requirements for a closed meeting, and requirements for minutes of a meeting.

Definition of a Meeting. The Mississippi Supreme Court interpreted the Open Meetings Act's definition of a meeting to include all meetings where deliberations relating to an issue occurs regardless of whether a vote is taken and a telephone conference or voting is prohibited.[49] The state's attorney general advised that all meetings must be public ones with the exceptions of social gatherings and chance meetings.[50]

The New York Open Meetings Law originally defined a meeting of a public body in terms of "officially transacting public business." Questions were raised whether this definition was limited to meetings where voting occurred or whether this definition covered meetings where public issues were discussed. In 1978, the Appellate Division of the Supreme Court rejected the argument of the Newburgh City Council that work sessions involving no votes were exempt from the law and opined that when a quorum of a public body is present and discusses public matters, the gathering is a meeting under the Open Meetings Law.[51] The decision was affirmed by the court of appeals, the state's highest court.[52]

The decision in the above case did not address the question of what constitutes a public body. In 1979, the Appellate Division of the Supreme Court was asked to determine whether committees of a board of education with advisory powers only could hold executive sessions. The Court opined that the committees could meet in closed sessions without a quorum of the committees or of the board of education present and were not public bodies capable of transacting public business, since their role was entirely advisory.[53]

The 1979 New York State legislature reversed the Court's decision by changing the definitions of "public body" and "meeting." The latter was redefined as the "official convening of a public body for the purpose of conducting public business."[54] The revised definition made clear that the definition of a meeting subject to the Open Meetings Law was not dependent upon whether votes were taken. The 1979 law redefined a "public body" as "any entity, for which a quorum is required in order to conduct public business and which consists of two or more members, performing a governmental function. . . ."[55] Hence, committee meetings were brought under the definition of the law.

Statutory Exemptions. With these legislative changes, litigation under the Open Meetings Law dealt with statutory exemptions. In 1980, the one Republican member of the Rochester City (New York) Council sought to attend executive meetings of the council's Democratic caucus which discussed matters coming before the council. The Supreme Court and its Appellate Division opined that the Republican council member had the right to attend the caucus.[56] The latter Court explained the political caucus exemption in the Open Meetings Law was designed:

to prevent the statute from extending to the private matters of a political party, as opposed to matters which are public business yet discussed by political party members. To allow the majority party members of a public body to exclude minority members, and thereafter conduct public business in closed sessions under the guise of a political caucus, would be violative of the statute.[57]

To avoid complying fully with the Court's decision, the Democratic council members subsequently divided the caucus into two groups with rotating members between meetings to ensure that a quorum of council members would not be present at a caucus meeting.[58]

Prior to this court decision, the state legislature always had amended the Open Meetings Law to expand the rights of citizens to attend meetings. Although the state legislature did not amend the law immediately, an advisory opinion of the Committee on Open Government in 1985 prompted the state legislature to modify the law and narrow its scope. The committee, basing its opinion on the *Sciolino* decision, advised the *New York Post* that caucuses or conferences held by members of the majority of either house of the state legislature for the purpose of conducting public business are covered by the Open Meetings Law.[59] In response, a bill quickly was introduced, enacted by the state legislature, and signed into law by Governor Mario M. Cuomo. The law exempts from the Open Meetings Law all "private meeting(s) of members of the Senate and Assembly or of the legislative body of a county, city, town, or village, who are members or adherents of the same political party. . . ."[60] The amendment specifically stipulated applies to the caucuses

without regard to (i) the subject matter under discussion, including discussions of public business, (ii) the majority or minority status of such political committees, conferences, and caucuses, or (iii) whether such political committees, conferences, and caucuses invite staff or guests to participate in their deliberations.[61]

The State of New York Commission on Government Integrity in 1987 recommended that the 1985 amendment be repealed relative to governing bodies of local governments because

the public is entitled to make an informed decision about the quality of its representatives, and can not do so if the significant deliberations of those representatives are held behind closed doors . . . discussions of most difficult and controversial issues are precisely those that legislators might most want to hold in private—such as the location of low-income housing or a major waterfront development, removal of asbestos from schools, solid waste disposal, or increases in their salaries. These are discussions in which the public has great interest and which should clearly be held in public.[62]

In 1991, the Georgia Supreme Court affirmed the decision of the trial court that an inquest was required to be open under the state's open meetings law and rejected the argument of the coroner of Muscogee County that the inquest could be closed because it involved a pending criminal investigation.[63] The court specifically held that the inquest did not fall under the section of the law exempting a law enforcement agency since the coroner has no law enforcement authority and the verdict of a coroner's inquest is solely advisory and does not constitute a formal charging or indictment.

The County Court for Broward County in 1991 interpreted the Florida Sunshine Law broadly. The court held that a meeting of an ad hoc advisory board of the City of Hollywood was subject to the law and specifically opined that "the fact that the final decision rested with the City Commission neither justifies nor excuses this private meeting."[64] The court added: "Nor can the Sunshine Law be evaded by characterizing this group as a 'staff meeting.' It is the nature of the act performed, not the make-up of the group, that determines the application of the statute."[65]

In Alabama, the attorney general in 1991 advised that a county board of education may evaluate the superintendent in executive session to the extent that the evaluation involves the superintendent's character or good name.[66]

An unusual case was decided in 1991 by the U.S. District Court for the Middle District of Alabama. A member of the Clio City Council sued the city and its mayor and police chief alleging violations of his first and fourth amendment rights under the U.S. Constitution because the mayor forbade the member to tape record sessions of the council and ordered the police chief to seize the tape recorder and hold it outside the council chambers until the conclusion of the meeting. The court agreed that the member's first and fourth amendments rights had been violated, but opined that the member's rights under the Alabama Open Meetings Law had not been violated:

The law thus guarantees citizens the right to attend certain government proceedings, but does not limit the conditions which government bodies may place upon such attendance. The "open meetings" law did not grant Thompson the right to record the council session, only to be present. Thus, defendants did not violate the law by insisting he put aside his tape recorder, regardless of whether the basis for this demand was reasonable or not.[67]

In New York State, on the other hand, a bylaw of a board of education forbidding the use of recording devices at board meetings was struck down as violating the open meetings law.[68]

Convening an Executive Session. All public meetings must commence as open meetings. To enter into an executive session, the open meetings laws specify that a majority or an extra majority of the members of a collegial body must vote to close a meeting and the vote must be recorded and included in the minutes of the meeting. The laws typically forbid a body to schedule closed meetings on a regular basis or to vote to have an executive session prior to a meeting. The public must be informed why an executive session will be held. The Mississippi statute requires a three-fifths vote of the membership to close a meeting and stipulates "the reason for holding such an executive session shall be stated in an open meeting, and the reason so stated shall be recorded in the minutes of the meeting."[69] The Mississippi Supreme Court in 1989 expanded the basic requirement for a reason for closing a meeting as follows:

It must be more than some generalized term which in reality tells the public nothing. To simply say, "personnel matters," or "litigation," tells nothing. The reason stated must be of sufficient specificity to inform those present that there is in reality a specific, discrete matter or area which the board had determined should be discussed in executive session.[70]

Notice and Minutes. New York courts have ruled that there must be strict compliance with the notice requirements of the open meetings law for an executive session to be valid. Simply including a statement that a town board will hold "discussions regarding proposed, pending or current litigation" is too general a reason for holding an executive session.[71] In 1980, all actions taken at a meeting of a board of education were invalidated by the Appellate Division of the Supreme Court because members of the board violated the notice requirement by failure to give notice to the extent practicable to the news media and to post conspicuously a notice in one or more designated public locations within a reasonable time period prior to the meeting.[72] Notice consisted of one typewritten announcement posted on the bulletin board in the offices of the board of education.

The New York Open Meetings Law requires that minutes must be taken at an executive session of any action taken by formal vote, but "such summary need not include any matter which is not required to be made public by the freedom of information law. . . ."[73] The Mississippi statute specifically requires a recording of the votes of individual members within thirty days after conclusion of a closed meeting.[74]

Enforcement

A person denied permission to attend a meeting of a public body in Mississippi may seek injunctive relief in the Chancery Court by filing suit in the county where the members of the board reside.[75] The statute does not contain provisions for the award of penalties or attorneys' fees, but the Mississippi Supreme Court has upheld the award of attorneys' fees for violations of the law.[76]

The New York Open Meetings Law grants citizens standing to enforce any provision of the law against a public body, but stipulates that "an unintentional failure to fully comply with the notice provisions required by this article shall not alone be grounds for invalidating any action taken at a meeting of a public body."[77] In addition, the law stipulates that failure to comply with its provisions does "not affect the validity of the authorization, acquisition, execution, or disposition of a bond issue or notes."[78]

Since the New York Open Meetings Law provides no remedy for a violation other than a court proceeding to invalidate the actions of a violating public body, members of public bodies are free to violate the law without fear of consequences. Furthermore, an action invalidated by a court on the ground of violating the law can be taken again at a public meeting. The supreme court ruled that a board of education decision taken at an open meeting was valid because "a prior violation of the Open Meetings Law does not taint a subsequently held legal meeting at which the action is taken."[79]

The State of New York Commission on Government Integrity in 1987 recommended the following amendment to the Open Meetings Law:

In such action or proceeding, the court shall also have the power to impose a fine upon any member of the public body who had knowingly and intentionally violated any provision of this article. Such fine shall not exceed $100 for the first violation and $200 for each succeeding violation committed within a period of eighteen months. Notwithstanding any provision of law to the contrary, no government entity shall indemnify any such member for payment of any such fine.[80]

The commission also recommended an amendment granting courts the power to invalidate an action taken at a public meeting if the action was taken "after substantial deliberations held in violation of the law."[81] No action has been taken on these proposed amendments by the New York State legislature.

SUMMARY AND CONCLUSIONS

The operations of the national, state, and local governments, with enumerated exceptions, have become subject to additional sunlight with the enactment of open meetings laws. The latter are based upon the checks and balances principle which seeks to ensure that meetings of public bodies are not subject to undue pressure by special interest groups and that decisions made are ethical ones. In common with other laws regulating an activity for the first time, there have been problems of definitions and exclusions. In general, legislative bodies have amended the statutes to define more carefully the terms *public body* and *meetings*.

Although it is essential to include enumerated exceptions in an open meetings statute, the exceptions create enforcement problems because action may be taken at a closed session beyond the permitted ones. A solution to this problem is a statutory requirement that each in camera session be audio or video taped.

The granting of standing to citizens to bring an action in court to force enforcement of the law has not been effective in most instances because of the cost involved in bringing an action. Furthermore, courts are limited to invalidating an action taken at an illegally held closed meeting and the concerned body subsequently can take the identical action at a public meeting.

The State of New York Commission on Government Integrity reported that public bodies continue to consider many important matters in private without violating the Open Meetings Law and added:

There is little logic in requiring a public hearing (where the public can ask questions and demand answers) when a local law is being passed which may be of minor significance, but requiring only an open meeting where decisions are being made which may be of maximum significance. For example, we question why a public hearing must precede passage of a local law requiring a minor increase in fees or fines, while a municipality can commit to spend millions of dollars on a new project without public participation.[82]

In sum, open meetings laws have dispelled to a great extent the rumors and associated citizen distrust of public officers flowing from closed meetings, reduced the opportunities for unethical conduct by public officers, and improved the decision-making process.

Conflict-of-interest statutes, codes of ethics, mandatory disclosure laws, and open meetings laws help to ensure that the public's business is conducted in an ethical manner. These laws, however, need to be supplemented by other actions. Of particular importance in detecting and preventing unethical behavior are internal controls which are the subject of Chapter 7.

NOTES

1. Government in the Sunshine Act of 1976, 90 Stat. 1241, 5 U.S.C. § 552b note (1977 and 1993 Supp.); and New York Public Officers Law, § 100 (McKinney 1988).

2. Rules of the House of Representatives (Washington, D.C.: 1993), Rule XXIX; and Standing Rules of the Senate (Washington, D.C.: United States Government Printing Office, 1992), Rule XXIX.

3. Subcommittee on Reorganization, Research, and International Organizations, United States Senate, *Government in the Sunshine: Responses to Subcommittee Questionnaires* (Washington, D.C.: United States Government Printing Office, 1974).

4. Government in the Sunshine Act of 1976, 90 Stat. 1241, 5 U.S.C. § 552(a)(2) (1977 and 1993 Supp.).

5. Ibid., 90 Stat. 1241-242, 5 U.S.C. §§ 552 and 554.

6. Ibid., 90 Stat. 1244, 5 U.S.C. § 554 (1977 and 1993 Supp.).

7. Theodore J. Jacobs, "The Federal Sunshine Act is Paying Off," *The New York Times*, June 7, 1980, p. 22.

8. Ibid.

9. Government in the Sunshine Act of 1976, 90 Stat. 1245, 5 U.S.C. § 554 (1977 and 1993 Supp.).

10. Ibid., 90 Stat. 1247, 5 U.S.C. § 557(2)(d) (1977 and 1993 Supp.).

11. *Federal Communications Commission v. ITT World Communications, Incorporated*, 466 U.S. 463 (1984).

12. *ITT World Communications, Incorporated v. Federal Communications Commission*, 699 F.2d 1219 (D.C. Cir. 1983).

13. *Federal Communications Commission v. ITT World Communications, Incorporated*, 466 U.S. 463 at 473 (1984).

14. Ibid. at 473-74 and 469-70.

15. David A. Barrett, "Facilitating Government Decision-Making: Distinguishing Between Meetings and Nonmeetings Under the Federal Sunshine Act," *Texas Law Review*, vol. LXVI, 1988, p. 1224.

16. *Clark-Cowlitz Joint Operating Committee v. Federal Energy Regulatory Commission*, 798 F.2d 499 (D.C. Cir. 1986).

17. *City of Bountiful, Utah et al.*, 11 FERC (CCH), par. 61,337 (1980).

18. *Alabama Power Company v. Federal Energy Regulatory Commission*, 685 F.2d 1311 (11th Cir., 1982).

19. *Clark-Cowlitz Joint Operating Committee v. Federal Energy Regulatory Commission*, 798 F.2d 499 (D.C. Cir. 1986).

20. Committee on Governmental Affairs, United States Senate, *Government in the Sunshine Act: History and Recent Issues* (Washington, D.C.: United States Government Printing Office, 1989), p. 32.

21. *Hunt v. Nuclear Regulatory Commission*, 468 F. Supp. 817 (N.D. Okla. 1979).

22. *Hunt v. Nuclear Regulatory Commission*, 611 F.2d 332 (10th Cir. 1979).

23. *Symons v. Chrysler Corporation Loan Guarantee Board*, 488 F. Supp. 874 at 876 (D.D.C. 1980).

24. *Symons v. Chrysler Corporation Loan Guarantee Board*, 670 F.2d 238 (D.C. Cir. 1981).

25. *Communications Systems v. Federal Communications Commission*, 595 F.2d 797 at 801 (D.C. Cir. 1978).

26. *Common Cause v. Nuclear Regulatory Commission*, 674 F.2d 921 (D.C. Cir. 1982).

27. Ibid. at 934-35.

28. *Time v. United States Postal Service*, 667 F.2d 329 at 334 (2d Cir. 1981).

29. *A.G. Becker, Incorporated v. Board of Governors*, 502 F.Supp. 378 (D.D.C. 1980).

30. Ibid. at 385.

31. *Pan American World Airways v. Civil Aeronautics Board*, 684 F.2d 31 at 36 (D.C. Cir. 1982).

32. *Information Disclosure: Government in the Sunshine Act Compliance at Selected Agencies* (Washington, D.C.: United States General Accounting Office, 1988), p. 1.

33. Ibid, pp. 11 and 14.

34. Rogelio Garcia, *Government in the Sunshine: Public Access to Meetings Held Under the Government in the Sunshine Act, 1979-1984* (Washington, D.C.: Congressional Research Service, 1986), p. 4.

35. Ibid., p. 7.

36. Ibid., pp. 12–13.

37. New York Public Officer Law, § 103(a) (McKinney 1988).

38. Ibid., § 102; and *Orange County Publications v. Council of the City of Newburgh*, 60 A.D.2d 409 at 419 (2nd Dept. 1978).

39. New York Public Officers Law, § 105 (McKinney 1988).

40. Ibid., § 106(2).

41. Ibid., § 108 (1-3).

42. Ibid., §§ 89(1)(a) and 109.

43. Ibid., § 107.

44. Mississippi Code Annotated, § 25-51-5 (1989 Supp.).

45. Ibid., § 25-41-3(a) (1989 Supp.).

46. Ibid., § 25-41-3(b) (1989 Supp.).

47. Ibid., § 25-41-7(4)(a-k) (1990 Supp.).

48. *Right to Know Law Memorandum* (Concord: The Attorney General, 1980), pp. 9–10. See also New Hampshire Revised Statutes, § 91-A:3, II(a-g) (1990 and 1993 Supp.).

49. *Board of Trustees v. Mississippi Publishers*, 478 So.2d 278-79 (Miss. 1985).

50. *Opinion of Mississippi Attorney General Franklin C. McKenzie*, August 22, 1984.

51. *Orange County Publications v. Council of the City of Newburgh*, 60 A.D.2d 409 (1978).

52. *Orange County Publications v. Council of the City of Newburgh*, 45 N.Y.2d 949 (1978), 383 N.E.2d 1157 (1978).

53. *Daily Gazette v. North Colonie Board of Education*, 67 A.D.2d 803 (1979).

54. New York Laws of 1979, chap. 704; and New York Public Officer Law, § 102(1) (1988).

55. New York Laws of 1979, chap. 704; and New York Public Officer Law, § 102(2) (1988).

56. *Sciolino v. Ryan*, 103 Misc.2d 1021 (Sup. Ct., Monroe County, 1980); and *Sciolino v. Ryan*, 81 A.D.2d 475 (1981).

57. *Sciolino v. Ryan*, 81 A.D.2d 475 at 479.

58. *Open Meetings Law: Report and Recommendations* (New York: State of New York Commission on Government Integrity, 1987), p. 13.

59. *Advisory Opinion Number OML-AO-1158* (Albany: New York State Committee on Open Government, April 11, 1985).

60. New York Laws of 1985, chap. 136, § 2; and New York Public Officers Law, § 108(2)(b) (1988).

61. Ibid.

62. *Open Meetings Law: Report and Recommendations*, pp. 19–20.

63. *Kilgore v. R.W. Page Corporation*, 261 Ga 410 405 S.E.2d 655 (1991).

64. *Florida v. Chiaro*, Florida County Court for Broward County, Case No. 90-39277 TI40A, January 24, 1991, p. 8.

65. Ibid., p. 9. See also *Cape Publications, Incorporated v. City of Palm Bay*, 473 So.2d 222 (Fla. 5th DCA 1985).

66. *Opinions of the Attorney General of Alabama*, April 1990-March 1991, opinion no. 91-00120.

67. *Thompson v. City of Clio*, 765 F.Supp. 1066 at 1081-182 (M.D.Ala, 1991).

68. *People v. Ystueta*, 99 Misc.2d 1105, 418 N.Y.S.2d 508 (1979).

69. Mississippi Code Annotated, § 25-41-7(1)(3) (1991).

70. *Hinds County Board of Supervisors v. Common Cause of Mississippi*, 551 So.2d 107 at 111 (Miss. 1989).

71. *Daily Gazette Company v. Town Board of Cobleskill*, 111 Misc.2d 303, 444 N.Y.S.2d 44 (1981).

72. *White v. Battaglia*, 79 A.D.2d 880, 434 N.Y.S.2d 537 (1980).

73. New York Public Officers Law, § 106(2) (1988).

74. Mississippi Code Annotated, § 25-41-11 (1989 Supp.).

75. Ibid., § 25-41-15 (1989 Supp.).

76. *Hinds County Board of Supervisors v. Common Cause*, 551 So.2d 107 at 125-26 (Miss. 1989).

77. New York Public Officers Law, § 107(2) (McKinney 1988).

78. Ibid.

79. *Dombroske v. Board of Education*, 118 Misc.2d 800 at 804 (Sup. Ct., Onondata County, 1983).

80. *Open Meetings Law: Report and Recommendations*, p. 38.

81. Ibid., pp. 40–41.

82. Ibid., pp. 41–42.

Chapter 7

Internal and External Oversight

Conflict-of-interest laws, codes of ethics, mandatory disclosure acts, freedom of information statutes, and open meetings laws can help to eliminate malversation in public office by raising behavioral norms and serving as a basis for disciplinary action. Nevertheless, these statutory requirements need to be supplemented by organizational changes and administrative actions removing or reducing the opportunity or temptation for unethical conduct, and increasing the risks of detection for officials engaged in unethical behavior.

The structure of a government has an important bearing on the maintenance of high ethical standards. A structure, relatively common on the local government plane, diffusing authority makes it extremely difficult to pinpoint responsibility for many actions and facilitates impropriety by impeding detection of wrongdoing. Consequently, modernization of the structure and procedures of a government may be essential if opportunities for unethical behavior by officials and employees are to be reduced or eliminated.

The New York State Commission on Government Integrity, for example, reported that New York City's

contracting system is fragmented and chaotic. The City's contracting operations are awash in a sea of paper, plagued by inordinate delays, and clouded by unclear and inconsistent rules and procedures which slow City business to a crawl and discourage vendors from stepping forward to bid. As a result, the City often pays far more than it should for goods and services, wasting millions of taxpayer dollars. At the same time, the widespread reluctance of vendors to do business with the City offers opportunities for bid rigging and corrupt side deals.[1]

Fortunately, the City charter was amended by the voters in 1989 to provide for a Procurement Policy Board to centralize the contracting.[2]

The organizational principles of unity of command and functional organization are not obsolete and their employment is essential if internal oversight is to be effective. The executive branch of a government should be organized on the hierarchical principle, with a single chief executive at the top of the pyramid responsible for ensuring accountability and responsiveness of government officers and employees to the policy dictates of elected officials and the general public. Functional organization also is essential because organizing a government in accordance with this principle facilitates the pinpointing of responsibility for all governmental actions taken by administrators.

A particularly difficult ethical problem is the *ultra vires* problem; that is, public officials and employees exceeding their legal authority. In certain instances, officials exceed their authority through ignorance of the law. In other instances, government officials and employees knowingly exceed their authority, convinced that they will not be challenged and that the average citizen will assume any "reasonable" action taken by a government official or employee is legal. The Geneva, New York, Code of Ethics addresses this problem directly by stipulating that "officials and employees should not exceed their authority or breach the law. . . ."[3]

The purposes of internal oversight and external oversight are to ensure that all public officials and employees do not exceed their authority and all government operations are conducted ethically in the most economical and efficient manner without favoritism to any individual or organization. This chapter reviews internal controls in the national government and the New York State government, inspectors general, chief executive oversight, and external oversight in the forms of legislative oversight, comptrollers, independent counsels, and ombudsmen.

INTERNAL CONTROLS

The adoption of adequate control devices by a government can help to establish and maintain high moral standards in the public service. Making a rigorous screening of applicants a part of the recruitment process, for example, will reduce the number of individuals with a proclivity to unethical conduct who are hired. Furthermore, good central purchasing, reporting, record keeping, and accounting systems will remove or reduce the opportunities or temptations for unethical behavior. These systems also can reveal improprieties, thereby permitting initiation of corrective action. Special controls should be applied to officers and employees with inspection or regulatory responsibilities as they have a greater opportunity than others to engage in unethical behavior. And senior officers may abuse the awarding of bonuses, travel expenses, official entertainment funds, and unvouchered expenditures if there are no internal controls.

Internal controls seek to reduce the opportunities for malfeasance, including bribery, kickbacks, and discounts on purchases; misfeasance; and nonfeasance, and to increase the risk of detection of such behavior. Purchasing officials have the opportunity to engage in bid rigging unless the purchasing system has special controls, and officials with regulatory responsibilities can be tempted to take advantage of their positions. A building inspector, for example, may delay action on a building permit application to the point that the applicant offers a bribe to the inspector or a person known to have influence with the inspector to expedite action on the application.

Federal Government Internal Controls

Top national government administrators have been directed by various statutes over the years to install certain types of internal controls and in 1950 were directed by the Accounting and Auditing Act to establish and maintain adequate systems of internal control.[4] These directives were supplemented by Office of Management and Budget (OMB) Circulars, such as Circular A-123 of 1981, specifying standards for evaluating, improving, and reporting on systems of internal controls. The circular also requires that specific officers throughout each department and agency must be assigned internal control responsibilities and vulnerability assessments were to be completed by each agency by December 31, 1982, and at least biennially subsequently.

The Congress in 1982 amended the 1950 statute by providing that the internal controls of each executive department and agency must be established in accordance with standards prescribed by the Comptroller General which are designed to ensure that:

i. obligations and costs are in compliance with applicable law

ii. funds, property, and other assets are safeguarded against waste, loss, unauthorized use, or misappropriation; and

iii. revenues and expenditures applicable to agency operations are properly recorded and accounted for to permit the preparation of accounts and reliable financial and statistical reports and to maintain accountability over the assets.[5]

The act also requires the head of each agency to prepare an annual statement that the agency's system of internal controls complies fully with the requirements of the act or fails to comply fully. In the latter event, the statement must identify weaknesses in the system and plans, and establish schedules for corrective action. The statement is transmitted to the president and the Congress.

OMB Circular A-127 makes each agency head responsible for establishing and ensuring the proper maintenance of a financial control system and requires the designation of a senior officer to be responsible for coordinating the agency's "effort of reviewing, improving, and reporting on the financial systems" to ensure compliance with the circular. The agency's inspector general is directed to provide technical assistance relative to efforts to review and improve the systems, and to inform the agency head whether the review has been carried out in compliance with OMB guidelines.

In compliance with the 1982 Act, the comptroller general prescribed the following general standards for internal controls:

1. *Reasonable Assurance.* Internal control systems are to provide reasonable assurance that the objectives of the systems will be accomplished.
2. *Supportive Attitude.* Managers and employees are to maintain and demonstrate a positive and supportive attitude toward internal controls at all times.
3. *Competent Personnel.* Managers and employees are to have personal and professional integrity and are to maintain a level of competence that allows them to accomplish their assigned duties, as well as understand the importance of developing and implementing good internal controls.
4. *Control Objectives.* Internal control objectives are to be identified or developed for each agency activity and are to be logical, applicable, and reasonably complete.
5. *Control Techniques.* Internal control techniques are to be effective and efficient in accomplishing their internal control objectives.[6]

While these general standards are reasonable and helpful, it is apparent that more detailed standards are necessary to guide federal government departments and agencies. To fill this need, the comptroller general prescribed the following specific standards:

1. *Documentation.* Internal control systems and all transactions and other significant events are to be clearly documented, and the documentation is to be readily available for examination.

2. *Recording of Transactions and Events.* Transactions and other significant events are to be promptly recorded and properly classified.

3. *Execution of Transactions and Events.* Transactions and other significant events are to be authorized and executed only by persons acting within the scope of their authority.

4. *Separation of Duties.* Key duties and responsibilities in authorizing, processing, recording, and reviewing transactions should be separated among individuals.

5. *Supervision.* Qualified and continuous supervision is to be provided to ensure that internal control objectives are achieved.

6. *Access to and Accountability for Resources.* Access to resources and records is to be limited to authorized individuals, and accountability for the custody and use of resources is to be assigned and maintained. Periodic comparison shall be made of the resources with the recorded accountability to determine whether the two agree. The frequency of the comparison shall be a function of the vulnerability of the asset.[7]

The comptroller general's standards also require each department and agency to group its activities into one or more cycles such as management, financial operations, and administrative support. By identifying cycles, appropriate controls can be developed, including secured procedures and physical facilities with fire alarms and locks.

A good internal control system ensures that required financial disclosure statements are filed, reviewed, and corrective action initiated if necessary. Each unit in the U.S. Department of Justice, for example, is "responsible for (1) notifying their employees who are required to file public disclosure reports, (2) assuring that the reports are filed on time, (3) reviewing the reports, and (4) certifying that the reports were reviewed and any apparent or potential conflict of interest [has been] resolved."[8] An ethics education program also is essential to ensure that all officers and employees are informed fully regarding potential unethical actions.

Protection of public employees against abuses in the merit system is an important governmental goal. The U.S. Merit Systems Protection Board was established by Reorganization Plan number 2 of 1978 and codified by the Civil Service Reform Act of 1978.[9] The board reviews significant actions initiated by the Office of Personnel Management and hears employee appeals. The board's administrative judges in regional offices issued 8,388 decisions during fiscal year 1991, "including decisions on initial appeals, stay requests, and addendum cases (requests for attorney fees, petitions for enforcement, and remands)."[10] The board hears appeals from decisions of administrative judges. In 1991, for example, the board upheld the decision of an administrative judge reversing the appellant's separation from government service because the concerned agency violated the employee's due process rights by failing to provide prior notice of the charges, and explanation of its evidence, and an opportunity to respond.[11]

The 1978 Act also created the Office of Special Counsel which investigates allegations of prohibited personnel practices, prosecutes employees violating civil service rules and regulations, and enforces the Hatch Act's ban on partisan political activities by government officers and employees, including macing.

The central management agency of a government should initiate a program to identify areas where the government is vulnerable to employee abuse, fraud, and waste. A program of this nature permits the development of countermeasures. It is essential, however, in a large government to establish departmental offices responsible for identifying the areas at risk and monitoring the effectiveness of counter measures.

In 1989, the Director of the U.S. Office of Management and Budget (OMB) initiated a high-risk program and directed deputy secretaries of departments and deputy administrators of administrations, such as the Environmental Protection Administration, to initiate a high-risk assessment program in conjunction with their respective inspectors general, assistant secretaries or administrators for management, and principal financial officers.

The director receives weekly status reports relative to progress made in protecting selected high-risk areas. The ratings assigned to high-risk areas and additions or deletions of areas from the list of high-risk areas are subject to the approval of the director and the Deputy Director for Management. In 1992, the deputy director commenced to send letters to high-level department and agency officials providing feedback on their high-risk efforts, including the proposed addition of areas to the list or deleting areas.

A 1992 assessment of the program by the U.S. General Accounting Office revealed mixed results. On the positive side, the report noted:

Agency officials have generally reacted positively to OMB's high risk program and feel it has helped focus a high-level interest on the program. For example, inspector general staff at one agency stated that they have seen increased accountability, more monitoring, and direct management involvement in high risk areas.

In another instance, an agency administrator expressed appreciation for the efforts made by the OMB staff in monitoring the agency's corrective action progress and stated that with OMB's assistance the agency had made progress. Further, an official in another agency told us that if top agency management had not been interested in the high risk issue, it would have gone to the bottom of the agency's priority list. [12]

The assessment added that the reported progress in some high-risk areas was misleading or overly optimistic, and that material weaknesses remain in a number of areas deleted from the original list of high-risk areas. [13] The executive budget submitted by the president annually to the Congress contains information on the status of the high-risk areas and progress made in reducing risks. Relative to deleted areas, the General Accounting Office reported that the executive budget fails to distinguish between areas deleted because effective corrective actions were taken and areas deleted which continue to contain material weaknesses. [14]

New York State Internal Controls

A 1990 survey revealed that fourteen states had established formal internal control systems, and other states reported that the state auditor conducted an internal control system review as part of the financial audit. [15]

The 1987 New York State legislature enacted an internal control law for executive agencies, public authorities, the state legislature, and the judiciary. [16] The law defines internal controls as encompassing "the plan of organization and all of the coordinate methods and measures adopted within an organization to safeguard its assets, check the accuracy and reliability of its accounting data, promote operational efficiency and encourage adherence to prescribed managerial policies."

Each head of an agency or public authority is directed to develop internal control guidelines, install a system of internal controls and a system for reviewing the controls, provide employees with a concise statement of applicable management policies and standards, designate an internal control officer, provide a program of internal control education, and evaluate periodically the need for an internal audit function.

State agencies and public authorities are directed to design and maintain their internal controls systems in conformance with standards promulgated by the comptroller general of the United States as modified by the New York state comptroller.

In developing internal controls, each agency or authority must identify activity cycles. Certain activities—such as budgeting, timekeeping, and personnel services—typically are performed by all units while other activities are performed only by one unit. Examples of the latter include payrolls and cash disbursement. Each activity cycle must be documented by reviewing records, observing the activity, and interviewing employees. The documentation identifies the purpose of the activity cycle personnel involved, procedures employed, and records maintained. An evaluation of existing internal controls is critical. The state-owned and operated Metro-North Commuter Railroad suggests that the following evaluation questions should be asked:

1. What could go wrong: Would the related internal control techniques prevent it from happening?
2. If it happened, would it be normally detected? How and when?
3. If not detected on time, how will it impact the department's operations, Metro-North's financial statement, and goals and objectives?[17]

A critical part of the internal controls process is the conduct of a vulnerability assessment to determine the agency's relative susceptibility to risk. The organizational structure, management's attitude toward an internal control system, reporting systems, span of control, and organizational checks and balances influence the vulnerability of an agency. Furthermore, an agency may be susceptible to external pressures to evade regular procedures. Hence, it is important to ensure that no one individual controls all key aspects of an activity.

The competitive bidding process can be undermined by bid rigging involving identical bids, penny or unbalanced bidding, front loading, and bid rotation. Identical bids on a standardized product are not unexpected, but identical bids on nonstandardized products or operations raise questions of bid rigging. Penny bidding refers to a business firm submitting a bid containing one or more specific items at a ludicrously low dollar amount such as one cent. Other items in the bid are inflated and a government accepting a bid containing penny items may pay an excessive amount for the entire contract. Front loading refers to the practice of including in the bid a provision that the contractor will receive most of the money from the government at the commencement of work under the contract instead of throughout the contract as work is completed. Under bid rotation, private firms agree to take turns in submitting the lowest bid for a contract.

To address the problem of rigged bidding, the New York State attorney general in 1980 initiated a bid-monitoring program involving the use of computers to analyze bids and detect patterns of collutions in the submittal of bids. Since firms bidding on New York State contracts often bid on Massachusetts contracts, the New York State attorney general entered into an agreement with the Massachusetts attorney general for a joint bid-monitoring program which operates as follows:

First, computer codes were assigned to political sub-divisions, products purchased, and vendors doing business with governmental entities.

Second, new computer programs designed to detect collusive patterns were developed. These programs can discover patterns of collusion which will ordinarily elude detection by manual inspection. For example, a pattern whereby vendors collusively allocate cities, towns, villages, or school districts may often be detected manually, but less obvious are markets allocated on the basis of zip codes or time sequences. These can be easily detected by computer.

Third, roughly fifty products and services were selected for initial bid analysis. Among the criteria were the importance of the product in dollar terms . . . , whether it was a standardized product . . . , and any historical or other data which provided a pre-existing basis for suspicion of collusion.[18]

INSPECTORS GENERAL

Formal systems of internal control have been supplemented by the legislative or executive creation of the positions of inspectors general (IG) responsible for conducting continuous investigations of alleged unethical behavior in executive departments and agencies. The federal Inspector General Act of 1978 established a system of twenty-five inspectors general who are required to submit semiannual reports to the Congress on their activities and findings, and the Intelligence Authorization Act for fiscal year 1990 established an inspector general in the Central Intelligence Agency.[19] These inspectors general are appointed by the president with the advice and consent of the Senate. The Inspector General Act Amendments of 1988 created the Office of Inspector General in thirty-three other federal units and the Government Printing Office Inspector General Act of 1988 created the office in the Government Printing Office.[20] These inspectors general are appointed by the agency heads and have the same duties as presidentially appointed inspectors general.

The Federal Managers' Financial Integrity Act of 1982 directs the president to provide a congressional committee, at its request, the amount of appropriations requested originally by each office of inspector general.[21]

The inspector general of the Department of Transportation, for example, has organized his office into three sections—investigations; auditing; and policy, planning, and resources—each headed by an assistant inspector general.[22] The inspector general is charged with the duties:

- To conduct and supervise audits and investigations relating to the programs and operations of the Department;
- To provide leadership and coordination and recommend policies for the Department designed to promote economy, efficiency, and effectiveness in the administration of programs and operations and also prevent and detect fraud and abuse in such programs and operations; and
- To keep the Secretary and Congress fully and currently informed about problems and deficiencies relating to the administration of such programs and operations and the necessity for and progress of corrective action.[23]

The importance of the office is indicated by its 473 member staff as of September 30, 1991 and the following accomplishments in the period from April 1, 1991 to September 30, 1991:

- Issued 884 audit reports—$717.1 million in funds to be put to better use, $74.2 million in questioned costs, and $4.7 million in unsupported costs.
- Obtained management decisions to seek recoveries, or more effective use of resources amounting to $259.9 million.
- Opened 110 reactive investigative cases, closed 140 cases, and 394 cases are pending.
- Completed investigations resulting in 39 convictions; 43 indictments; $6.5 million in fines, court-ordered restitutions, administrative recoveries, and cost avoidance; 61 years in sentences; 97 years probation; 9 suspensions and debarments; and 42 administrative actions.
- Recommended recovery of Federal funds when transit authorities prematurely removed buses from revenue service without reimbursing the Urban Mass Transportation Administration (UMTA) for its proportionate investment. . . .[24]

Table 7.1 contains data on protective audits designed to assess administrative management practices at approximately 2,800 smaller department facilities. These audits identified weaknesses in internal controls and the resulting misuse of governments benefits, missing equipment and other property, loss of department funds, and improper small purchases. Disciplinary action was initiated against officials and employees responsible for the abuses.

Table 7.1
Summary of Protective Audit Deficiencies, U.S. Department of Transportation,
April 1, 1991 through September 30, 1991

ORGANIZATION	Number of Audits	Deficiencies								Total
		Time and Attendance	Travel	Inventory Control	Vehicle Utilization	Small Purchases	Property Records	Imprest Fund	Other Areas	
Federal Aviation Administration	12	12	10	2	6	3	5	4	4	46
Coast Guard	10	6	4	1	5	5	9	3	7	40
Federal Highway Administration	2	2	2	0	2	1	1	1	1	10
Office of Secretary	2	2	2	1	0	0	0	0	0	6
National Highway Transportation Safety Administration	1	1	1	1	0	0	0	0	0	3
Urban Mass Transportation Administration	1	1	1	0	1	0	1	0	1	5
Totals	28	24	20	5	14	10	16	8	13	110

Source: Inspector General Semiannual Report to the Congress, April 1, 1991–September 30, 1991 (Washington, D.C.: United States
Department of Transportation, 1991), p. 4.

Requests for an inspector general investigation can be made by members of the Congress. Allegations by a whistleblower relative to defects in radiographs of welds at the Seabrook nuclear power station in New Hampshire led Senator Edward M. Kennedy of Massachusetts to forward on February 27, 1990, a copy of the allegations to the Chairman of the U.S. Nuclear Regulatory Commission (NRC) along with fifteen questions. On March 7, 1990, Representative Peter Kostmayer of the U.S. House of Representatives wrote to the chairman and raised additional questions about defects in radiographs of welds. The chairman responded with answers to the questions on March 15, 1990. Unsatisfied with the answers, Senator Kennedy and Representative Kostmayer, joined by four other members of Congress, requested that the commission's Office of the Inspector General (OIG) conduct an investigation of the matter.

The inspector general reported that his investigation revealed no "attempt to mislead the Congress by providing false or inaccurate information" but found:

1. The OIG investigation determined that Inspection Report 84-07 did not support the NRC's representation to Congressman Kostmayer about the 100% review of all safety-related weld radiographs.

2. Contrary to the NRC's response to Congressman Kostmayer, the OIG investigation found that during NRC Inspection 84-07, YAEC [Yankee Atomic Electric Company] did not have a written procedure that required the review of all safety-related vendor and site generated radiographs.[25]

The performance of the inspectors general is subject to congressional oversight. In December 1991, the chairman of the Subcommittee on Federal Services, Post Office, and Civil Service of the U.S. Senate issued a staff report critical of the use of contractors by inspectors general. In particular, the staff report criticized (1) use of contractors to conduct "such sensitive work as criminal investigations, determinations regarding compliance with laws and rules, and targeting subjects for investigation," (2) failure of inspectors general to require the contractors to provide information on related work they are performing for other clients, and (3) additional costs associated with use of contractors instead of federal government employees.[26]

The staff report also questioned whether the reliance upon contractors violated two circulars issued by the U.S. Office of Management and Budget. Circular A-76 stipulates "certain functions are inherently governmental in nature, being so intimately related to the public interest as to mandate performance only by federal employees" and Circular A-120 stipulates "advisory and assistance services shall not be . . . used in performing work of a policy, decision-making, or managerial nature which is the direct responsibility of agency officials. . . ."[27]

In addition, the report identified a conflict of interest when an inspector general employed a contractor who also is a contractor for another unit in the agency and stressed that reliance on contractors results in the loss of institutional memory that is essential if an inspector general is to perform adequately in the future.[28]

The head of each federal department or agency rates the performance of the inspector general and the possibility exists that an inspector general who is highly critical of aspects of an agency's operations may receive a low performance rating. The chairman of the Farm Credit Administration, for example, rated the administration's inspector general's performance as "minimally successful" during federal fiscal year 1990. This rating prompted the chairman and the ranking minority member of three congressional committees to request the Comptroller General of the United States, an employee of the Congress, to conduct an investigation of the rating.

The comptroller general's report concluded that the performance rating of the inspector general was not substantiated by the record.[29] The report concluded that thirty-one of thirty-six examples cited by the chairman to support the rating "did not demonstrate a lack of compliance with government auditing standards, and the remaining examples contained minor deviation from standards but contained sound conclusions and recommendations."[30]

Governor Mario M. Cuomo of New York in 1986 issued Executive Order Number 79 creating the position of State Inspector General with authority to investigate and make recommendation to prevent and detect abuse, corruption, and fraud in state agencies whose heads are nominated or appointed by the governor. The state inspector general is directed to receive and investigate complaints; notify federal, state, or local government agencies when evidence is uncovered that nonstate agency personnel have engaged in criminal activities, periodically review agency policies and procedures; and monitor their day-to-day operations and make recommendations for improvement.

A 1989 report of the state inspector general revealed major ethical breaches by certain members of the New York State Labor Relations Board who were political appointees of the governor.[31] In particular, the report found that the governor's counsel's office failed to use available information on the nominees to detect and prevent conflicts of interest from arising following their nomination by the governor and confirmation by the state senate.[32] Problems of the board were brought to the attention of the inspector general when the board was scheduled to vote on the findings of an administrative law judge involving organizing activities at a pub and it was disclosed that the brother of a commissioner is the business manager of the union involved in the dispute.[33]

In 1991, the state inspector general released two reports involving the State Department of Social Services. The first report found that the department's Office of Human Resources Development lacks monitoring procedures to ensure that contractors claim only actual expenditures as reimbursable contract costs, fails to verify adequately contractors' indirect cost rates, and "does not maintain an arm's length relationship with training contractors."[34]

The second report revealed that a number of individuals in the same office were aware that a contract had been reassigned without official approval, yet took no action to demand that such approval be sought.[35]

In a state such as New York, it is apparent that the duties of the inspector general overlap in part the duties of other state officers or bodies including the ethics commission, attorney general, and state comptroller, and it is essential that the activities of these bodies and officers be coordinated.

Local governments also have established inspector general's offices and special investigating bodies. A special Commissioner of Investigation for the New York City School District replaced the former inspector general in 1991 and received numerous complaints alleging that personnel in the Division of School Safety were guilty of serious misconduct. The special commissioner's report found that retired government employees were allowed to collect a salary and pension in violation of the City charter and state law, the School Safety's Chief of Operations made false statements relative to his prior criminal record, the executive director and chief of operations entered into an illegal business arrangement, and the division hired twelve relatives of the deputy executive director.[36]

As noted, opportunities for corruption abound in governmental agencies with regulatory responsibilities. To investigate complaints against their members, police departments have established internal affairs units or complaint review boards. Approximately 15,000 allegations of unethical behavior are filed annually against the 27,500-member New York City Police force.[37] An internal investigation conducted by the police commissioner in 1992 revealed poor methods of investigations and inadequate coordination within the department's Division of Internal Affairs which has approximately 300 field investigators and 150 investigators assigned to headquarters of the division. Investigators anonymously telephone police precincts and file false reports of corruption in order to determine whether the reports are transmitted to the Internal Affairs Division.

Whether a police department can investigate adequately allegations of serious misconduct against its members is a topic of intense debate. Critics allege that an independent body is essential if such allegations are to be investigated impartially and public confidence in the police is to be maintained. Nevertheless, few cities have established independent police complaint review boards.

CHIEF EXECUTIVE OVERSIGHT

The chief executive of a government, particularly one endowed with strong formal powers, can use his/her supervisory and budget powers to detect wrongdoing or inefficiencies in executive departments and agencies. Required reports can be useful in ensuring that all administrative actions are efficient and ethical provided the reports contain critical information and are reviewed carefully.

The executive budget process is a valuable tool for detecting unneeded programs, inefficiencies, and wrong-doing. The head of each department or agency is required to justify in writing each requested appropriation and also is subject to direct questioning by the chief executive or budget office officials. Furthermore, budget examiners can exercise continuous oversight over the departments and agencies.

A number of state legislatures have enacted statutes empowering the governor to appoint a special commission to investigate a state agency or department and report findings and recommendations to the governor and the legislature. In 1907, for example, the New York State legislature enacted the Moreland Act, authorizing the governor to appoint an investigating commission at any time.[38] The first commission appointed by the governor was charged in 1907 with examining the Department of Insurance. A second commission was appointed the following year to investigate the state Board of Embalming Examiners. Scandals involving nursing and residential homes and the bankruptcy of the state Urban Development Corporation induced Governor Hugh L. Carey in 1975 to appoint two Moreland Act commissions.

A governor also may create an investigating commission by executive order. In 1987, Governor Mario M. Cuomo of New York issued Executive Order Number 88 establishing the New York State Commission on Government Integrity. A 1989 commission report was highly critical of the New York City mayor's Talent Bank which sought, among other things, to promote hiring of women and members of certain minority groups. The commission found that the Talent Bank primarily placed "candidates with political pedigrees. . . ."[39]

EXTERNAL OVERSIGHT

Legislatures historically have exercised general oversight to ensure that executive departments and agencies follow legislative intent; manage programs in an economical, efficient, and ethical manner; achieve mandated goals; and respond to the legitimate grievances of citizens. Oversight is exercised directly by legislatures and indirectly through legislatively created offices such as auditors, independent counsels, and ombudsmen.

Legislative Oversight

Standing committees of state legislatures date to the 1780s but were little used during the late eighteenth and early nineteenth centuries as reliance was placed upon the committee of the whole. A more active standing committee system developed in the nineteenth century as industrialization and urbanization produced a sharp increase in the number of bills introduced.

When allegations of unethical behavior were made in the nineteenth century, such as the canal and railroad scandals, a legislative body would establish a select (special) committee to conduct an investigation of the allegations and report to the legislative body. Such committees continue to be appointed. An investigating committee can be a single house committee or a joint committee.

Standing committees and subcommittees of legislatures also conduct special investigations. The U.S. Senate Committee on the Judiciary, for example, released a major investigative report in 1992 containing its findings and conclusions relative to whether the U.S. Department of Justice converted, stole, or misappropriated the Promis computer software developed by INSLAW, Incorporated and attempted to put INSLAW out of business. The committee concluded there was "strong evidence" to support the allegations.[40]

The committee included harsh criticism in its investigative report because the Department of Justice is responsible for ensuring that wrongdoing will be punished.

The history of the Department's behavior in the INSLAW case dramatically illustrates its (1) reflexive hostility and "circle the wagons" approach toward outside investigations; (2) inability or unwillingness to look objectively at charges of wrongdoing by high level Justice officials, particularly when the agency itself is a defendant in litigation; and (3) belligerence toward Justice employees with views that run counter to those of the agency upper management. The fact that the Department failed to recognize a need for an investigation of the INSLAW matter for more than 7 years is remarkable. Failure to do so has effectively shielded officials who may have committed wrongdoing from investigation and prosecution.[41]

Recognizing the need for a permanent program auditing body, the 1969 New York State legislature established the first such body in the United States—the Legislative Commission on Expenditure Review. Composed of the leader of each house and other key leaders, including the chairmen of the Senate Finance Committee and the Assembly Ways and Means Committee, the commission did excellent work in identifying program inefficiencies and mismanagement. Nevertheless, the commission was eliminated for political reasons in 1992. However, several other states have established similar program audit commissions.

Legislative bodies rely heavily upon two other mechanisms to exercise oversight. Departments and agencies are required to submit periodic reports on specified activities which enable the legislatures to determine whether corrective action is necessary. The appropriation process allows committees to investigate in-depth the activities of executive agencies and question their heads relative to the spectrum of activities under their control. For these mechanisms to be effective, it is essential that the legislatures have adequate staff competent in various functional areas.

A state legislature can conduct an investigation jointly with the governor. The New York State legislature has relied for decades upon "temporary state commissions" to conduct studies of major problems. Each commission is composed of an equal number of members appointed by the governor, the Senate President Pro Tempore, and the Speaker of the Assembly.

Comptrollers

Each of the fifty states has an auditor or controller (often officially spelled comptroller) whose function is to scrutinize the state's financial transactions and accounts; twenty-four states have both an auditor and a controller. Twenty-nine auditors and ten controllers are popularly elected. The remaining ones are selected by the state legislature. The U.S. Comptroller General, who heads the General Accounting Office, is selected by the Congress. Although the terminology of statutes sometimes confuses and even juxtaposes the distinction between the two officers, properly speaking an auditor has the function of post-auditing and a controller has the function of conducting a current audit.

In current auditing, the controller examines vouchers submitted by spending agencies and, before monies can be disbursed, must certify that the expenditure is covered by a legislative appropriation made in accordance with law. In post-auditing, the auditor examines accounts to determine whether they have been kept accurately and whether officers have been honest and have conformed to law in spending the state's money. The auditor is granted access to the accounts, books, and other records of all state departments and agencies.

Auditors and comptrollers originally conducted only financial audits. In the twentieth century, auditors commenced to conduct program audits and to question the judgment of executive officers. The New York State comptroller is an unusual constitutional elected officer in that he/she is authorized to conduct pre-audits and post-audits, and to prescribe accounting methods that must be followed by all state and local governmental departments and agencies. The state comptroller also conducts critical program audits which are made public.

In 1992, the New York state comptroller released an audit report on internal controls employed by the Division of Meter Collections (DMC) of the New York City Department of Transportation (DOT). Findings included:

- Metal detectors used to prevent the theft of coins from DMC's coin processing areas were inaccurate.
- DMC has no video monitoring system to deter theft, as do other similar facilities . . . ,
- DMC's computerized Parking Information Management Systems does not compare actual revenue collections to revenue targets by collection area as a means of identifying potential thefts. Our analysis identified 36 significant decreases in revenue which we referred to DOT for investigation.
- Controls over subway tokens which are accepted by certain meters were weak. We identified a potential shortage of 1,800 tokens.
- DMC's inventory of master keys which open meter coin boxes was short 69 keys.[42]

The comptroller of the United States reported to the Congress in 1992 that the U.S. Department of Transportation had been appropriated more than thirty-six billion dollars in federal fiscal year 1992, but lacked a single consolidated accounting system, has made limited progress in correcting accounting weaknesses, and has made little progress in providing departmental managers and the Congress with financial information essential for overseeing programs and operations.[43] The comptroller general also reported in 1992 that the Drug Enforcement Administration has failed to correct serious computer security weaknesses and the failure poses a significant risk to the integrity of the administration's computer system.[44]

In 1993, the Comptroller General reported that numerous employees of the Internal Revenue Service (IRS), who opened mail, had access to and could utilize the Integrated Data Retrieval System to adjust taxpayer accounts.[45] In addition, the comptroller general discovered that IRS "management manipulated performance statistics by closing cases prematurely to meet deadlines or to increase statistics in a particular area and leaving known input errors in reports to portray favorable measurements."[46]

Auditors and controllers can detect the need for new laws or amendments of existing ones. The Presidential Records Act of 1978 stipulates that specified reports of departing presidents and their staffs are government property that will be retained by the National Archives and Records Administration.[47] No federal law, however, establishes procedures for the removal of materials by departing agency heads. In 1991, the comptroller general reported:

some classified information that was removed did not receive required security protection. Also, agencies did not always know what information was removed by departing agency heads. Further, documents, including original documents and classified information, were removed without agency knowledge. Once these documents are removed, the government's access to them is not ensured.[48]

The Independent Counsel or Commission

President Richard M. Nixon's discharge of Special Prosecutor Archibald Cox, who was investigating the Watergate scandal, provoked a reaction in the Congress which in 1978 enacted the Ethics in Government Act containing a provision for the appointment of an independent counsel (termed Special Prosecutor until 1983) by a three-judge panel to investigate allegations of criminal wrongdoing by senior members of the executive branch—the president, vice president, members of the Cabinet, senior officers of the Justice Department, and certain political party officials.[49] The constitutionality of the act was upheld by the U.S. Supreme

Court and the act was extended in 1982 and in 1987, but an extension bill died in the Senate in October 1992 in the face of a threatened filibuster.[50] Eleven independent counsels were appointed and four filed indictments.

Independent Counsel Lawrence E. Walsh completed eleven prosecutions and won eight convictions or guilty pleas and was prosecuting former Defense Secretary Caspar W. Weinberger when the law expired in 1992. Although investigations underway could continue after the expiration of the law, President George Bush on December 24, 1992, granted a pardon to Mr. Weinberger and five other convicted or indicted federal government officers involved in the arms for hostages agreement with Iran.

The independent counsel was authorized by the Congress because it was convinced that the Justice Department, a unit of the executive branch, could not be trusted to investigate thoroughly allegations of wrongdoing by high administration officials and seek indictments for criminal offense if the evidence warranted indictments. The statute authorizing the office was criticized strongly by officials of the Reagan and Bush administrations. Three major arguments were employed against congressional extension of the authorizing statute. First, the independent counsels exercise their prosecutorial powers without accountability and effective review. Second, the office is unnecessary since allegations of wrongdoing by high administration officials can be investigated and, if need be, prosecuted by the Justice Department. Third, investigations by an independent counsel are extremely expensive since the counsel is not subject to ordinary governmental financial controls.

Deputy Attorney General George Terwilliger testified in 1992 that "an independent counsel is unsupervised in the exercise of prosecutorial discretion, which is broad in the normal case, but virtually unchecked in the case of an Independent Counsel."[51] He added the department brought public corruption indictments in 1991 against 803 federal officials, 115 state officials, 242 local officials, and 292 others, and that high-ranking officers including a U.S. attorney, assistant U.S. attorneys, an assistant to the attorney general, a U.S. marshal, and several Federal Bureau of Investigation and Drug Enforcement Administration special agents were convicted.[52]

Terrence O'Donnell, a former general counsel of the Department of Defense, testified that "the Independent Counsel is actually a corps of vigilante prosecutors formed after the targets are identified. Once the targets are identified, the search for a crime begins. This is fundamental distortion of the normal prosecution process. It turns things upside down to the great prejudice of the targets."[53] He also was critical of the fact that Independent Counsel Walsh at one time had three full-time press aides who "helped to shape the story in the halls during the breaks with the press, putting a spin on the testimony and the trial."[54]

Terry Eastland, a former official of the Justice Department, criticized the law because it "invites the President and Congress, in effect, to join in a handshake of irresponsibility and leave the issue of executive malfeasance to Independent Counsels who are politically account-able . . . to no one, except perhaps the elite political culture of Washington, D.C."[55]

Suzanne Garment, a resident scholar at the American Enterprise Institute, reported that Independent Counsel Leon Silverman twice ended his investigation of Ray Donovan, a member of President Ronald Reagan's cabinet, "only to be forced to reopen it. The publicity surrounding the investigation had produced an unending stream of new charges against Donovan, and the law required investigation of these charges, even though they were virtually all unprovable."[56]

The U.S. General Accounting Office is required by law to audit the expenditures of the independent counsels. In 1992, the Office released a highly critical report relative to the expenditures of nine independent counsels.[57] The report revealed five independent counsels did not provide reports of all their expenditures, serious internal control weaknesses exist, several expenditures were inconsistent with statutes and regulations, and there was noncompliance with pay and travel requirements.

The Ombudsman

The first "Justitieombudsman" office was created by an 1809 amendment to the Constitution of Sweden as a mechanism for ensuring that all laws and ordinances were observed by civil servants, military officers, and judges.[58] The ombudsman's office in particular was designed to enable the Riksdag (parliament) to balance the powers of the king. Sweden currently has two additional ombudsmen—the Antitrust Ombudsman and the Consumer Ombudsman. Both are appointed by the Government in contrast to the "Justitieombudsman" who is elected by the Riksdag for a four-year term.

An ombudsman possesses a most important power that an individual legislator lacks, that is, authority to examine *all* records of an agency. An ombudsman can not initiate corrective action and must rely upon the prestige of the office to convince an executive agency to take corrective action.

The Irish Oireachtas (parliament) in 1980 created the Office of Ombudsman, but the first ombudsman did not assume office until 1984.[59] The ombudsman is another official to whom a citizen aggrieved by an administrative decision can turn to for assistance, and provides the parliament with another mechanism for controlling the executive branch. In contrast to the Parliamentary Commissioner (ombudsman) in the United Kingdom who can investigate a complaint only if it is forwarded by a member of Parliament, the Irish ombudsman can accept and investigate complaints received directly from citizens.[60]

The Irish ombudsman conducts investigations in secret and an executive organization and/or concerned individual must be given the opportunity to comment on the action in question. A recommendation for corrective administrative action typically is sufficient to persuade the concerned department or other body to accept the recommendation, but the ombudsman may issue a special report to the Oireachtas should the department fail to initiate corrective action. Although the ombudsman is not specifically charged with investigating unethical conduct, he has stressed that civil servants "have a special responsibility to ensure that the information and advice they give to members of the public is accurate."[61]

Representative Henry Reuss of Wisconsin introduced the first ombudsman bill in the Congress in 1963 providing for the appointment of a congressional ombudsman appointed by the Speaker of the House of Representatives and the president pro tempore of the Senate. Under the Reuss bill, the congressional ombudsman would gain jurisdiction over a citizen complaint only if the complaint was forwarded by a member of Congress. Senator Edward V. Long of Missouri in 1967 introduced a bill establishing an Office of Administrative Ombudsman authorized to receive complaints directly from citizens. The Congress, however, has not created an ombudsman office.

Several governors and mayors of large cities in the United States have established an ombudsman office, but these offices are not genuine independent investigating agencies, since the ombudsmen are appointed by the chief executives to investigate departments and agencies under their control. To ensure independence for an ombudsman, the office must be created and invested with broad powers by a legislative body to investigate complaints by citizens against executive officers.

Four state legislatures—Hawaii, Nebraska, Alaska, and Iowa—have created a classical position of ombudsman. The Hawaii state legislature in 1967 was the first legislative body in the United States to create an ombudsman-type office.[62] The state legislature appoints the ombudsman by a majority vote of each house for a six-year term and a two-thirds vote is required for the removal of the ombudsman from office. The ombudsman is charged with investigating administrative acts or inaction of state and local government agencies, departments, and officers involved with an aggrieved citizen. He also may initiate an investigation and has access to all internal documents of agencies. The ombudsman lacks the power to prosecute wrongdoers, but may refer evidence of malfeasance, misfeasance, or nonfeasance to appropriate officers. He submits annual reports to the state legislature and the governor.

Table 7.2 reveals that 67.1 percent of the inquiries received by the Hawaiian ombudsman between July 1991 and June 1992 were complaints, 25.3 percent involved requests for information, and 7.1 percent were outside the jurisdiction of the ombudsman.

Table 7.2
Numbers and Types of Inquiries, Fiscal Year 1991–92

Month	Total Inquiries	No Jurisdiction	Information	Complaint
July	674	45	181	448
August	663	35	135	493
September	584	45	136	403
October	593	42	148	403
November	535	44	144	347
December	549	46	135	368
January	602	45	152	405
February	567	34	153	380
March	574	43	143	388
April	580	57	165	358
May	607	49	174	384
June	534	50	119	365
TOTAL	7,062	535	1,785	4,742
% OF TOTAL INQUIRIES	100%	7.6%	25.3%	67.1%

Source: *Report of the Ombudsman* (Honolulu: State of Hawaii, 1992), p. 17.

The 1969 Nebraska state legislature created an ombudsman-type position entitled the Office of Public Counsel.[63] The public counsel is appointed by a two-thirds vote of the unicameral state legislature for a six-year term and may be removed from office by a two-thirds vote. The chief duty is to investigate citizen complaints against state executive agencies and to negotiate remedial action by agencies as necessary. The public counsel has no jurisdiction over local governments. A second duty is to provide answers to citizen questions and to assist citizens experiencing problems with a government. In common with the Hawaiian ombudsman, the public counsel has access to all internal documents of executive departments and agencies, but lacks the power to prosecute.

SUMMARY

Conflict-of-interest laws, codes of ethics, and various sunshine statutes help to raise ethical standards in the public service by providing guidance relative to acceptable and unacceptable behavior by public officials and employees, and facilitating the detection of unethical actions. Unfortunately, these statutes are not totally self-enforcing. Hence, it is essential that each government establish systems of internal and external oversight of the activities of public employees.

An effective system of internal controls reduces the opportunities for malfeasance in public office and identifies system failures that need to be corrected. In designing an internal controls system, it is essential that special precautions be taken by a government to prevent abuses by officials with regulatory powers. The first step in installing an internal controls system is a vulnerability assessment to determine high-risk areas of activities.

An important internal controls official is the inspector general who is authorized to conduct investigations of alleged unethical behavior and to initiate investigations on his/her own initiative. The performance of an inspector general should be subject to legislative oversight to ensure that he/she is performing assigned duties competently and free from undue pressure by agency officials not to issue a critical report or be punished in some manner for issuing such a report.

Internal oversight of administrative activities may not be fully effective unless there is external oversight. Legislative investigating committees should play a major oversight role in ensuring that administrative departments and agencies conduct their activities in accordance with high ethical standards. The work of these committees can be supplemented on a continuing basis by auditors who conduct program reviews as well as financial audits.

In cases where allegations against high level officials are very serious, a legislative body can create an office of independent counsel to conduct investigations and prosecute wrongdoers. The independent counsel can play a most useful role in the national government by ensuring fairness in investigations and prosecutions of allegations of wrongdoing in the executive branch. The independent counsel in particular is viewed as a neutral official in these cases in contrast to a U.S. Department of Justice prosecutor who is employed by the attorney general, who is appointed by the president with the advice and consent of the Congress.

Although there is only a relatively small number of offices of the ombudsman created by legislative bodies in the United States, serious consideration should be given to the creation of such an office by the Congress, state legislatures lacking an ombudsman, and the councils of large cities. The primary function of an ombudsman is to investigate citizen grievances against administrative officials and employees. In the process of conducting an investigation, the ombudsman may uncover evidence of unethical actions which can be turned over to prosecutors.

Internal oversight and external oversight are most effective if the oversight bodies receive information relative to unethical behavior from citizens and public employees. The latter, of course, face the possibility of retaliation by their governmental superiors if wrongdoing is reported to appropriate officials. To encourage whistleblowing and to protect whistleblowers, governments have enacted whistleblower protection statutes which are examined in Chapter 8.

NOTES

1. *A Ship Without a Captain: The Contracting Process in New York City* (New York: New York State Commission on Government Integrity, 1989), p. 1.

2. New York City Charter, § 311(a) (1989).

3. Geneva, New York, Code of Ethics, art. 15, § 15.2.

4. Accounting and Auditing Act of 1950, 31 U.S.C. § 66a (1983 and 1992 Supp.).

5. Federal Managers' Financial Integrity Act of 1982, 96 Stat. 814, 31 U.S.C. § 65 note (1983 and 1992 Supp.).

6. *Standards for Internal Controls in the Federal Government* (Washington, D.C.: United States General Accounting Office, 1983), p. 2.

7. Ibid., p. 3.

8. *Ethics: The Department of Justice's Ethics Program* (Washington, D.C.: United States General Accounting Office, 1988), p. 5.

9. Civil Service Reform Act of 1978, 92 Stat. 1111, 5 U.S.C. § 2302 (1992 Supp.).

10. *Annual Report for Fiscal Year 1991* (Washington, D.C.: U.S. Merit Systems Protection Board, 1991), p. 15.

11. *Stephen v. Department of the Air Force*, BN315H8710028 (April 26, 1991), 47 M.S.P.R. 672 (1991).

12. *OMB High Risk Program: Benefits Found But Greater Oversight Needed* (Washington, D.C.: United States General Accounting Office, 1992), p. 5.

13. Ibid., pp. 6–7.

14. Ibid., p. 8.

15. David J. Kidera and Stephen M. Fletcher, "New York Takes the Pulse: Internal Control in State Government," *Government Finance Review*, August 1991, p. 7.

16. New York Laws of 1987, chap. 814; and New York Finance Law, § 2-a (McKinney 1989).

17. *Internal Control Review Handbook* (New York: Metro-North Commuter Railroad, n.d.), p. 3.

18. *Bid Rigging in the Competitive Bidding Process* (Albany: New York State Department of Law, 1985), p. 8.

19. Inspector General Act of 1978, 92 Stat. 1101, 5 U.S.C. App. § 1 (1993); and Intelligence Authorization Act for Fiscal Year 1990, 102 Stat. 1904.

20. Inspector General Act Amendments of 1988, 102 Stat. 2515, 5 U.S.C. § 5315 (1980); and Government Printing Office Inspector General Act of 1988, 102 Stat. 2515, 44 U.S.C. § 3901 (1993 Supp.).

21. Federal Managers' Financial Integrity Act of 1982, 96 Stat. 815, 31 U.S.C. § 1105 (1983 and 1992 Supp.).

22. *Inspector General Semiannual Report to the Congress: April 1, 1991-September 30, 1991* (Washington, D.C.: United States Department of Transportation, 1991), p. 37.

23. Ibid.

24. Ibid., p. v.

25. *Office of the Inspector General, Review of the NRC Staff's Responses to Congressional Inquiries Regarding Joseph Wampler and the Welding Program at Seabrook Nuclear Station* (Washington, D.C.: United States Nuclear Regulatory Commission, 1990), pp. 17 and 30.

26. *The Inspectors General Use of Contractors* (Washington, D.C.: Subcommittee on Federal Services, Post Office, and Civil Service, United States Senate, 1991), pp. 1–2.

27. Ibid., pp. 9–10.

28. Ibid., pp. 18 and 24.

29. *Inspectors General: Issues Involving the Farm Credit Administration's Chairman and IG* (Washington, D.C.: United States General Accounting Office, 1991), pp. 1–2, and 6–7.

30. Ibid., pp. 1–2.

31. *Report of Investigation Concerning Operation of the New York State Labor Relations Board* (Albany: Office of the State Inspector General, 1989).

32. Ibid., pp. 39–40.

33. Ibid., p. 4.

34. *Report Concerning Management of Training Contracts: New York State Department of Social Services* (Albany: Office of Inspector General, 1991), p. ES-3.

35. *Report Concerning Improper Assignment of Training Contract-Office of Human Resources Development, New York State Department of Social Services* (Albany: Office of Inspector General, 1991), p. 1.

36. *Private Interest Over Public Trust: An Investigation into Certain Improprieties by the Leadership at the Division of School Safety* (New York: City of New York Special Commissioner of Investigation, 1992), p. 1.

37. Sam Dillon, "Fighting Police Department Corruption Amid Distrust," *The New York Times*, December 7, 1992, p. B1.

38. New York Laws of 1907, chap. 539; and New York Executive Law, § 6 (McKinney 1982).

39. *"Playing Ball" with City Hall: A Case Study of Political Patronage in New York City* (New York: New York State Commission on Government Integrity, 1989), p. 5.

40. Committee on the Judiciary, United States Senate, *The INSLAW Affair* (Washington, D.C.: United States Government Printing Office, 1992), p. 3.

41. Ibid., p. 13.

42. *Internal Controls and Accountability over Meter Revenue, New York City Department of Transportation Division of Meter Collections* (New York: Office of the State Comptroller, 1992), pp. S-1 and S-2.

43. *Financial Management: DOT's Accounting and Financial Information System Can be Improved* (Washington, D.C.: United States General Accounting Office, 1992), pp. 1–2.

44. *Computer Security: DEA is Not Adequately Protecting Sensitive Drug Enforcement Data* (Washington, D.C.: United States General Accounting Office, 1992), p. 3.

45. *Tax Administration: Examples of Waste and Inefficiency in IRS* (Washington, D.C.: United States General Accounting Office, 1993), p. 8.

46. Ibid., p. 17.

47. Presidential Records Act of 1978, 88 Stat. 1695, 44 U.S.C. § 3315 (1991).

48. *Federal Records: Document Removal by Agency Heads Needs Independent Oversight* (Washington, D.C.: United States General Accounting Office, 1991), p. 5.

49. Ethics in Government Act of 1978, 92 Stat. 1867, 28 U.S.C. §§ 591-99 (1992 Supp.).

50. *Morrison v. Olson*, 487 U.S. 654 (1987); and "Independent Counsel Reauthorization Act," *Congressional Record*, September 29, 1992, p. S15604.

51. "Statement of George Terwilliger, Deputy Attorney General, before the Subcommittee on Oversight of Government Management, Committee on Governmental Affairs, United States Senate, Concerning Reauthorization of the Independent Counsel Statute on August 11, 1992," p. 2.

52. Ibid., p. 4.

53. "The Constitutionality of the Independent Counsel Statute," *Congressional Record*, September 18, 1992, p. E2697.

54. Ibid., pp. E2697-698.

55. "Independent Counsel Law," *Congressional Record*, September 25, 1992, p. E2808.

56. Ibid.

57. *Financial Audit: Expenditures by Nine Independent Counsels* (Washington, D.C.: United States General Accounting Office, 1992), pp. 1–18.

58. Constitution of Sweden, art. 96. See also "The Swedish Ombudsmen," *Facts on Sweden* (Stockholm: The Swedish Institute 1992), p. 1.

59. The Ombudsman Act, 1980; and The Ombudsman (Amendment) Act, 1984 (Republic of Ireland). See also Statutory Instrument Number 332 of 1984: Ombudsman Act First Schedule (Amendment) Order, 1984.

60. For an in-depth report on the United Kingdom Parliamentary Commissioner, see Roy Gregory and Peter Hutcheson, *The Parliamentary Ombudsman: A Study in the Control of Administrative Action* (London: George Allen & Unwin, 1975).

61. *Annual Report of the Ombudsman* (Dublin: The Stationery Office, 1987), p. 13. For additional details, see Joseph F. Zimmerman, "The Office of Ombudsman in Ireland," *Administration*, vol. XXXVII, no. 3, 1989, pp. 258–72.

62. Hawaii Laws of 1967, chap. 306; and Hawaii Revised Statutes, §§ 96.1-96.19 (1992).

63. Nebraska Laws of 1969, chap. 762; and Nebraska Revised Statutes, §§ 81-8,240 to 81-8,254.

Chapter 8

Whistleblowing

If conflict-of-interest laws, codes of ethics, and internal and external controls were fully effective in ensuring that all government officers and employees performed their duties in accordance with the highest ethical standards, there would be no need for whistleblowing. This term has been defined by the U.S. Office of the Special Counsel as a government employee who provides information to the Special Counsel, agency officials, an inspector general, or individuals outside of government service relative to "a violation of any law, rule, or regulation; or mismanagement, a gross waste of funds, an abuse of authority, or a substantial and specific danger to public health or safety."[1] However, this definition does not include disclosures prohibited by statutes or executive orders if the information relates to national defense or conduct of foreign policy.

The Campaign for Freedom of Information in the United Kingdom maintains that whistleblowing is legitimate in order:

a. To expose illegal acts or corruption.

b. To expose the unfitness for office of someone in a position of public responsibility.

c. To disclose information of public concern to an appropriate person; *e.g.*, the Director of Public Prosecutions or the Chairman of a Select Committee.[2]

Whistleblowing, which indicates the lack of or failure of internal control systems, is in the tradition of the muckrakers, such as Lincoln Steffans and

Upton Sinclair, who exposed corruption in cities and certain industries. The whistleblower may report unethical behavior anonymously or publicly. The whistleblower revealing his/her identity suffers the possibility of reprisal in the form of blacklisting, firing, demotion, harassment, intimidation, and transfer. Hence, there is a tendency for the whistle to be blown anonymously if the whistleblower is still in government service.

The organizational culture of a government agency or department establishes the ethical climate and either encourages or discourages whistleblowing. The culture in some agencies places priority on protecting the agency at all costs and frowns upon whistleblowing which besmirches the agencies' reputation. A survey of 161 whistleblowers, 80 percent of whom were or are government employees, revealed they "are not only committed to certain values but that they are capable of acting on this sense of obligation even when there are strong organizational situational pressures to the contrary."[3]

Nevertheless, if whistleblowing is to be encouraged, it is essential that the culture is one that encourages collegial support for the whistleblower. Furthermore, protection of the whistleblower against retaliation must be a key ingredient of a government program to encourage public officers and employees to report malfeasance, misfeasance, and nonfeasance.

Whistleblower protection laws have been enacted by the Congress, thirty-five state legislatures, and local government legislative bodies. There is considerable variation among the laws with one group protecting whistleblowers who report unethical behavior to a specific officer or agency, a second group not specifying to whom reports should be made, and a third group providing financial incentives for whistleblowers.

This chapter traces briefly the history of federal laws designed to protect public officers and employees who blow the whistle, and reports the results of studies of the effectiveness of the laws and surveys of government employees relative to their perceptions of the degree of protection offered by the statutes. The chapter also examines the New York State whistleblower protection statute.

LEGAL PROVISIONS

The United States inherited a spoils system from Great Britain. Both nepotism—the appointment of relatives—and patronage—the employment of friends or dependents—were practiced freely in the colonial and early national periods. When the American two-party system arose, it became customary for the winners to dismiss incumbents from office and fill the vacant positions from among their friends and followers. In 1832, the practice was justified in a high-sounding statement by Senator William L. Marcy of New York: "To the victor belongs the spoils of the enemy." Unfortunately, the victors dismissed honest and capable officials as well as "enemy spoilsmen." The appointment of inefficient and often dishonest party hacks contributed to the degeneration of the public service and the corruption of the democratic process.

The antithesis of the spoils system is the merit system under which persons seeking public employment must demonstrate their capacity to fill a position before they can be appointed. Advocates of the merit system made little headway until 1881 when the assassination of President James A. Garfield by a disappointed office-seeker shocked the public conscience into action. Within three years the Congress enacted the Pendleton Act, which remains the fundamental federal law on the subject; the New York State legislature created separate civil service commissions for the state and New York City; and Massachusetts established a merit system for the selection of state employees. The system was adopted by other states, in part in response to a 1939 congressional stipulation that state and local governments would not be eligible to receive federal grants-in-aid unless public officers and employees administering the programs were chosen under a merit system.

Public officers and employees possess the right to blow the whistle on wrongdoing as guaranteed by the U.S. Constitution and statutes, and state constitutions and statutes. Initially, the First Amendment to the U.S. Constitution and the Fourteenth Amendment offered the public employee little protection against arbitrary discharge from his/her position. In 1968, however, the U.S. Supreme Court opined that a public school teacher could not be discharged for writing a letter to the editor of a newspaper criticizing the policy of the school board.[4] In 1976, the Court held that patronage dismissals of non-policy-making public employees is violative of the guarantees of the First and Fourteenth Amendments because such dismissals severely restrict political beliefs and the right of association.[5] As the result of these and other decisions, the public employee is protected against arbitrary discharge. Nevertheless, a whistleblower can be subject to reprisal.

National Laws

The most major change in the national civil service system was effectuated by the Civil Service Reform Act of 1978, which is the first national statute specifically to protect a whistleblower by prohibiting reprisals against any employee disclosing information he/she believes is evidence of "(i) a violation of any law, rule, or regulation, or (ii) mismanagement, a gross waste of funds, an abuse of authority, or a substantial and specific danger to public health or safety. . . ."[6]

The act abolished the Civil Service Commission and created three new agencies—Federal Labor Relations Authority, Office of Personnel Management, and Merit Systems Protection Board. The latter investigates complaints filed by government employees and protects whistleblowers. Presidential Reorganization Plan No. 2 of 1978, issued by President James E. Carter, created the Office of Special Counsel (OSC) within the Merit Systems Protection Board (see Chart 8.1).

As explained in Chapter 7, the Congress in 1978 enacted the Inspector General Act establishing the position of inspector general in each of twelve departments and agencies.[7] A whistleblower can request an Inspector general to investigate activities which the whistleblower believes to be unethical.

The failure of the protection offered by the Civil Service Act of 1978 to whistleblowers induced the Congress to enact the Whistleblower Protection Act of 1989 expanding the personnel actions that may result in an appeal to the Merit Systems Protection Board if a prohibited personnel practice complaint has been filed with the special counsel, and the special counsel did not seek corrective action from the board. These complaints include appointments, details, promotions, reassignments, transfers, and decisions relative to awards, benefits, education, pay, and training.

The declared purposes of the act are to establish:

a. That the primary role of the Office of Special Counsel is to protect employees, especially whistleblowers, from prohibited personnel practices;
b. That the Office of Special Counsel shall act in the interests of employees who seek assistance from the Office of Special Counsel; and
c. That while disciplining those who commit prohibited personnel practices may be used as a means by which to help accomplish that goal, the protection of individuals who are the subject of prohibited personnel practices remains the paramount consideration.[8]

The Whistleblower Protection Act of 1989 removed the Office of Special Counsel from the Merit Systems Protection Board and established OSC as an independent agency charged with protecting employees, whistleblowers in particular, from prohibited personnel practices and assisting employees. The 455 allegations of reprisal for whistleblowing

Chart 8.1
Organization of the Office of Special Counsel

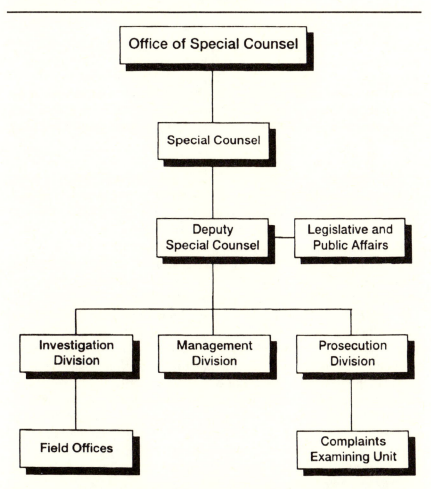

Source: A Report to Congress from the U.S. Office of Special Counsel, Fiscal Year 1991 (Washington, D.C.: United States Government Printing Office, 1992), p. 21.

was the largest category (18.6%) of complaints filed with the Office of Special Counsel during the fiscal year ending September 30, 1991.[9]

The act lowers the burden of proof for an employee alleging that retaliation has been taken against her/him for whistleblowing and expanded the rights of employees to seek an independent hearing by the board if they failed to obtain relief through OSC for an alleged retaliation.

As of 1992, members of the Congress expressed disappointment with the protection offered whistleblowers by the Office of the Special Counsel. Senator Carl Leven stated:

Although OSC has achieved some form of corrective action for about 70 whistleblowers over the last 2 years, many others have not received the Office's help. In too many cases, OSC has shied away from providing the kind of aggressive assistance that some whistle-blowers really needed. Indeed, the Office has only once made a determination under the statute that there were reasonable grounds to believe that a prohibited personnel practice had taken place.[10]

Until enactment of the Military Whistleblower Protection Act of 1988, members of the armed forces were not protected by statute against reprisal for blowing the whistle on wrongdoing.[11] The act affords protection only if the disclosures were made to the Department of Defense Inspector General, a military service inspector general, or a member of the Congress. In 1991, the Congress directed the Department of Defense to issue regulations to expand whistleblower protection to auditors, inspectors, investigators, and other law enforcement officers.

In 1989, the Congress enacted the Major Fraud Act Amendments authorizing a monetary reward, not to exceed $250,000 per case, for whistleblowers providing information relative to a possible prosecution for fraud.[12] An individual is not eligible for an award if he/she furnishes information in the performance of official duties or failed to provide the information to the individual's employer prior to providing the information to law enforcement authorities, or the information is based on public disclosure of allegations in a legislative hearing or government report.

The U.S. Department of Justice has misgivings regarding the *qui tam* provisions of the act which allow government employees the right to sue in the name of the United States and to receive a percentage of the amount recovered by the United States Treasury. Assistant Attorney General Stuart M. Gerson testified in 1992 that

We also must forestall any incentive for government employees to misappropriate government audits, investigative reports, and other documents that could provide the basis for a personal *qui tam* suit before the case has been referred to the Department of Justice and before a considered decision can be made about whether the case warrants criminal, civil, or administrative action.[13]

Views of Federal Government Employees

In 1981, the Merit Systems Protection Board released a report revealing 45 percent of the surveyed employees observed one or more instances of illegal or wasteful activities during the past year with the percentage of employees observing such instances varying from agency to agency.[14] More than 70 percent of the employees observing an illegal or wasteful activity did not report it to any officer.[15] Relative to employees who reported such activities, twenty-eight percent reported such activities because it was part of their job, such as auditing.

With respect to employees who reported a serious abuse, 24 percent indicated they were not identified as a whistleblower and 55 percent of the employees identified as whistleblowers reported that they experienced no retaliation. On the other hand, "over a third of the identified reporters believe that reporting the incident resulted in some form of 'negative experience' for them."[16] Reprisals reported included transfers to less desirable assignments, lowered performance evaluations, and denial of promotion.

A high percentage of the surveyed employees feared that their immediate supervisors would take reprisal action against them, with the percentage varying from 47 to 62 percent in the different agencies.[17]

A follow-up survey of federal government employees was conducted by the Merit Systems Protection Board in 1983. Findings, with one major exception, were very similar to the earlier findings:

- One quarter of the respondents admitted knowledge of at least one illegal or wasteful activity.
- The percentage of employees with such knowledge varied from 9 percent in one agency to 36 percent in the agency at the other extreme.
- Fifty-three percent of the respondents with knowledge of illegal or wasteful activities reported that poor program management and purchase of unnecessary goods or services were the cause of waste.
- Forty-seven percent of respondents claiming knowledge of wrongdoing estimated that the cost of each such observed activity exceeded $1,000 in funds or property.[18]

The major difference between the 1980 and 1983 findings is the decline in the percentage (45 to 23) of respondents reporting personally to have observed illegal or wasteful activity during the preceding year.[19] The board's report did not indicate a reason for the decline other than to note the reason "is beyond the scope of this particular study to ascertain."[20]

The board cautions in its report that the percentage of employees in an agency acknowledging observation of an illegal or wasteful activity is not necessarily indicative of the incidence of wrongdoing, since a single incident might be so blatant that it was observed widely by employees.

Chart 8.2 reveals there is a direct correlation between an employee's pay grade level and observation of illegal or wasteful activities. Employees at the GS-9 through 12 grade levels claimed the most knowledge of wrongdoing and were followed by employees at the GS or GM-13 through 15 grade levels. The report also reveals that 29 percent of the employees reporting observation of wrongful activities were men compared to 20 percent who were women.[21] This finding may reflect the composition of the employees at various pay grades with women concentrated in the lower pay grades, but the report does not make this association.

The report quotes two respondents who reported how they arrived at their estimates of waste:

A contractor was paid to do work that could have been done in house with [the] skill mix of Federal employees. After the expenditure of approximately $200,000 for contractor support, the contractor was unable to satisfactorily complete the work. [The] task was then completed by one government employee in a 3-month period (Grade GS-13) while simultaneously performing on-going work assignments.

Approval of a loan pay-off and subsequent reinstatement that resulted in approving an additional $900,000 at a substantially *below* market interest rate and providing additional rent subsidies to off-set the increased amortization.[22]

Disturbed by the high percentage of employees observing but not reporting illegal or wasteful activities in 1980, the board surveyed employees in 1983 and added a number of demographic questions to provide additional insight into the survey findings which are summarized below:

- Sixty-nine percent of employees reporting personal knowledge of wrongdoing did not report the wrongdoing.
- Thirty-four percent of male employees and 22 percent of female employees observing an illegal or wasteful activity reported it.
- Forty percent of the employees in the 50-59 age group reported observed incidents, but only 18 percent in the 20-29 age group reported observed incidents.
- The most common reason for not reporting an illegal or wasteful activity was the belief that no corrective action would be initiated.

Chart 8.2
Observed Activity by Pay Grade

1980
Survey

1983
Survey

Question 15: Regardless of whether or not it is part of your job, during the last 12 months have you personally observed or obtained direct evidence of the following activity?

Question 14: During the last 12 months, did you personally observe or obtain direct evidence of one or more illegal or wasteful activities involving your agency?

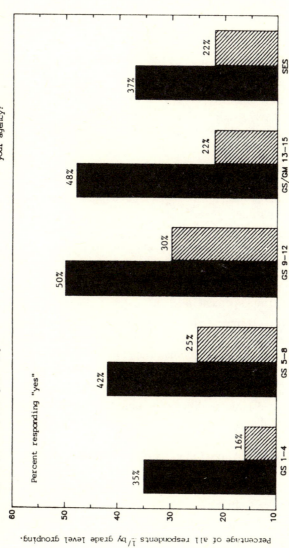

Percent responding "yes"

	GS 1–4	GS 5–8	GS 9–12	GS/GM 13–15	SES
1980	35%	42%	50%	48%	37%
1983	16%	25%	30%	22%	22%

Percentage of all respondents 1/ by grade level grouping.

1/Respondents: Restricted to employees within the 14 agencies surveyed in both 1980 and 1983.
Number of respondents: 7,271 for 1980 survey; 2,243 for 1983 survey.

Source: Blowing the Whistle in the Federal Government: A Comparative Analysis of 1980 and 1983 Survey Findings (Washington, D.C.: United States Merit Systems Protection Board, 1984), p. 15.

- The percentage of employees not reporting an illegal or wasteful activity because of fear of reprisal increased from 20 percent in 1980 to 37 percent in 1983.
- The percentage of employees observing an illegal or wasteful activity reporting an incident varied from 30 percent with less than one-year to less than four-year service compared to 42 percent with thirty or more years' service.[23]

With respect to the last finding, the board suggested that employees near retirement age are more apt to report incidents because they have less to fear in terms of reprisal. However, these employees also tend to be in the higher pay grades with management responsibilities.

Major findings of the 1983 survey include:

- Forty-one percent of the 1983 respondents, compared to 24 percent of the 1980 respondents, indicated they were not identified as the source of a report of an illegal or wasteful activity, thereby suggesting an increased wish for anonymity in reporting abuses.
- Approximately the same percentage of employees in 1983 and in 1980 (slightly more than one-half) indicated they were not subject to retaliation for reporting incidents.
- The percentage of employees reporting reprisals increased from 20 percent in 1980 to 23 percent in 1983.
- The most common forms of reported reprisal in 1980 and 1983 were subjective ones, "such as being assigned the less desirable or less important duties, being given a poorer performance appraisal than that which would otherwise have been received," or denied a promotion that had been expected.
- The least frequently employed types of reprisal were ones that can be documented more readily—demotion, geographic reassignment, and suspension from duties.[24]

The board concluded its report with the following observation:

Of particular concern to the Board is the finding in 1983 that more than one out of every five employees who said they reported fraud, waste, or abuse also said they were the victim of a reprisal or the threat of a reprisal as a result. Even though in many cases the reprisal reported experienced is not in the form of an official personnel action, the apparent odds in favor of experiencing some type of negative consequence if one reports an illegal or wasteful activity are high enough to discourage many employees from taking the chance.[25]

In 1993, the board released a follow-up report summarizing the responses of more than 13,000 employees.[26] The key findings were similar to the findings of the 1983 survey, although the percentage of employees reporting they had observed or obtained direct evidence of illegal or wasteful activities declined from 23 to 18 percent. Most respondents (63%) reported that the illegal or wasteful activities occurred in other units within their agencies. Forty-four percent estimated that the costs involved in the illegal or wasteful activity exceeded $1,000.

Perceptions of wasteful activities were subjective. The report quotes two respondents who viewed affirmative action programs as wasteful and notes, "these same programs are probably seen very differently by policymakers and others developing and administering them (and by employees benefitting from them)."[27]

Respondents identified as the most important factor in encouraging them to report an illegal or wasteful activity concern that it might endanger lives. Only 10 percent of the respondents viewed a cash award for whistleblowing as a very important motivator and 59 percent reported they did not report illegal or wasteful activities because they were convinced no corrective action would be initiated.[28] Eighty-seven percent of the observers of such activities reported that their agencies had not specifically informed them of their rights in the event they encountered retaliation for blowing the whistle.[29] Chart 8.3 contains data on the effect of whistleblowing on the reporter, and Chart 8.4 summarizes the types of reprisals whistleblowers reported they experienced or were threatened with.

The survey data reveal that the goal of the Civil Service Reform Act of 1978 to encourage employees to report wrongdoing and waste by protecting the employees against reprisal has not been achieved. A key question in need of an answer is: why do such a high percentage of federal employees fear possible retaliation for blowing the whistle?

The Government Accountability Project, initiated by the Institute for Policy Studies, has published a guide urging that a whistleblower:

1. Retain a lawyer, union representative, or other legal counsel.
2. Petition agency for pertinent documents. If necessary, file under the Privacy and Freedom of Information Acts.
3. Keep detailed reports of what is said and done.
4. Find a trustworthy co-worker to be a witness and have important documents co-signed.[30]

Chart 8.3
Effect of Reporting Illegal or Wasteful Activity on the Reporter

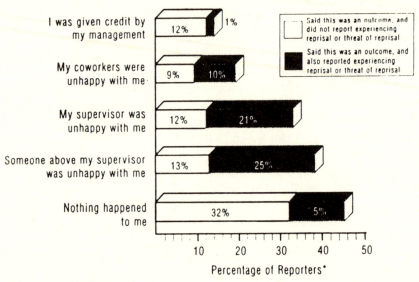

* Reporters could select more than one response

Source: *Whistleblowing in the Federal Government: An Update* (Washington, D.C.: United States Merit Systems Protection Board, 1993), p. 20.

GAO Reports

In response to a request by the chairman of a senate committee, the U.S. General Accounting Office (GAO) investigated the manner in which the Office of the Special Counsel (OSC) of the Merit Systems Protection Board performs its mission and reported that the Office does not view its role as an employee advocate or ombudsman and that whistleblower reprisal complainants rarely qualify for special counsel protection.[31]

The U.S. Court of Appeals for the District of Columbia Circuit in 1983 reviewed the legislative history of the Civil Service Reform Act of 1978 and opined the Office's primary role is that of a prosecutor.[32] More specifically, the court pointed out that the Office's congressionally assigned duty is to protect the merit system and not to remedy the grievances of individual employees.

The special counsel is quoted in the GAO report as stating his role is not "to gratify the individual's personal wishes as to what he or she believes

Chart 8.4
Types of Reprisal Reporters Said They Were Threatened with or Experienced

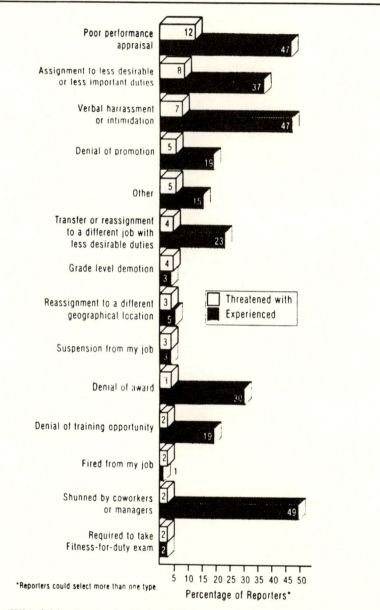

Source: *Whistleblowing in the Federal Government: An Update* (Washington, D.C.: United States Merit Systems Protection Board, 1993), p. 22.

ought to be done for them," but noted that corrective action settlements instituted by his office may benefit a whistleblower by "revising adverse personnel actions."[33] The interviewed special counsel and his predecessor deliberately sought to emphasize the prosecutorial role of the Office. Organizations of whistleblowers and a number of attorneys argue that the legislative history of the Office can be read to require the Office to protect whistleblowers.

The Office closes its investigation after screening the following types of complaints if there is no evidence of a prohibited personnel practice:

- Matters pending before appeal bodies such as the MSPB, the Office of Personnel Management, the Equal Employment Opportunity Commission (EEOC), the Federal Labor Relations Authority, or an agency grievance proceedings.
- Allegations which do not involve defined "personnel actions," but other complaints against agency management.
- Matters in which an administrative appeal has been completed.
- Allegations from employees of agencies not within OSC's jurisdiction, including government corporations, intelligence agencies, the Postal Service, the General Accounting Office, or the Federal Bureau of Investigations.
- Matters alleging violations in connection with a promotion action, or non-selection for a vacancy, where no prohibited personnel practice is evident.
- Allegations of discrimination, in which OSC normally "defers" to agency investigatory bodies or the EEOC.
- Allegations of unfair labor practices, in which OSC normally defers to the Federal Labor Relations Authority.[34]

The overwhelming majority of incoming complaints after screening are closed by the Office and each complainant, as required by law, receives a letter containing reasons for the closure. The GAO report quotes the following letter posted to a complainant:

Our investigation revealed that your non-promotion in June, 1983 was due to the fact that you lacked the requisite number of years of nursing experience for promotion. We also determined that your non-promotion in September, 1983 was the result of performance problems made known to you well before you made disclosures to your Congressman. As a consequence, we are unable to conclude that your non-promotion constituted reprisal for your disclosure.[35]

Although whistleblower reprisal cases constituted 42 percent of matters under OSC's investigation at the time of the GAO audit, relatively few cases qualified for prosecution by OSC. The Merit System Protection Board has ruled that to make a *prima facie* case of a prohibited reprisal, the special counsel must be able to show that (1) the whistleblower was engaged in an activity protected by statute, (2) he/she subsequently was subjected to adverse treatment by the agency, (3) the decision-making official had knowledge of the protected activity, and (4) a causal connection existed between the protected activity and the agency's treatment of the employee.[36]

To examine the special counsel's disposition of allegations of whistleblower reprisals, GAO reviewed a random sample of 76 to 401 allegations closed during the period from August 31, 1982 to August 31, 1984. Cases were closed because (1) the personnel actions were not taken within the OSC's jurisdiction, (2) the cases were withdrawn, mooted, or abandoned by the complainants, (3) the responsible official was outside OSC's jurisdiction, (4) the complainants' disclosures were not protected by law, (5) there were independent grounds for disciplinary action, (6) there were documented performance problems, (7) legitimate management reasons existed for a transfer or reduction in force, (8) the timing of the disclosure did not precede the personnel action, and (9) the official initiating the personnel action did not have knowledge of whistleblowing or a motive for reprisal.[37] GAO did not disagree with the special counsel's decisions to close the reviewed cases.

The General Accounting Office also examined nine of the ten most recently completed settlement actions at the agency level. Case 2 in Table 8.1 involved an auditor for the Defense Contract Audit Agency who was denied a waiver of the agency's mandatory rotation policy in light of his planned retirement. The special counsel found that the denial was retaliation for public whistleblowing by the auditor relative to cost overruns and unjustified expenditures on defense contracts. The special counsel's letter to the secretary of defense recommended that the auditor be allowed to remain in his position until his retirement at the end of the year and to cease discrimination and harassment against the auditor. The department complied with the corrective action recommendations.[38]

Cases 7 and 8 involved a supervisory construction analyst in the Department of Housing and Urban Development who alleged that his detail out of a branch chief position and a marginally satisfactory performance rating were reprisals for his whistleblowing relative to processing irregularities and major management problems to the department's inspector general and Washington, D.C., office. Although the

Table 8.1
Agency Disciplinary and Corrective Action in Recent OSC Settlements

	Prohibited Personnel Practice	Settlement Date	Disciplinary Action	Corrective Action
1.	Nepotism	March, 1984	Letter of reprimand and hiring approval authority revoked	
2.	Reprisal for whistle-blowing	December, 1983		Inform management officials that such reprisal is prohibited.
3&4.	Nepotism[a]	November, 1983	Father to be suspended 14 to 30 days[b]	Son's employment terminated.
5.	Unauthorized preference	October, 1983	• 60-day suspension • $1,000 civil penalty	
6.	Reprisal for whistleblowing	August, 1983		Reassignment rescinded.
7&8.	Reprisal for whistleblowing[a]	June, 1983	Letter of admonishment	• Agency directive supporting CSRA and communications with inspector general. • Upgrade performance rating. • Restore 16 hours leave. • Reassignment. • Attorneys fees[c]
9.	Reprisal for whistleblowing	April, 1983		• Reassignment rescinded. • Secretarial protective notices.
10.	Reprisal for whistleblowing	August, 1982		• Reassignment rescinded. • Within-grade salary increase. • Upgraded performance appraisal

[a]Combined because only one investigation was involved.
[b]Suspension had not been imposed as of September 5, 1984.
[c]Corrective action rejected by complainant as unsatisfactory.

Source: Whistleblower Complainants Rarely Qualify for Office of the Special Counsel Protection (Washington, D.C.: United States General Accounting Office, 1985), p. 31.

department proposed removing the employee for breach of department conduct regulations, OSC petitioned the Merit System Protection Board for a stay of the removal action and the department subsequently withdrew the proposed action.

The 1983 settlement agreement included a letter of admonishment issued to the supervisor of the complainant for engaging in an illegal reprisal, a directed assignment of the complainant, a partial upgrading of his performance rating, payment of his attorney's fees, and restoration of sixteen hours of leave taken by the whistleblower to prepare his response to his proposal removal.[39] The department also agreed to issue a directive to all managers stressing that employee communications with the inspector general were to be unhindered and personnel practices prohibited by the Civil Service Reform Act of 1978 will not be tolerated.

GAO examined three proposed statutory amendments to enhance OSC's role to protect whistleblowers. The first proposal would allow OSC to appeal decisions of the Merit System Protection Board to the U.S. District Court and is based upon the belief the court "would be more receptive to OSC's legal arguments than was the MSPB."[40] GAO doubts that enactment of such an amendment would offer significant protection to whistleblowers because of OSC's orientation toward prosecution and not to protection of whistleblowers.

Although the special counsel suggested that his office would be more effective if it was transferred to the Department of Justice, GAO concluded OSC's "function of investigating prohibited personnel practices could be overshadowed by Justice's other priorities," and transfer of OSC to the department would make it subject to control by the administration which would lessen the Office's independence.[41]

The third statutory proposal is the abolition of the Office and the transfer of its Hatch Acts, Freedom of Information Act, and whistleblower referral functions to the Office of Personnel Management and Merit System Protection Board. GAO concluded that enactment of this proposal into law probably would allow more litigation by the board and the courts by aggrieved employees because "the Special Counsel now acts as an effective screening mechanism to limit the volume of complaints that reach the stage of adjudication."[42]

The General Accounting Office concluded the existing law was imperfect in terms of protecting whistleblowers and stressed:

Many forms of harassment and resentment by fellow employees and supervisors would be difficult to define and prohibit even if OSC's powers were not limited to official personnel actions. A clever, patient, and circumspect agency official can conceal evidence of his or her prohibited motive so that even malevolently inspired actions can be plausibly defended as a legitimate exercise of managerial discretion.[43]

As noted, the Whistleblower Protection Act of 1989 expanded protection for federal government employees reporting wrongdoing. At the request of the Chairman of the Subcommittee on the Civil Service of the U.S. House of Representatives, the General Accounting Office conducted a review of the processing of whistleblower reprisal complaints and the effectiveness of OSC in protecting whistleblowers against retaliation.

GAO in 1992 analyzed the questionnaire responses of 1,055 employees covered by the Whistleblower Protection Act and made the following findings:

- The bulk (83%) of the employees were aware that a law protected them against reprisals for whistleblowing, but 73 percent lacked information relative to the protection afforded them by the law and 70 percent did not have sufficient information with respect to where to report misconduct.

- Seventy-six percent of the respondents did not receive information relative to whistleblower protection from their respective agencies and approximately 46 percent reported they received information about such protection from newspapers, radio, television, and word of mouth.

- Nearly one-half of the responding employees were unaware of the extent to which whistleblower protection was supported by their agencies. One-third of the respondents did not know what their agency reactions would be if they reported misconduct. Approximately one out of every six respondents was of the opinion that their agencies strongly supported the policy of protecting whistleblowers against reprisals.

- Approximately 93 percent of the responding employees moderately or strongly supported employees in their units reporting misconduct. Fifty-seven percent of the employees responded that they would report misconduct.

- More than one-third (36%) of the respondents were convinced that there was inadequate protection against retaliation for whistleblowers compared to only 13 percent who indicated that the protection was adequate. Approximately one-fourth of the respondents feared that their agencies would retaliate against them if they reported misconduct and about the same percentage indicated their agencies would support them.

- The bulk of the respondents indicated they would be encouraged to blow the whistle if action was taken on the reported problem, the misconduct was very serious, the reporting employee would be protected against retaliation, and the whistleblower would remain anonymous.[44]

In 1992, GAO released a report on whistleblower protection for members of the armed forces revealing impediments to implementation of the Military Whistleblower Protection Act of 1988. The report noted:

- Members of the armed forces may be excluded from certain protections offered by the Act if they do not follow the procedure of reporting the reprisal complaint directly to the Department of Defense Inspector General.

- The Act does not contain criteria for proving military whistleblower reprisals.

- There is no process established by the Act to resolve whistleblower retaliation complaints outside the service member's department or agency.

- Members of the armed forces until recently were not informed on a routine basis about whistleblower protection.

- Even under the current policy, the Department of Defense Inspector General does not notify whistleblowers that they have the right to have their allegations reviewed by a Board for the Correction of Military Records and by the Secretary of Defense.

- A review of thirty-five whistleblower reprisal cases conducted by service Inspectors General revealed that eight cases were incomplete and five of these cases "had significant omissions that might have affected the conclusion of the investigation."[45]

New York State Whistleblower Protection

The 1984 New York State legislature amended the Civil Service Law to protect whistleblowers by prohibiting the discharge of or other disciplinary action against a state or local government employee for blowing the whistle on violations of a law or regulation presenting "a substantial and specific danger to the public health or safety," provided the employee is convinced the violation is an improper action.[46] The whistleblower is required, prior to blowing the whistle, to notify "the appointing authority or his or her designee" of the information proposed for disclosure and to afford "the appointing authority or designee a reasonable time to take appropriate action unless there is imminent and serious danger to public health or safety."[47]

If the employee is subject to dismissal or other disciplinary action under a final and binding arbitration provision, the employee may assert his/her discharge or other disciplinary action is a reprisal for blowing the whistle and the arbitrator is required to determine the merits of the assertion.[48] If the arbitrator determines the allegation has merit, he/she is directed to dismiss or recommend dismissal of the disciplinary proceeding and reinstate the whistleblower with back pay. If the employee is not subject to a binding arbitration provision, he/she may commence a court action to block the disciplinary action.[49]

In 1991, the Appellate Division of the Supreme Court ruled that a county associate public health engineer's employment was not terminated because he attempted to inform the county executive of violations allegedly committed by the engineer's superior.[50] The Court found that the engineer had been discharged for insubordination, including acts of insubordination occurring prior to his attempt to inform the county executive of the violations.

A whistleblower who was discharged the year before the whistleblower protection law was enacted sought a remedy in a civil suit filed in the U.S. District Court. In 1991, a district court jury awarded the plaintiff $300,000 in punitive damages against the two officials of the State Department of Education who had fired him.[51]

The State-City Commission on Integrity in Government reviewed the whistleblower protection law and advanced three recommendations to enhance protection for public employees blowing the whistle. First, the commission recommended amendment of the Civil Service Law to "(i) protect an employee who is requested to, and who does, participate in an investigation or court proceeding" and "(ii) protect an employee who objects to participating, or who refuses to participate in illegal activity by the employer."[52] Second, the commission recommended amendment of the Civil Service Law and the Labor Law "to provide express protection to employees who disclose violations of anti-corruption laws, such as laws to bar the purchase of favors through improper campaign contributions, activities that involve conflicts of interest that render certain government contract unlawful, and similar breaches of integrity of government or abuses of power."[53]

Third, the commission recommended that the state legislature enact an amendment authorizing the whistleblower to register a complaint directly with the State Commission on Ethics and, if there is no prompt or reasonable response, to notify the media.[54]

SUMMARY AND CONCLUSIONS

Extensive whistleblowing is evidence of systemic government failure to ensure that governmental activities are conducted in accordance with the highest ethical principles and should be interpreted by chief executives and legislators as a call for a review of governmental organization, policies, and procedures. Dedicated government officers and employees exhibit great courage in blowing the whistle on wrongdoing because of the possibility of immediate and/or future reprisal.

The Congress, state legislatures, and local governing bodies have enacted statutes to protect whistleblowers. Experience with congressional statutes reveals that a declaration of protection for officers and employees blowing the whistle does not guarantee that they will be afforded sufficient protection. The inadequacy of the Civil Service Act of 1978 led to enactment of the Whistleblower Protection Act of 1989 which offers additional protection. Nevertheless, a 1992 report issued by the U.S. General Accounting Office revealed that 36 percent of federal government employees responding to a questionnaire believe there is inadequate protection against reprisals for whistleblowing.

In addition to availing themselves of the protections provided by statutes, whistleblowers should seek the support of individual legislators, the Government Accountability Project, the media, public interest groups, professional associations, and unions as appropriate. In certain instances, the whistleblower should seek the assistance of an attorney to ensure that his/her due process of law rights are not violated.

Although the importance of providing adequate protection for whistleblowers cannot be denied, recognition must be accorded the fact that such protection may affect adversely the authority and account-ability of managers if insubordination and dissidence increase sig-nificantly. A number of whistleblowers have a history of disciplinary and performance problems, and may be troublemakers instead of genuine whistleblowers.

Whereas whistleblowing may result in the termination of unethical behavior in government, the revolving door described in Chapter 9 facilitates such behavior.

NOTES

1. *For Merit and Honesty in Government: The Role of the Special Counsel* (Wash-ington, D.C.: United States Office of the Special Counsel, 1980), p. 3.

2. Treasury and Civil Service Commission, *Civil Servants and Ministers: Duties and Responsibilities* (London: Her Majesty's Stationery Office, 1986), vol. II, p. 30.

3. Philip H. Jos, Marke E. Tompkins, and Steven W. Hays, "In Praise of Difficult People: A Portrait of the Committed Whistleblower," *Public Administration Review*, November/ December 1989, p. 557.

4. *Pickering v. Board of Education*, 391 U.S. 563 (1968).

5. *Elrod v. Burns*, 427 U.S. 347 (1976).

6. Civil Service Reform Act of 1978, 92 Stat. 111, 5 U.S.C. § 2302(b)(8) (1993 Supp.).

7. Inspector General Amendments Act of 1978, 92 Stat. 1101, 5 U.S.C. § 5315 (1992 Supp.).

8. Whistleblower Protection Act of 1989, 103 Stat. 17, 5 U.S.C. § 1201 note (1993 Supp.).

9. *A Report to Congress from the U.S. Office of Special Counsel, Fiscal Year 1991* (Washington, D.C.: United States Government Printing Office, 1992), p. 12.

10. Carl Leven, "U.S. Office of Special Counsel Authorization Act," *Congressional Record*, September 25, 1992, p. S. 15113.

11. Military Whistleblower Protection Act of 1988, 102 Stat. 2027, 10 U.S.C. § 1034 (1992 Supp.).

12. Major Fraud Act Amendments of 1989, 103 Stat. 759, 18 U.S.C. § 1001 note (1993 Supp.).

13. "Statement of Assistant Attorney General Stuart M. Gerson before the Subcommittee on Civil and Constitutional Rights of the United States House of Representatives concerning the *Qui Tam* provisions of the False Claims Act and H.R. 4563 on April 1, 1992."

14. *Whistleblowing and the Federal Employee* (Washington, D.C.: United States Merit Systems Protection Board, 1981), p. 7.

15. Ibid., p. 33.

16. Ibid.

17. Ibid., p. 44.

18. *Blowing the Whistle in the Federal Government: A Comparative Analysis of 1980 and 1983 Survey Findings* (Washington, D.C.: United States Merit Systems Protection Board, 1984), p. 12.

19. Ibid., p. 13.

20. Ibid.

21. Ibid., p. 19.

22. Ibid., pp. 17 and 21.

23. Ibid., pp. 24 and 30.

24. Ibid., p. 38.

25. Ibid., p. 43.

26. *Whistleblowing in the Federal Government: An Update* (Washington, D.C.: United States Merit Systems Protection Board, 1993).

27. Ibid., p. 5.

28. Ibid., p. 9.

29. Ibid., p. 15.

30. *A Whistle-Blower's Guide to the Federal Bureaucracy* (Washington, D.C.: Institute for Policy Studies, 1977), p. 10.

31. *Whistleblower Complainants Rarely Qualify for Office of the Special Counsel Protection* (Washington, D.C.: United States General Accounting Office, 1985), p. 4.

32. *Frazier v. Merit Systems Protection Board*, 672 F2d 150 (D.C. Cir. 1983).

33. *Whistleblower Complainants*, p. 5.

34. Ibid., p. 10.

35. Ibid., p. 12.

36. See *Frazier*, 1 MSPB 159 (1979); *Gerlach v. FTC*, 8 MSPB 499 (1981); and *Rohrmann*, 9 MSPB 14 (1982).

37. *Whistleblower Complainants*, pp. 20–25.

38. Ibid., pp. 32–33.

39. Ibid., p. 33.

40. Ibid., p. 38.

41. Ibid., p. 39.

42. Ibid., p. 40.

43. Ibid.

44. *Whistleblower Protection: Survey of Federal Employees on Misconduct and Protection from Reprisal* (Washington, D.C.: United States General Accounting Office, 1992), pp. 3–4.

45. *Whistleblower Protection: Impediments to the Protection of Military Members* (Washington, D.C.: United States General Accounting Office, 1992), pp. 2–3.

46. New York Laws of 1984, chap. 660; and New York Civil Service Law, § 75-b(2)(a)(i-ii) (McKinney 1993 Supp.).

47. Ibid., § 75-b(2)(b).

48. Ibid., § 75-b(3)(a-b).

49. Ibid., § 75-b(4).

50. *Plante v. Buono*, 576 N.Y.S.2d 924 (1991).

51. Dan Janison, "Whistle-Blower Wins $300G," *The Times Union* (Albany, New York), June 7, 1991, p. 1.

52. *Report and Recommendations on Whistleblowing Protection in New York* (New York: State-City Commission on Integrity in Government, 1986), p. 3.

53. Ibid., p. 4.

54. *The Quest for an Ethical Environment* (New York: State-City Commission on Integrity in Government, 1986), p. 10.

Chapter 9

Postemployment Restrictions

Governments had little need to impose restrictions upon their former officers and employees when their numbers were small and many were employed by governments on a part-time basis. With the development of big government with large numbers of full-time officers and employees, governments began to become concerned with the problems associated with the revolving door, that is, individuals working for private firms who enter government service, depart such service after a period of time to join private firms, and subsequently reenter government service. The revolving door is not necessarily bad. Persons moving from the private sector to the government can bring new perspectives and similarly can bring new perspectives to their private firms upon returning after government service.

When a government officer resigns his/her position in order to join a private firm, the possibility exists that the individual may utilize knowledge gained and contacts made in government service for private gain. It is particularly important that former government officers respect their fiduciary duty to keep confidential information confidential. Similarly, the former government officer may have special access to government officers because of their prior service together. Criticism in particular has been directed at the close association between officers of the U.S. Department of Defense and defense contractors, and between attorneys who leave government service to join private firms and subsequently rejoin the government service. The revolving door can destroy the competitive equality of private firms bidding on government contracts and destroy the general public's confidence in the integrity of a government. Postgovernment employment restrictions seek to ensure that there is equal access by all citizens and firms to government information and equal treatment by government departments and agencies.

Key questions involve (1) whether all government employees should be subject to postemployment restrictions, (2) the scope and length of the restrictions, (3) tailoring the restrictions to classes of employees, and (4) applications to consultants. Relative to the latter, a 1961 U.S. Senate Subcommittee report asked: "When does the postemployment period begin for a standby consultant who may advise the Government four or five times a year? More important, why should he accept a consultancy if he thereby runs the risk of disruptions in his regular business?"[1]

NATIONAL LAWS

The first congressional postgovernment service restriction upon an executive branch officer was contained in a rider attached to the Post Office Appropriation Act of 1872. The rider prohibited an executive branch officer from acting as a counsel for a party bringing a claim against the United States during the officer's service in the government and for two years after departing government service.[2] The officer, however, was not prevented from appearing before an agency, provided the appearance was unrelated to a claim against the government. The rider provided no penalty for its violation. The Congress in 1948 expanded the restrictions to commissioned officers and authorized criminal penalties: a $10,000 fine, imprisonment for one year, or both.[3]

President John F. Kennedy in 1961 appointed an advisory body to study and recommend amendments of the postgovernment employment laws. In 1962, the Congress enacted most of the recommended amendments into law.[4] The act expanded the prohibitions to cover all executive branch employees, but exempted consultants and part-time employees. The amendments narrowed the previous law by prohibiting only postgovernment employment service relating to the matters and specific parties with whom the former employee dealt. The statutes also imposed a one-year ban on postgovernment employment involvement with matters within the official responsibilities of the former employee, but was restricted to a former employee acting in a representative capacity before an agency of the federal government. The former officer was not forbidden to provide advice to a colleague who would appear before a government agency.

Although President Lyndon B. Johnson issued Executive Order Number 11222 on the subject of ethics in government in 1965, the order contained no reference to postemployment restrictions.[5] Dissatisfaction with the existing statues continued and charges were made that an incestuous relationship had developed between a number of federal government officers employed by regulatory agencies and the firms they intended to join upon leaving government service.

Only one statute contains a complete ban on a former government employee working for certain private firms. The Consumer Products Safety Act of 1972 forbids senior Consumer Product Safety Commission officers from working for manufacturers subject to the act during the first year after departure from the commission.[6]

Two acts require former employees of specified agencies to file reports on their employment by private contractors. Former National Aeronautics and Space Administration (NASA) employees must file reports relative to their work for NASA contractors.[7] Similarly, former Senior Defense Department officials working for firms holding contracts with the department must file reports.[8] Another method employed to restrict the use of information by a former government employee is the Central Intelligence Agency's secrecy agreements.[9]

Continuing public concern with the level of ethical conduct in the federal government resulted in the enactment of the Ethics in Government Act of 1978 which extended the restriction on postgovernment service to "aiding and assisting" by personal presence in addition to direct representation before the department or agency which had employed him/her and applied the restriction for a period of two years to officers at GS-17 level or higher and comparable ranks in the armed forces.[10] A "cooling-off" period of one year prevented a former government officer at the GS-16 level or higher from contacting employees of the department or agency where the former employee worked. The act, however, exempted from its prohibitions uncompensated appearances and communications to a department or agency involving scientific or technical information. The act authorized the head of a department or agency, after notice and a hearing, to ban a former employee from future contacts with the department or agency if he/she had violated the postgovernment employment restrictions.

There was strong bureaucratic opposition to the new law and a significant number of public officers announced their intention to resign from government service. This opposition generated responses in the Congress as the chairmen and ranking minority members of the concerned House and Senate committees wrote to the director of the Office of Government Ethics, an office created by the act, that the section of the law relating to "aiding and assisting" should be interpreted narrowly, and the Office issued regulations with a narrow interpretation limiting the section to representational activities only.[11]

Prior to the effective date of the act, the Congress amended the act by modifying the "aiding and assisting" section to provide it applies only to a former employee providing assistance by "personal presence" at the appearance before a department or agency.[12] The act applied the prohibition only to persons who were in a position with "significant decision-making or supervisory responsibility, . . ." and exempted one- and two-star generals and former officers employed by state and local governments, higher education institutions, and medical research organizations.[13]

In 1985, the Congress attached a rider to the Department of Defense Authorization Act restricting the employment of presidential appointees after they left government service if they had negotiated contracts with defense firms.[14] The following year, the Congress attached a rider to the Omnibus Continuing Appropriations Act repealing the 1985 restriction, placing postgovernment employment restrictions on specified Department of Defense employees, imposing reporting requirements on defense contractors, and making contractors civilly liable for violations of the revolving door prohibition.[15]

Ethics Reform Act of 1989

Continuing public concern with ethical problems associated with the postgovernment service employment of former public officers led to the introduction of several bills in the Congress placing additional restrictions upon public officers leaving government service. In particular, release of information on former national government officials representing foreign interests led to the introduction of H.R. 1231 providing for a four-year prohibition being placed on former officers representing a foreign interest for compensation. H.R. 1231 was unusual in that its prohibition applied to members of Congress as well as executive branch officers.

Although H.R. 1231 was not enacted into law, the bill influenced H.R. 5043—the Post-Employment Restrictions Act of 1988—which was approved by the Congress but pocket vetoed by President Ronald Reagan on the ground the bill was enacted hurriedly. He expressed concern that signing the bill into law would limit the national government's ability to attract highly qualified persons to its service.

Members of Congress continued to introduce bills on ethics in the national government service, and in 1989 the Congress enacted the Ethics Reform Act which revised drastically the 1978 Ethics in Government

Act.[16] One of the most major changes made by the 1989 Act was the extension of postgovernment employment restrictions to the Congress which results in a more evenhanded application of the restrictions and recognizes the possibility of former members and staff abusing their influence for personal gain.[17]

The Congress decided that the restrictions should not apply uniformly to all members and their staffs because of the varying amounts of influence that could be exerted after leaving the Congress. A fivefold classification scheme is applied to determine the nature of the postemployment restrictions: (1) members of Congress, (2) personal staff of members, (3) staffs of standing, select, and joint committees, (4) leadership staff, and (5) all remaining congressional employees. The latter include employees of the Congressional Budget Office, Architect of the Capitol, Botanic Garden, General Accounting Office, Government Printing Office, Library of Congress, Technology Assessment Office, Capitol Police, and Copyright Royalty Tribunal.

Leadership staff in the House of Representatives include employees who work for the Speaker, majority leader, minority leader, majority and minority whips, chief deputy majority and minority whips, chairman of the Democratic Steering Committee, chairman and vice chairman of the Democratic Caucus, chairman, vice chairman, and secretary of the Republican Conference, chairman of the Republican Research Committee, chairman of the Republican Policy Committee, and any leadership position subsequently created.[18]

Leadership staff in the Senate include employees who work for the vice president, president Pro Tempore, deputy president Pro Tempore, majority and minority leaders, majority and minority whips, chairmen and secretaries of the Majority Conference and the Minority Conference, chairman and cochairman of the Majority Policy Committee, chairman of the Minority Policy Committee, and any leadership position subsequently created.[19]

Former members of the Congress are forbidden for one year to knowingly make any communication with or appearance before a member of the Congress, an officer of the Congress, or an employee of the Congress with the intent to influence an action by the person.[20] Personal staff members paid at the GS-17 level or higher are subject to a similar one-year restriction relative to intentionally contacting—by a communication with or personal appearance—the member formerly employing them or an employee of the member.[21] There is no prohibition relative to contacting other members of the Congress or staff members of various committees. Since employees typically interact with other employees including staff members of committees, this limited prohibition may prove to be inadequate in curbing abusive influence.

Former employees of standing, select, and joint committees also are under a one-year restriction, but it applies only to contacting an employee, member, or former member of a committee who was a committee member during the year preceding the former employee's departure from congressional service.[22] A similar restriction applies to former members of the leadership staff and questions can be raised as to the adequacy of the limited restriction in view of the widespread interaction of such staff with other members and staff of the Congress.[23] All other former employees are subject to a one-year prohibition on communications with or appearance before the offices which had employed them.[24]

All of the above former members and employees also are subject to a one-year prohibition relative to advising or representing persons or organizations, except the United States, with respect to current trade or treaty negotiations with which they were involved.[25] In addition, the act prohibits all members of the Congress, congressional employees, and senior-level executive branch officers during the year after termination of their government service from knowingly advising or representing foreign entities—governments or political parties—with the intent to influence a decision to be made by an officer or employee of any United States department or agency.[26]

The act specifically provides that employees detailed from one department or agency to serve with another department or agency are deemed employees of the two departments or agencies.[27] A former government employee, however, may provide advice to or appear before a current government officer during the first year after termination of government service provided no compensation is involved.[28] This exception facilitates the briefing of incoming staff members by department staff members and smoothes the transfers of responsibilities.

The addition by the 1989 Act of civil penalties to the criminal penalties provided by the 1978 Act is a major change which may result in more effective enforcement of the postemployment restrictions.[29] The 1978 Act provided for a fine of $10,000, imprisonment for two years, or both for violations of the act, and these sanctions may be responsible for the relatively lax enforcement of the act and low conviction rate for violations. The difficulty of proving criminal intent hampered enforcement of the 1978 Act.

Franklyn Nofziger, a former adviser to President Reagan, was convicted of contacting officials in the White House on behalf of clients during the one-year postemployment prohibition period. The U.S. Court of Appeals, however, overturned the conviction on the ground the government had not proven criminal intent on the part of Nofziger beyond a reasonable doubt. Civil penalties are more effective in achieving convictions since the government does not have to prove a knowing and intentional violation of the prohibition beyond a reasonable doubt. The civil remedy facilitates a civil action by the U.S. attorney general, since a violation may be proved by a preponderance of the evidence. The act also authorizes the attorney general to seek injunctive relief from a court to prevent a former employee from violating the postgovernment service prohibition.

The act also provides an exception for testimony and allows a former member of the Congress or employee of the executive or legislative branches, including the vice president, to give testimony under oath or statements required to be made under the penalty of perjury.[30] Nevertheless, a former officer of an executive department or agency subject to permanent restrictions on representation on particular matters may serve as an expert witness for a party other than the United States only pursuant to a court order.[31]

Concerned that a blanket one-year restriction placed on certain senior personnel of the executive branch and independent agencies would make it difficult for the concerned departments and agencies to recruit qualified personnel, a provision was added to the act authorizing the director of the Office of Government Ethics to waive the restriction relative to officers paid at the GS-17 level or higher and commissioned officers in pay grade 0-7 and higher at the request of a department or agency, provided "granting the waiver would not create the potential for use of undue influence or unfair advantage."[32]

The coverage of the postemployment restrictions was broadened on January 20, 1993, when President William J. Clinton issued Executive Order Number 12834—"Ethics Commitments by Executive Branch Appointees"—expanding the coverage of the Ethics Reform Act of 1989 to include approximately 1,100 noncareer presidential appointees.

Congressional Standing Rules

Standing rules of the U.S. Senate and House of Representatives also contain postemployment restrictions applicable to former members and former employees. Senate Standing Rule XXXVII forbids a former member for a period of one year after leaving office to lobby members, officers, or employees, if the former member becomes a lobbyist required to register under the Federal Regulation of Lobbying Act of 1946 or is retained by a registered lobbyist to influence proposed legislation.[33]

Similarly, an employee of the Senate who leaves his/her position and becomes a registered lobbyist under the Federal Regulation of Lobbying Act of 1946—2 U.S.C. §§ 262-70—or is retained by a registered lobbyist to influence proposed legislation is forbidden to lobby the member for whom he/she worked or the member's staff for a period of one year.[34] If a staff employee of a committee leaves his/her position and becomes a registered lobbyist or is retained by a registered lobbyist for the purpose of influencing Senate action on bills, the former employee may not lobby the members or staff of the committee for a period of one year.

Rules of the House of Representatives address the postemployment question in a different manner. No time restriction is placed on lobbying before their former colleagues and the rule only forbids former members to enter the House if their only reason for being in the House is to lobby for the approval or defeat of a bill or an amendment.[35]

STATE LAWS

Statutes enacted by state legislatures contain various types of postemployment restrictions that apply to former state officers and employees. The Hawaii state legislature in 1972 enacted a statute relative to former legislators and legislative employees stipulating:

a. No former legislator or employee shall disclose any information which by law or practice is not available to the public and which he acquired in the course of his official duties or use the information for his personal gain or the benefit of anyone. . . .
c. No former legislator or employee shall, within twelve months after termination of his employment, assist any person or business or act in a representative capacity for a fee or other consideration, on matters involving official action by the particular state agency or subdivision thereof with which he had actually served.
d. This section shall not prohibit any agency from contracting with a former legislator or employee to act on a matter on behalf of the State within the period of limitations stated herein, and shall not prevent such legislator or employee from appearing before any agency in relation to such employment.[36]

Similarly, Minnesota statutes forbid a former commissioner or deputy commissioner of a department to appear or participate in proceedings of the department on behalf of a private person for a period of one year.[37]

The New York State legislature enacted a restrictive law applicable to the postgovernment service activities of members of the state legislature, legislative employees, and executive employees. For a period of two years after termination of his/her service, a member of the state legislature may not render lobbying services for compensation on behalf of any individual or firm involving the approval of any bill or resolution by either house.[38]

No legislative employee required to file an annual financial disclosure statement may receive compensation for lobbying the state legislature or its members during the remainder of the legislative term after leaving the employment of the legislature relative "to any matter with respect to which such person was directly concerned and in which he personally participated during the period of his service or employment."[39] However, a former legislative employee who acted in a supervisory capacity with respect to a specific matter or "who was not personally involved in the development, negotiation, or implementation of the matter to an important and material degree" may lobby for compensation with the approval of the Legislative Ethics Committee.[40]

The law forbids any former state officer or employee to appear before, communicate with, or render services before a state agency on behalf of any person or firm for compensation relative to any matter "with which he personally participated during the period of his service or employment, or which was under his or her active consideration."[41] The law also stipulates that a state agency may adopt more restrictive provisions concerning practice before it by a former officer or employee.[42]

Exceptions are provided by the statute. Members of the State Board of Regents, officers of boards who are unpaid or paid on a per diem basis, and members of public authorities with at least one member appointed by the governor who are unpaid or paid on a per diem basis are exempt from the postemployment restrictions.[43] In addition, former members of the state legislature and former state employees may appear before, practice, or communicate with a state agency for compensation for service rendered "while carrying out official duties as an elected official or employee of a federal, state, or local government, or one of its agencies."[44]

A 1987 amendment to the Public Officers Law specified that the postemployment restrictions on legislative employees would apply only to employees terminating their employment prior to January 1, 1989.[45] A group of former state attorneys sought a preliminary injunction on the grounds the revolving door provisions of the act were unconstitutional because they violated the equal protection of the law and ex post facto clauses and included unconstitutional delegation of legislative powers. The Appellate Division of the Supreme Court dismissed the suit and its decision was upheld by the court of appeals in 1989.[46]

In 1990, the court of appeals upheld the constitutionality of the revolving door provisions and rejected the argument that the prohibition violated due process of law by forbidding former officers and employees from exercising the right to pursue their professional career and opined the prohibition did not violate any protected interest and was related reasonably to the goal of restoring public confidence in the integrity of government.[47]

The New York State attorney general in 1988 issued an advisory opinion that a local government possesses the authority to include provisions in its code of ethics governing or prohibiting appearances before the local government by its former officers and employees.[48]

Enactment of postemployment restrictions by a state legislature leads to efforts to have laws enacted excepting specified individuals or groups of former employees from the restrictions. The 1992 New York State legislature enacted such a bill, but it was vetoed by Governor Mario M. Cuomo who wrote:

The process of restoring the public's trust is a slow and deliberate one. To threaten this process by creating an exemption from the application of reasonable, consistently applied ethical standards will feed the public perception that government can not comply with ethical rules which are aimed at eliminating conflicts of interest.[49]

The bill would have allowed laid-off state employees to seek positions with firms which conduct business with the former employees' state agencies.

In 1992, the New York State Ethics Commission expanded the revolving door coverage by prohibiting a former state labor commissioner from lobbying the state legislature.[50] The Public Service Law specifically forbids former state employees to lobby a state agency relative to issues they were personally involved with while state employees. The commission held "the agenda of state government is an integrated whole, the Legislature enacts law, many of which are implemented and enforced by state agencies."[51]

The State Ethics Commission in 1993 forbade a former counsel to Governor Mario M. Cuomo to lobby the state legislature and state agencies relative to issues he dealt with while in government service.[52] The former counsel was employed by four groups to lobby for the defeat or weakening of a law he helped to draft. In 1991, the former counsel obtained an advisory, nonbinding opinion from an ethics commission counsel to the effect it was lawful for the former counsel to lobby provided he did not lobby his former employer.[53]

Massachusetts Lieutenant Governor Paul Cellucci as Acting Governor in 1992 signed an executive order prohibiting private firms from hiring state officials who negotiate, prepare, or supervise contracts the firms hold with the Commonwealth.[54] The executive order specifically provides:

I. In the preparation of Requests for Proposals (RFPs) for privatization projects, there shall be specifically included language which puts all bidders on notice of both the conflict-of-interest law and this order; and includes limitations regarding the hiring of state employees by private companies contracting with the Commonwealth.

II. All contracts for the privatization of services shall contain a specific prohibition against the hiring at any time during the term of the contract, and for any position in the contractor's company, any state management employee who is, was, or will be involved in the preparation of the RFP, the negotiation leading to the awarding of the contract, the decision to award the contract, and/or the supervision or oversight of performance under the contract.[55]

AN ASSESSMENT

How broad should statutory subject matter provisions restricting the postemployment activities of government officers be? Are time restrictions placed on postgovernment employment activities realistic in terms of achieving their stated goals? Should a former government officer be subject to restrictions because he/she acquired information outside of his/her job responsibilities? To what extent should a former public officer be allowed to maintain social contacts with his/her former colleagues if the former officer currently works for a firm that conducts business with or bids on contracts advertised by his/her former agency? Should private parties injured by the postgovernment service of a former public officer be allowed to institute a private course of action?

Subject Matter Restrictions

Statutes limiting postemployment activities of former public officers to specified matters obviously restrict the statutes' coverage. The federal ethics law defines a "particular matter" as one involving any application, contract, controversy, charge, claim, arrest, investigation, request for a ruling, rule making, or judicial or other proceeding.[56]

To qualify as a "particular matter" under federal law, the subject must be one in which the United States has a direct and substantial interest, the former officer must have had a personal and substantial participation in the matter, and the matter had to have involved a specific party or parties during the former officer's participation.[57] Furthermore, the former officer must have known or reasonably known that the matter was under his/her official responsibilities.

The ethics acts restrict only a communication with the former officer's or employee's department or agency or an appearance before it. The former officer or employee is not prohibited from lobbying other departments and agencies.

Current ethics laws place no restrictions upon the use by former officers of nonclassified information gained in the public service for private gain. As W.J.M. Cody and R. R. Lynn pointed out in *Honest Government*, "there is a great deal of valuable but confidential information that is not classified."[58] A government officer obviously may acquire confidential information on a matter even if he was not concerned personally and directly with the matter as part of his/her official duties.

Subject matter prohibitions and restrictions may penalize unfairly a former officer who gained information and/or sharpened his/her skills on his/her own time while in government service in order to improve job performance. Although the information was not gained as the result of public service, a subject matter prohibition or restriction could be a restraint upon the individual's postgovernment service career.

Joseph I. Hochman contended that "postemployment lobbying restrictions may infringe personal petition rights when lobbyists' interests coincide with clients' interests. For example, former Members who personally are interested in liberalizing American banking laws can not lobby Congress on this issue if they are paid by a bank with identical interests."[59]

Time Restrictions

The provisions of ethics statutes prohibiting postemployment representation of private interests before the officer's former agency are based upon the assumption that the information obtained in government service will decline in value within one or two years. The private value of confidential information acquired during public service, however, may not lose its value within a short period of time. As a note in the *Yale Law Journal* stressed:

restrictions fail to prohibit the use of confidential information when characteristics of contact, particular matter, prior participation, and, in some instances, time are not present. Yet the same restrictions may bar activities that exhibit those characteristics but that include no undue influence or use of confidential information. One consequence of these limited and inconsistent rules is the knowledge that one will be restricted in his career after leaving government, despite the absence of any wrongdoing.[60]

One can argue that a one- or two-year restriction is inadequate in ensuring that in all cases confidential information and personal contacts with former department or agency officers no longer will benefit the former employee. It is evident that certain types of information retain value over a relatively long time period. A case in point would be the testing of new drugs over several years by the Food and Drug Administration. Knowledge of early test results might benefit the private interests of a former officer. Regulations limit public access to department information in the National Archives for a number of years because the information has long-term value.

Although information gained in government service may deteriorate in value with time, contacts with other government officers while in public service may prove to be of value to a former government officer for years. In other instances, the former public officer may receive no special treatment or information from his/her former colleagues, yet he/she may hint to potential clients that a special relationship exists with the former colleagues. Cody and Lynn pointed out:

The danger is that employees may think they are buying greater access when someone is hired fresh from government service or that clients or customers will choose an attorney or lobbyist based on a perception that the recency or importance of the former government job gives him or her an advantage. The other possibility is that the former official will make those claims either directly or indirectly. The former official who picks up the phone in the client's presence and whose call is answered immediately by a current official may not be told anything confidential, but the client has an impression of real power.[61]

A difficult question to answer is whether a former government official should be prohibited from paying social visits to his/her former department or agency for a specified period of time if his/her firm conducts business with the department or agency. Four days before the Metropolitan Transportation Authority in New York City was scheduled to vote in 1991 on a $111 million contract, former Authority Chairman Robert R. Kiley paid a social visit to the authority. His firm was one of the bidders on the contract.

Mr. Kiley was dressed casually "and apparently had the day off when he stopped by on December 16," said M.T.A. officials, who insisted that the contract was not discussed.[62] As noted, the New York Public Officers Law prohibits a former state officer from conducting business with his/her former agency for a period of two years subsequent to termination of employment with the agency. Although the contract was not awarded to Mr. Kiley's firm, this incident raises the question whether a former officer should terminate all contacts with former colleagues during the post-employment time restriction period. An official of the New York State Ethics Commission stated "social visits are acceptable. However, I think someone with a contract before an agency should be particularly careful about the appearance of propriety."[63]

Hochman argued that there are differences between executive branch employment and congressional employment since the latter lacks civil service tenure protection and hence the Congress may experience difficulty in recruiting competent employees if they are subject to postemployment restrictions for a long period of time.[64] He pointed out that the bicameral structure of the Congress reduces the amount of influence that a former member of one house or a former staff member may exercise on the congressional action taken on a bill.[65]

Hochman recognized that it is important to place restrictions on former congressional employees and argued that a one-year restriction is adequate to deal with the following potential problem:

Congressional personnel who leave Congress during mid-session and become lobbyists within the same session know who is vulnerable to pressure or wavering on specific issues. They know the intricacies of bargaining sessions between members. The entire process of drafting, introducing, amending, and adopting a piece of legislation creates incalculable amounts of information, all of which would be valuable to partisan lobbying interests. When congressional personnel move into private sector in mid-session with such fresh information, they possess tools that are neither available to other lobbyists nor to the general public.[66]

Wendy L. Gerlach argued for a broader restriction to be placed on former congressional staff personnel because they develop close relations with other congressional staff and members, yet a former staff member is not restricted in contacting members and staff other than the ones he/she worked for.[67] She recommended that "a one year restriction should be added prohibiting business contacts with congressional employees, members, or offices with which the former employee had personal and substantial dealings."[68]

An argument can be made that the time restriction placed upon former members of the Congress should be extended to two years to bring their restriction into conformance with the restriction placed upon former high-ranking officials of the executive branch. As noted, the New York

Public Officers Law places a two-year restriction upon former members of the state legislature contacting members or staff of the legislature.

A Private Cause of Action

Gerlach argued the postemployment restrictions statutes should be amended to authorize parties "who are economically injured by a former government employee's misuse of confidential information or influence" to institute a private cause of action.[69] Governments prosecute only a small number of cases involving violation of the postemployment restrictions and prohibitions, and it is apparent that private business firms often have the resources to institute an action if the firms have been injured financially by the actions of a former government officer.

Gerlach is convinced that a private cause of action is apt to be more efficient than an action initiated by a government because "a private party who is harmed will necessarily be better informed regarding the particular facts of the case than the government. Also, the private party would bear the cost of such a lawsuit, unless attorney's fees were awarded to the prevailing party to compensate it for any harm."[70]

It is apparent that authorization of a private cause of action may engender other problems. Gerlach recognized that the authorization may be used to harass competitors, but is convinced that requiring the plaintiffs to pay court costs and attorney fees in frivolous cases is an adequate safeguard.[71] She also noted that a private cause of action may result in the abuse of the discovery process because "a party might seek confidential information being used by the company employing the former government employee."[72] A protective order issued by the court, she maintained, would solve this potential problem.

SUMMARY AND CONCLUSIONS

The United States has a long history of government service on a part-time or full-time basis by citizens who subsequently depart government service for a private career and at a later date reenter the service. These citizens can bring new perspectives and approaches to solving problems to the attention of career bureaucrats. Unfortunately, the revolving door can be abused for private gain and it is essential to place postgovernment service restrictions upon certain government officers and employees who should be encouraged to avoid the appearance of an impropriety after leaving government service relative to their contacts with the government. These restrictions create a conflict with the right to petition the government guaranteed by the First Amendment to the U.S. Constitution and courts have been called upon to determine the reasonableness of the restrictions.

Stringent, uniform, postemployment prohibitions and restrictions will make the recruitment of talented individuals by governments difficult. Hence, it is essential that restrictions be tailored in coverage and time to classes of public officers and employees in terms of their ability personally to profit in their private careers from their government service. The Massachusetts total prohibition of the hiring by a private firm of a state official involved in the process of privatizing government services is a reasonable prohibition in the light of the potential abuse that otherwise might occur. On the other hand, a law prohibiting private firms to hire any government officer for a stated period of time would be unreasonable.

In certain instances, a requirement that former government officers file reports on their private sector interactions with their former government department or agency will be an adequate safeguard to protect the public against abuses. In all instances, it would be desirable to have the postemployment statute authorize a private cause of action.

The postemployment statutes should provide an appeals mechanism to be utilized by departments and agencies experiencing difficulties in recruiting competent personnel because of the postemployment restrictions. The board of ethics should be authorized to grant waivers from the restrictions upon the request of a department or agency.

Chapter 10 reviews the actions that have been taken by governments or proposed to ensure that unethical behavior is eliminated from the public service and presents a model ethics program.

NOTES

1. Subcommittee on National Policy Machinery, United States Senate, *The Private Citizen and the National Service* (Washington, D.C.: United States Government Printing Office, 1961), p. 3.

2. 17 Stat. 202. The act was repealed in 1962.

3. Crimes and Criminal Procedures Act of 1948, 62 Stat. 698. The act was repealed in 1962.

4. Bribery, Graft, and Conflicts of Interact Act of 1962, 76 Stat. 1123, 18 U.S.C. §§ 201-18 (1969 and 1993 Supp.).

5. 30 *Federal Register* 6569 (1965).

6. Consumer Product Safety Commission Improvement Act of 1976, 90 Stat. 503, 15 U.S.C. § 2053(g)(2) (1982 and 1993 Supp.).

7. Ethics in Goverment Act of 1978, 92 Stat. 1824, 42 U.S.C. § 2462(b)(1) (1973).

8. Defense Technical Correction Act of 1987, 101 Stat. 273, 10 U.S.C. § 2397 (1993 Supp.).

9. See *Snepp v. United States*, 444 U.S. 507 (1980), dealing with the enforcement of such an agreement.

10. Ethics in Government Act of 1978, 92 Stat. 1824. The act's provisions have been codified in various sections of titles 2, 5, 18, 20, 28, and 42 of the United States Code.

11. *Congressional Record*, February 21, 1979, p. S1613; and 44 *Federal Register* 19,974 (1979).

12. Ethics in Government Act of 1978, 93 Stat. 76, 18 U.S.C. § 207(b) (1993 Supp.).

13. Ibid., 18 U.S.C. § 207(d)(1)(C).

14. Department of Defense Authorization Act of 1985, 99 Stat. 582.

15. Defense Acquisition Improvement Act of 1986, 100 Stat. 1783-130, 10 U.S.C. § 2937(b-c) (1993 Supp.).

16. Ethics Reform Act of 1989, 103 Stat. 1716, 5 U.S.C. app. § 101 note (1993 Supp.).

17. Ibid., 103 Stat. 1719, 18 U.S.C. § 207(e).

18. Ibid., 103 Stat. 1721, 18 U.S.C. § 207(e)(4).

19. Ibid.

20. Ibid., 103 Stat. 1719, 18 U.S.C. § 207(e)(1)(A).

21. Ibid., 103 Stat. 1720, 18 U.S.C. § 207(e)(6).

22. Ibid., 103 Stat. 1719-720, 18 U.S.C. § 207(e)(3).

23. Ibid., 103 Stat. 1720, 18 U.S.C. § 207(e)(4).

24. Ibid., 103 Stat. 1720, 18 U.S.C. § 207(e)(5).

25. Ibid., 103 Stat. 1717, 18 U.S.C. § 207(b)(1).

26. Ibid., 103 Stat. 1722, 18 U.S.C. § 207(f)(1-2).

27. Ibid., 103 Stat. 1722, 18 U.S.C. § 207(g).

28. Ibid., 103 Stat. 1723, 18 U.S.C. § 207(j)(4).

29. Ibid., 103 Stat. 1717, 18 U.S.C. § 216.

30. Ibid., 103 Stat. 1724, 18 U.S.C. § 207(j)(6).

31. Ibid.

32. Ibid., 103 Stat. 1718, 18 U.S.C. § 207(c)(2)(D).

33. *Standing Rules of the Senate* (Washington, D.C.: United States Government Printing Office, 1992), Rule XXXVII(8).

34. Ibid., Rule XXXVII(9).

35. *Standing Rules of the House of Representatives* (Washington, D.C.: United States Government Printing Office, 1993), Rule XXXII(2-3).

36. Hawaii Laws of 1972, chap. 163, § 1; and Hawaii Revised Statutes, § 78-6 (1985).

37. Minnesota Laws of 1977, chap. 305; and Minnesota Statutes Annotated, § 15.06(9) (1988).

38. New York Public Officers Law, § 73(8) (1993 Supp.).

39. Ibid.

40. Ibid.

41. Ibid.

42. Ibid.

43. Ibid., § 73(i and iii-iv).

44. Ibid., § 73(8).

45. New York Laws of 1987, chap. 813.

46. *Kuttner v. Cuomo*, 147 A.D.2d 215, 75 N.Y.2d 596, 554 N.E.2d 876 (1989).

47. *Forti v. New York State Ethics Commission*, 75 N.Y.2d 596, 554 N.E.2d 876 (1990).

48. *Opinions of the Attorney General for the Year Ending December 31, 1988* (Albany: New York State Department of Law, 1989), pp. 38–39.

49. *Disapproval Memorandum #22* (Albany: Executive Chamber, July 24, 1992).

50. "Hartnett Prohibited from Lobbying Before Legislature," *Times Union* (Albany, New York), December 29, 1992, p. B-2.

51. Ibid.

52. Tom Precious, "Panel Limits Lobbying by Former Cuomo Aide," *Times Union* (Albany, New York), January 29, 1993, p. 1.

53. Ibid.

54. Argeo P. Cellucci, *Executive Order No. 346* (Boston: Executive Department, December 2, 1992). See also Efrain Hernandez, Jr., "State Curbs Private Hiring of Its Workers," *The Boston Globe*, December 3, 1992, p. 1.

55. *Executive Order No. 346*, p. 2.

56. 18 U.S.C. § 207(i)(3).

57. 18 U.S.C. § 207(a)(1)(A-C).

58. W. J. Michael Cody and Richardson R. Lynn, *Honest Government: An Ethics Guide for Public Service* (Westport, Conn.: Praeger, 1992), p. 114.

59. Joseph I. Hochman, "Post-Employment Lobbying Restrictions on the Legislative Branch of Government: A Minimalist Approach to Regulating Ethics in Government," *Washington Law Review*, October 1990, p. 895.

60. "The Fiduciary Duty of Former Government Employees," *Yale Law Journal*, November 1980, pp. 196–97.

61. Cody and Lynn, *Honest Government*, pp. 111–112.

62. Alan Finder, "Visit by an Ex-M.T.A. Chief Raises the Issue of Propriety," *The New York Times*, December 24, 1991, p. B3.

63. Ibid.

64. Hochman, "Post-Employment Lobbying Restrictions," p. 900.

65. Ibid., p. 899.

66. Ibid., pp. 897–98.

67. Wendy L. Gerlach, "Amendment of the Post-Government Employment Laws," *Arizona Law Review*, Spring 1991, p. 421.

68. Ibid.

69. Ibid., p. 424.

70. Ibid.

71. Ibid., p. 425.

72. Ibid.

Chapter 10

Ethical Government

The pervasiveness of unethical behavior by a significant number of public officers and employees is a most serious problem which can be eliminated or ameliorated only by concerted actions to deter such behavior, and to detect and prosecute or otherwise discipline violators of ethical standards.

While it is easy to proclaim that the principle guiding all public servants must be *res publica* (the public good), determining when an action by a public servant runs counter to the ideal is problematical. How remote, for example, must an interest in a matter be to ensure a public officer will not gain personally from one of his/her actions?

The preceding chapters make clear that governmental corruption is a multifaceted problem and precise measurement of its extent and cost to the taxpayers is an impossibility. The nature of the problem in policy-making and administration, as well as its many subtle forms, are well known as is the difficulty of eliminating the problem. U.S. Senator Paul H. Douglas of Illinois in 1952 identified one subtle form by pointing out that the person seeking special benefits "does not generally pay money directly to the public representative. He tries instead by a series of favors to put the public official under such a feeling of personal obligation that the latter gradually loses his sense of mission to the public and comes to feel that his first loyalties are to his private benefactors and patrons."[1] The model ethical program contained in this chapter addresses this subtle form of corruption and other subtle forms.

The direct economic costs to the taxpayers of nefarious public servant behavior are obvious and justify vigorous efforts to root out unethical behavior. We must not, however, overlook the indirect costs of improper conduct, including pollution of the environment, and deaths and injuries resulting from the bribing of inspectors responsible for ensuring that bridges and buildings are constructed in accordance with building and fire safety standards.

As noted in Chapter 1, democratic governments rest upon a foundation of citizen participation in the decision-making process and citizen support for the implementation of public policies. Improper behavior by public officers and employees undermines democratic governing processes, which protect the interests of the citizenry, and public support for governmental programs. Corruption also can have a negative impact upon the morale of ethical public officers and employees, and encourage citizen disrespect for laws.

This chapter draws upon the ethical problems and the various approaches to eliminating corrupt behavior described and analyzed in the preceding chapters in order to develop a model program for guaranteeing that policy-making and administration comport with the highest ethical standards.

A MODEL FOR ETHICAL GOVERNMENT

Our model is designed to reduce the opportunities and incentives for corruption and to facilitate its detection. The model recognizes that a public servant cannot disassociate himself/herself totally from private activities that may constitute a conflict of interest, and that guidance must be provided to all public officers and employees to enable them to perform their duties in accordance with official standards and to avoid the appearance of an impropriety. The success of the model is highly dependent upon continuous, strong, executive and legislative leadership in implementing each element of the model.

The model calls for the enactment of statutes, and constitutional provisions where necessary, which:

- Centralize all executive authority in a single chief executive and provide for a uniformity of administrative structure and terminology.

- Require all executive departments and agencies to be organized by major function.

- Mandate the recruitment and promotion of personnel in accordance with the merit principle with the exception of top policy-makers.

- Make conflicts of interest illegal and provide severe penalties for violations.

- Establish a code of ethics addressing subtle ethical questions regarding the conduct of government officers and employees.

- Create a Board of Ethics to monitor compliance with the conflict-of-interest statutes, code of ethics, and mandatory disclosure statutes; investigate allegations of unethical behavior; and provide advice on ethical questions to public officers and employees.

- Require public officers and employees to disclose aspects of their personal finances, lobbyists to register and file financial disclosure statements, candidates for elective offices to reveal aspects of campaign finance and comply with campaign expenditure limits, and major contributors to election campaigns to file finance reports which are subject to in-depth audit and to comply with limits on campaign contributions.

- Make most government information available to the general public while protecting the privacy of citizens.

- Authorize citizens to attend meetings of collegial bodies with a few specified exceptions.

- Require each executive agency to adopt a system of effective internal controls to prevent unethical conduct and detect such conduct when it occurs.

- Install a system of rigorous external controls.

- Protect whistleblowers from retaliation.

- Prevent former public officers and employees for a period of time from benefiting indirectly from their government service.

For maximum effectiveness, the statutes implementing the model must be developed as an integrated whole since the key elements are closely related. The development and enforcement of clear and consistent ethical standards throughout a government is critical. If there is a patchwork of inadequate or overly restrictive or conflicting standards, the public servant will be confused and the standards probably will not be enforced fully.

The statutes ideally should be administered by a single independent board or commission with a guarantee of adequate funding. Typically, a separate board or commission is responsible for a specific regulatory function such as corrupt practices acts or lobbying. Because of the inter-relationships of these acts, enforcement will be more effective if such responsibility is confided in a single board.

A Single Chief Executive

The municipal reform and administrative management movements early in the twentieth century concluded that centralization of responsibility for all executive functions in a single chief executive officer would promote the provision of governmental services in the most economical and efficient manner, and also help to root out corruption. This conclusion is as valid today as when the conclusion first was reached.

A chief executive must be more than a chief executive in name. He or she must be granted authority commensurate with the responsibilities of the position. Clear lines of authority should run from the chief executive, at the apex of the hierarchical pyramid, through departments, divisions, bureaus, and offices, to the base of the structure. The chief executive should have complete power to appoint and remove department heads without legislative confirmation in order that he/she may enforce responsibility throughout the administration.

Many state and local governments unfortunately lack a single chief executive who could provide strong ethical leadership and ensure that all activities of bureaucrats are proper. The problem is particularly acute in jurisdictions where elected officers head departments, because there may be no general executive check on the performance of each department. At the local government level, it is not uncommon to have a governmental structure with executive and legislative powers confided in the same body. Where the governing body exercises executive as well as legislative powers, it is probable that there is no independent check on the performance of executive agencies, with the exception of a periodic financial audit.

Functional Organization

Departments should be organized according to major function, and all agencies concerned with a particular operation should be grouped together in one department. Successive subdivisions of departments should be composed of similar groups.

The concept of span of control influences the determination of the number of subdivisions to be created at each level. Depending upon the subject matter, experts estimate that one officer can supervise directly in an effective manner from three to seven immediate subordinates. However, the number of subordinates an executive can supervise properly depends upon the ability of both the executive and the subordinates.

Unless the executive branch of a government is organized by function, it will be difficult to ensure that all actions are ethical, because the governance process will not be visible as an integrated whole. A requirement, for example, that a permit must be obtained from more than one regulatory agency in a functional field creates opportunities for extortion and bribe giving.

Personnel Policies

All government personnel in the executive branch, with the exception of top policy-making departmental officers, should be hired and promoted in accordance with the merit principle. The recruitment and examination processes obviously must ensure that persons appointed are competent to perform their duties. Of equal importance is the weeding out of applicants who have a demonstrated proclivity for unethical behavior.

There is a positive correlation between employee morale and improper behavior. Many factors affect employee morale including the leadership provided by superiors and the salary plan.

The first step in developing an equitable salary plan is the classification of all positions according to the nature of work to be done and the responsibilities imposed on the officers and employees. A salary plan that rewards equally every officer and employee with identical duties and responsibilities will maintain high morale and prevent the development of disgruntled personnel who may engage in improper activities.

Supplemental approaches to solving ethical problems include recognition of the relationship between the salary schedule and public servant behavior. Logic suggests that low pay scales may be an incentive for corrupt conduct as officers and employees, particularly those with regulatory responsibilities, are tempted to supplement their salaries by accepting bribes in the form of money or gifts in return for a favor. It is, however, unrealistic to anticipate that a high salary schedule automatically will raise moral standards in a government.

Conflict-of-Interest Statutes

There must be a comprehensive statutory definition of the public interest which makes clear to public servants that they may not make private gains at the expense of taxpayers, if our model for ethical government is to achieve its goal, since the remaining elements of the model are based upon such a definition.

Drafters of conflict-of-interest statutes must consider the possibility that the statutes may make difficult the recruitment of the most competent personnel. Hence, statute drafters may have to strike a balance between highly restrictive standards and standards that will not deter personnel recruitment. The effectiveness of the statutes will not be diminished significantly if they include *de minimis* exceptions.

Experience reveals that these statutes can be successful in dealing with direct conflicts of interest, but are less effective in dealing with situations involving an indirect interest in a matter by a public officer. The effectiveness of these statutes in many governmental jurisdictions also is impeded by their complexity—direct, indirect, and remote interest—and the fact they tend to be scattered throughout the general laws, the constitutions of states, and the common law. Compounding the problem of guiding public officers and employees is the scattered interpretations of the statutes by courts and attorneys general.

The inadequacies of conflict-of-interest statutes in eliminating subtle forms of corruption became apparent with the great expansion of governmental regulatory activities and the resulting necessity of granting broad discretionary authority to many public officers which produced situations where the propriety of certain actions was questionable, although not a clear violation of the statutes.

Codes of Ethics

By the middle of the twentieth century, many legislative bodies began to recognize that the parameters of ethical behavior cannot be delineated precisely by statute or administrative rule and regulation. In consequence, they commenced to draft and adopt codes of ethics providing more detailed guidance relative to acceptable and unacceptable conduct by public servants.

The codes reflect the subtle nature of ethical problems and establish boards of ethics with the duties of monitoring compliance with ethical prescripts and providing advisory opinions to bureaucrats uncertain whether a contemplated action clearly would be ethical. Governing bodies also created committees to provide advisory opinions to legislators and their staffs. Boards frequently issue opinions in response to requests for a clarification whether a small gift or honorarium may be accepted under specified circumstances. Boards also are typically authorized to conduct investigations of charges of unethical behavior.

The board or legislative advisory committee is in a position to provide advice on unanticipated developments involving situations where a sharp line cannot be drawn between permitted and prohibited behavior. With the passage of time, the advisory opinions become a type of common law that provides guidance to all public servants. Furthermore, codes of ethics and boards of ethics help to remove public suspicions that government officers and employees are using their positions for private gain.

Mandatory Information Disclosure

Complementing conflict-of-interest statutes and codes of ethics are several types of mandatory information disclosure laws premised on the theory that public knowledge of certain types of information will deter wrongdoing by public servants and also facilitate detection of unethical behavior.

These statutes require candidates for elective office, lobbyists, and public officers and employees to file various types of reports containing information on their finances and the finances of family members. These "sunshine" laws have been adopted widely in the United States in the belief they will deter unethical behavior. Unfortunately, many laws have weak reporting requirements and often either are not enforced or are enforced inadequately.

Mandatory information disclosure statutes may invade unnecessarily the privacy of the covered public servants. Required financial disclosures preferably should be limited to a listing of sources of income and not specific amounts. It may be desirable to require each filer of a report to indicate whether a particular source of income exceeds specified figures such as $10,000, $25,000, $50,000, or $100,000.

The least effective disclosure laws tend to be the corrupt practices acts, which often contain loopholes and are enforced by a regulatory body that frequently is composed of political appointees with little interest in the rigorous enforcement of the laws. A compounding factor is the failure of many legislative bodies to provide adequate funding for full enforcement of the laws. Hence, a strong case can be made for the drafting and adopting of a single mandatory disclosure code with stringent requirements by an independent commission with guaranteed funding.

Freedom of Information

Closely related to mandatory disclosure requirements are freedom of information laws enacted with the conviction that an informed public is essential to proper functioning of the governance process, and availability of information to the public will deter unethical conduct and facilitate its detection, remedy inadvertent injustices, and encourage citizen participation.

The information must be systematized to increase its availability to the public. The Code of Federal Regulations, for example, was developed in the 1930s because of the proliferation of rules and regulations that were not readily accessible. Also helpful are requirements that each agency maintain an index of its documents and reasonable time limits for agencies to respond to requests for information.

Elected officials and bureaucrats have a natural penchant for secrecy and an extreme case is the Official Secrets Act in the United Kingdom. There admittedly is a legitimate reason for keeping a few types of information—such as medical or investigative files—secret, but a broad secrecy act may hide wrongdoing and inefficient performance of governmental functions. Related problems include unnecessary delays in releasing information to the public and issuance of reports containing obfuscate language.

In drafting a freedom of information statute, safeguards must be incorporated to ensure that the resulting "sunshine" does not invade personal privacy unnecessarily by authorizing the withholding of certain types of information and requiring deletion of details identifying individuals. A privacy act should be drafted in conjunction with a freedom of information act to eliminate unnecessary conflicting provisions and reduce the barriers to the release of data and information.

Protection of personal privacy will encourage individuals to provide more complete and accurate information to governmental agencies highly dependent upon such information. Since governments may maintain they are protecting privacy by not releasing information, provisions must be made for an independent body to review nonrelease decisions and to provide advice relative to whether the sought-after information should be released. Furthermore, the statute should contain a provision authorizing a citizen to bring suit to force the release of public information. The burden of proof should be placed on the agency withholding the requested information.

Open Meeting Laws

Citizen participation in the governance process is promoted if public bodies hold open meetings. Citizens attending meetings are able to suggest improvements to a proposed law or administrative action, and often are in a position to raise questions if there has been inadequate justification for the proposal under consideration. In addition, open meetings reduce the opportunities for unethical decision making and assist voters in evaluating the performance of elected officers.

These laws must be drafted carefully, particularly the definition of "meeting" and "public body," to guarantee that citizens have the right to attend meetings with a few specified exceptions which protect the public's interest and the privacy of individuals. The statute should authorize the convening of an executive session of a collegial body only by an extraordinary vote that must be included in the minutes of the meeting available to the public. The collegial body also should be required, except in emergency situations, to identify clearly in its required notice the specific purpose for the in camera session. In common with the freedom of information statute, an open meeting statute should be drafted in conjunction with the drafting of a privacy statute.

The cost of preparing an official transcript of all meetings of governmental bodies would be prohibitive, but the required recording of all meetings would be an inexpensive alternative. The audio or video recording of meetings would be of great value to individuals or groups challenging the legality of actions taken at a closed meeting, and also would be of benefit to citizens unable to attend an open meeting.

Internal Controls

The above elements of our model promote but do not guarantee ethical conduct by all public servants. Internal controls are vital supplements which will help to ensure that public officers and employees do not exceed their authority, reduce the opportunity for improprieties and facilitate their detection, and promote the most economical and efficient operation of an agency. These systems should place special emphasis upon public officers and employees with the greatest opportunities to engage in improper activities for personal gain.

Internal controls commence with a vigorous screening of applicants for appointed positions to ensure that persons with a record of ethical violations are not hired. Relative to the daily operations of an agency, all transactions must be documented and the documents must be available for inspection at any time. A classification system helps to make the documentation readily available. Access to many records must be restricted to the smallest number of officers and employees who have a demonstrated need for such access.

The internal control system must ensure that no one official is responsible for authorizing, processing, recording, and reviewing transactions. To the extent feasible, each of these subfunctions should be assigned to a different officer. Top-level supervisors must review the internal controls periodically to determine whether they are achieving their goals.

Each executive agency should have an internal controls officer or unit responsible for monitoring the system and ensuring compliance with all requirements, including the filing of mandatory information disclosure reports. The statute establishing the internal controls system must direct each agency's internal controls officer or unit to review carefully all filed disclosure reports and to conduct a vulnerability assessment on a periodic basis to permit the initiation of new controls and procedures to eliminate opportunities for corrupt behavior. Computerization of key records will permit analysts to detect unethical practices such as bid rigging. In particular, officers and units with broad discretionary authority should be subjected to the strictest internal controls which include a double and triple checking of certain activities.

Provision for inspectors general is a key ingredient of an effective internal controls system. An inspector general conducts continuous investigations to detect improper behavior, including allegations of unethical actions, and to identify weaknesses in the internal controls system to permit the initiation of corrective action. Since the duties of an inspector general overlap the responsibilities of other officers and boards, the statute creating the office should contain provisions for the coordination of the inspector general's activities with the activities of the other investigatory officers and boards. For maximum effectiveness, the inspector general must be protected against retaliation by superiors and granted security of tenure.

External Controls

Experience reveals that systems of internal controls are not completely successful in eliminating unethical behavior. Furthermore, the general public may view internal control systems as window dressing which hide more than what they uncover. The public also may be skeptical that an agency will conduct a vigorous investigation on a continuing basis.

Legislative oversight of the executive branch is an inherent feature of a system of government based upon the principles of separation of powers and checks and balances.

Legislatures, however, seldom conduct investigations for more than a year or two and tend to be reactive and create a special committee to investigate charges of unethical behavior or gross incompetence only when public and media pressure to do so becomes strong. Their investigations also may be hindered by the lack of an adequate and competent staff.

All states have a popularly elected or legislatively appointed auditor or comptroller who scrutinizes financial accounts and transactions. Initially, these officers conducted only postaudits to determine that all expenditures were authorized and spent in accordance with the law. In more recent years, many auditors conduct wide-ranging investigations of current agency performance of their responsibilities. All auditors, whether popularly elected or appointed by a legislative body, should be required by law to conduct performance evaluations.

Two relatively recent developments in the United States have been the appointment of independent counsels and ombudsmen. The former are special prosecutors with broad powers and a substantial staff to investigate allegations of criminal wrongdoing by executive branch officers. One reason for the creation of the position of special prosecutors has been the heavy workload of existing prosecutors who would be unable to devote sufficient time to the conduct of the necessary investigations of a complex case involving large sums of money and many individuals. A second reason for creating the position in some instances is the fear that the regular prosecuting attorney may have a conflict of interest if he/she was appointed by the chief executive whose agencies have been charged with unethical conduct.

Genuine ombudsmen are appointed by legislative bodies although several chief executives have appointed officers labeled ombudsmen. The ombudsman's principal function is to assist citizens who have been aggrieved by a governmental action. In the process of conducting investigations, the ombudsman may detect improper conduct. Although the ombudsman can not initiate corrective action, he/she can place public pressure on the responsible officer to initiate such action. In common with the independent counsel, the ombudsman must be guaranteed broad powers, an adequate staff, and security of tenure.

Protecting Whistleblowers

There would be no need for whistleblowing if the preceding elements of our model were totally effective in ensuring ethical governance. Surveys reveal that a significant percentage of governmental officers and employees have witnessed wasteful or unethical activities, but they may be deterred by loyalty to the agency and fear of reprisals from exposing wrongdoing.

Since societal norms and agency culture do not encourage public servants to be tattlers, there is little incentive for them to report unethical behavior by other public servants when the risks of reprisals—discharge, demotion, reassignment, lowered performance rating, ostracism—are great.

Governments must institute programs that protect whistleblowers against retaliation and that stress that public officers and employees have a duty to report improper behavior. As noted in Chapter 8, the national Whistleblower Protection Act of 1989 has not been effective in all agencies, in part because the agencies failed to inform their officers and employees of their protection rights and did not develop procedures for implementing the protection. To encourage whistleblowing, a statute should authorize a reward for information leading to the conviction of a government worker for an ethical violation.

Additionally, whistleblower laws should be enacted to protect officers and employees of private firms who report wrongdoing involving the firms' transactions with governments. Private firms always have provided services and constructed public works for governments, and scandals occasionally have been exposed. The recent trend involving governments contracting with firms to provide services previously provided by the governments has enlarged the opportunities for unethical actions by private firms.

The public must be assured that information provided by whistle-blowers will be examined carefully and appropriate corrective action initiated. If the concerned agency or the ethics board fails to act on the information provided, the whistleblower should be protected by law if he/she reveals wrongdoing to the media.

Postemployment Restrictions

Enactment of statutes containing postgovernment employment restrictions are an additional safeguard to prevent individuals from making personal gains as a direct consequence of their government service. A serious but not universal problem involves the revolving door. Media revelations of the movement of individuals between the U.S. Department of Defense and the defense industry highlight the nature of this problem, which is not limited to the national government.

A more common problem involves a government regulator resigning his/her position and accepting a position with a business firm he/she formerly regulated. The solution to this problem is the enactment of statutes prohibiting a former government officer from dealing with his/her former agency for a stipulated period of time.

To protect the public interest, postgovernment service statutes must require former public officers to keep confidential information confidential and not use such information for personal gain. The statutes typically prohibit a former officer for a period of one to two years to represent parties before the agency which employed the officer. These restrictions must be applied to former legislators and their staffs as well as to former bureaucrats. The statute specifically should forbid a private firm to hire a public officer who negotiated, prepared, or supervised contracts the firm holds with the government. Former legislators and legislative staff members should be forbidden to lobby the legislative body for compensation for a period of two years with respect to a matter that the former legislator or staff member was directly concerned.

Drafting an effective postemployment statute is a difficult task because it may restrict unfairly the activities of former government officers, make recruitment of officers more difficult, and fail to offer adequate protection to the public. The statute must be custom-tailored to certain classes of officials and consultants, as Congress did relative to former employees of the Department of Defense and the National Aeronautics and Space Agency.

If serious recruitment problems are encountered because of the postemployment restrictions, the statute should be amended to authorize the board of ethics under specified conditions to grant a waiver of the restrictions for an individual with a special talent the government is attempting to recruit.

Experience reveals that civil penalties are more effective for violations of the postemployment restrictions than criminal penalties, since courts have overturned convictions on the ground that criminal intent was not proved beyond a reasonable doubt.

CONCLUDING COMMENTS

It is difficult to argue with the conclusion of John C. Bollens and Henry J. Schmandt that "the degree of corruption in a political system reflects, in a sense, the public's tolerance of improprieties by its officials."[2] They referred specifically to "the widespread tendency of Americans to cheat; the lenient attitude of society toward white-collar crime in general; and popular cynicism about the integrity, honesty, and impartiality of government."[3]

Their explanation of why corruption exists in government is not universally applicable. As noted in Chapter 1, Daniel J. Elazar described three types of political culture. His individualistic culture would appear to encompass Bollens' and Schmandt's description. Elazar also noted the presence of a moralistic political culture which needs to be nourished and developed throughout the United States.

Unfortunately, there is no simple prescription for the development of a moralistic political culture. We know that legal sanctions do not develop such a culture and are inadequate to deter unethical behavior. Education, a long-term process, must play a key role in the development of such a culture. Our model recognizes that the individualistic political culture tends to be the prevailing one in many areas of the United States, and the ethical abuses associated with it must be addressed by a variety of counter measures.

If governing bodies fail to implement programs to ensure that the public's business is conducted in accordance with the highest moral precepts, voters must possess the ability to take direct action. Hence, it is desirable that state constitutions and local government charters authorize voters to employ the protest referendum, the initiative, and the recall to institute necessary corrective actions.[4]

The protest referendum, also labeled the citizen referendum, allows voters to collect a specified number of signatures in order to suspend implementation of a law until a referendum is held on the question of repealing the law. Similarly, the initiative allows voters by means of petitions to place a proposed law on the ballot in the event the legislative body refuses to consider the proposed law. And the recall permits voters by means of petitions to call a special election for the purpose of deciding whether an elected officer should be removed from office prior to the expiration of his/her term. These participatory devices are standby ones that should be available to the voters for use in the event the governing body is unresponsive to citizen concerns.

One can conclude with certainty that ethical problems will continue to exist in the public service and change in nature with the passage of time. Consequently, prevention and detection of improper behavior must be a continuing activity that periodically is adjusted to address newly emerging ethical problems.

NOTES

1. Paul H. Douglas, *Ethics in Government* (Cambridge: Harvard University Press, 1952), p. 44.

2. John C. Bollens and Henry J. Schmandt, *Political Corruption, Power, Money, and Sex* (Pacific Palisades, Calif.: Palisades Publishers, 1979), p. 238.

3. Ibid., p. 239.

4. Joseph F. Zimmerman, *Participatory Democracy: Populism Revived* (New York: Praeger, 1986), pp. 35–134.

Bibliography

Books

Alexander, Herbert E. *Financing Politics: Money, Elections, and Political Reform.* Washington, D.C.: CQ Press, 1992.

Al-Mulk, Nizam. *The Book of Government or Rules for Kings.* New Haven: Yale University Press, 1960. Translated by Hubert Darke.

Appleby, Paul H. *Morality and Administration in Democratic Government.* Baton Rouge: Louisiana State University Press, 1952.

Aristotle. *The Nicomachean Ethics.* Dordrecht, Holland: D. Reidel Publishing Co., 1975.

The Association of the Bar of the City of New York. *Conflict of Interest and Federal Service.* Cambridge: Harvard University Press, 1960.

Axelrod, Donald. *Shadow Government: The Hidden World of Public Authorities—and How They Control Over $1 Trillion of Your Money.* New York: John Wiley & Sons, 1992.

Becker, Lawrence D., and Becker, Charlotte B., eds. *Encyclopaedia of Ethics.* New York: Garland Publishing, 1992, 2 vols.

Bigelow, Page E., and Tullai, Margaret M., comps. *Citizenship and Ethics: An Annotated Bibliography,* 2d ed. New York: Institute of Public Administration, 1993.

Blum, Ann, and Apostolik, Elinid, eds. *The Right to Privacy Versus the Right to Know.* Athens: Institute of Government, University of Georgia, n.d.

Bollens, John C., and Schmandt, Henry J. *Political Corruption: Power, Money, and Sex.* Pacific Palisades, Calif.: Palisades Publishers, 1979.

Bowman, James S., and Elliston, Frederick A., eds. *Ethics, Government, and Public Policy: A Reference Guide.* Westport, Conn.: Greenwood Press, 1988.

Campaign Finance, Ethics & Lobby Law Blue Book, 1992-93. Lexington, Ky: The Council of State Governments, 1992.

Campaign Finance: A Model State Law. New York: National Municipal League, 1979.

Chapman, Richard A. *Ethics in the British Civil Service.* London: Routledge, 1988.

Childs, Richard S. *The First Fifty Years of the Countil-Manager Plan.* New York: National Municipal League, 1965.

——— . *The Short Ballot: A Movement to Simplify Politics.* New York: The National Short Ballot Organization, 1916.

City Management Code of Ethics. Washington, D.C.: International City Management Association, 1972.

Codes of Ethics and Implementation Guidelines. Washington, D.C.: American Society for Public Administration, 1984.

Cody, W.J. Michael, and Lynn, Richardson R. *Honest Government: An Ethics Guide for Public Service.* Westport, Conn.: Praeger, 1992.

Coleman, Ranson B., Jr. *Ethics in Alabama State Government.* University: Bureau of Public Administration, University of Alabama, 1972.

Cooper, Terry L. *Handbook of Administrative Ethics.* New York: Marcel Dekker, 1993.

——— . *The Responsible Administrator: An Approach to Ethics for the Administrative Role,* 3d ed. San Francisco: Jossey-Bass, 1990.

David, Irwin T.; Sturgeon, C. Eugene; and Adams, Eula L. *How to Evaluate and Improve Internal Controls in Governmental Units.* Chicago: Municipal Finance Officers Association, 1981.

Davis, Kenneth C. *Discretionary Justice: A Preliminary Inquiry.* Baton Rouge: Louisiana State University Press, 1969.

Denhardt, Kathryn G. *The Ethics of Public Service: Resolving Moral Dilemmas in Public Organizations.* Westport, Conn.: Greenwood Press, 1988.

Donagan, Alan. *The Theory of Morality.* Chicago: University of Chicago Press, 1977.

Douglas, Paul H. *Ethics in Government.* Cambridge: Harvard University Press, 1952.

Elazar, Daniel J. *American Federalism: A View from the States,* 3d ed. New York: Harper & Row, 1984.

Elliston, Frederick et al. *Whistleblowing Research: Methodological and Moral Issues.* New York: Praeger, 1985.

Ethical Insight, Ethical Action. Washington, D.C.: International City Management Association, 1988.

The Federalist Papers. New York: New American Library, 1961.

Fleishman, Joel L.; Liebman, Lance; and Moore, Mark H., eds. *Public Duties: The Moral Obligations of Government Officials.* Cambridge: Harvard University Press, 1981.

French, Peter A. *Ethics in Government.* Englewood Cliffs, N.J.: Prentice-Hall, 1983.

Gardner, John A., and Lyman, Theodore R. *Decisions for Sale: Corruption and Reform in Land-Use and Building Regulations.* New York: Praeger, 1978.

Gawthrop, Louis C. *Public Sector Management, Systems, and Ethics.* Bloomington: Indiana University Press, 1984.

Gilson, Lawrence. *Money and Secrecy: A Citizen's Guide to Reforming State and Federal Practices.* New York: Praeger, 1972.

Glazer, Myron P., and Glazer, Penina M. *The Whistle-blowers: Exposing Corruption in Government and Industry.* New York: Basic Books, 1989.

Golembiewski, Robert T. *Men, Management, and Morality: Toward a New Organizational Ethic.* New York: McGraw-Hill, 1965.

Gortner, Harold F. *Ethics for Public Managers.* Westport, Conn.: Praeger, 1991.

Gottfried, Frances. *The Merit System and Municipal Civil Service*. Westport, Conn.: Greenwood Press, 1988.

Green, Bruce A., ed. *Government Ethics for the 1990s: The Collected Reports of the New York State Commission on Government Integrity*. New York: Fordham University Press, 1991.

Gregory, Roy, and Hutcheson, Peter. *The Parliamentary Ombudsman: A Study in the Control of Administrative Action*. London: George Allen & Unwin, 1975.

Guide for Studying and Evaluating Internal Controls in the Federal Government. Washington, D.C.: Arthur Andersen & Co., 1986.

Gutman, Amy, and Thompson, Dennis. *Ethics and Politics*. Chicago: Nelson-Hall, 1984.

Hadden, Susan G. *A Citizen's Right to Know: Risk Communication and Public Policy*. Boulder, Colo.: Westview Press, 1989.

Hale, John. *The Whistle Blowers*. New York: Collier Books, 1988.

Harwell, Fred. *The Right to Be Able to Know: Public Access to Public Information*. Raleigh: North Carolina Center for Public Policy Research, 1978.

Hauth, Robert F. *"Knowing the Territory": Basic Legal Guidelines for Municipal Officers*. Seattle: Municipal Research and Services Center of Washington, 1987.

Jowett, Benjamin, trans. *Aristotle's Politics*. New York: Carlton House, n.d.

Kellar, Elizabeth K., ed. *Ethical Insight, Ethical Action: Perspectives for the Local Government Manager*. Washington, D.C.: International City Management Association, 1988.

Larrabee, Harold A., ed. *Bentham's Handbook of Political Fallacies*. Baltimore: Johns Hopkins University Press, 1952.

Lewis, Carol W. *The Ethics Challenge in Public Service*. San Francisco: Jossey-Bass, 1991.

———. *Scruples & Scandals*. Storrs: Institute of Public Service and Institute of Urban Research, University of Connecticut, 1986.

Light, Paul C. *Monitoring Government: Inspectors General and the Search for Accountability*. Washington, D.C.: The Brookings Institution, 1992.

Linowes, David F. *Privacy in America: Is Your Private Life in the Public Eye*. Urbana: University of Illinois Press, 1989.

Locke, John. *The Second Treatise of Government*. New York: The Liberal Arts Press, 1952.

Machiavelli, Niccolo. *The Prince and the Discourses*. New York: The Modern Library, 1940.

Madsen, Peter, and Shafrtiz, Jay M., eds. *Essentials of Government Ethics*. New York: Penguin Books, 1992.

Makinson, Larry. *Open Secrets: The Cash Constituents of Congress*. Washington, D.C.: CQ Press, 1992.

Malbin, Michael J. *Money and Politics in the United States*. Washington, D.C.: American Enterprise Institute, 1984.

McKinney, Jerome B., and Johnston, Michael, eds. *Fraud, Waste, and Abuse in Government*. Philadelphia: ISHI Publications, 1986.

Model City Charter, 7th ed. Denver: National Civil League, 1989.

A Model Ethics Law for State Government. Washington, D.C.: Common Cause, 1989.

Model State Conflict of Interest and Financial Disclosure Law. New York: National Municipal League, 1979.

Morgan, Thomas, and Rotunda, Ronald D. *Professional Responsibility*, 3d ed. Mineola, New York: Foundation Press, 1984.

Neely, Alfred S. IV. *Ethics-in-Government Laws: Are They Too "Ethical?"* Washington, D.C.: American Enterprise Institute for Public Policy Research, 1984.

Noonan, John T., Jr. *Bribes*. New York: Macmillan, 1985.

Peters, Charles, and Branch, Taylor. *Blowing the Whistle: Dissent in the Public Interest*. New York: Praeger, 1972.

Prescott, Richard. *A Practical Handbook on the Illinois Open Meeting Act*. Springfield, Ill.: House Republican Staff, 1982.

Rawls, John. *A Theory of Justice*. Cambridge: Belknap Press of Harvard University Press, 1971.

Rees, D. A., ed. *Aristotle The Nicomachean Ethics*. Oxford: Clarendon Press, 1951.

The Right to Privacy versus The Right to Know. Athens: Institute of Government, University of Georgia, n.d.

Roberts, Robert N. *White House Ethics: The History of the Politics of Conflict of Interest Regulation*. Westport, Conn.: Greenwood Press, 1988.

Rohr, John A. *Ethics for Bureaucrats*, 2d ed. New York: Marcel Dekker, 1989.

Rosen, Bernard. *Holding Government Bureaucracies Accountable*. New York: Praeger, 1982.

Sawyer, Lawrence B. *The Practice of Modern Internal Auditing*. New York: The Institute of Internal Auditors, 1973.

Selznick, Philip. *TVA and the Grass Roots*. Berkeley: University of California Press, 1949.

Sheeran, Patrick J. *Ethics in Public Administration: A Philosophical Approach*. Westport, Conn.: Praeger, 1993.

Steffens, Lincoln. *The Shame of the Cities*. New York: McClure, Phillips & Co., 1905.

Steinberg, Sheldon S., and Austern, David T. *Government, Ethics, and Managers*. Westport, Conn.: Praeger, 1990.

The Sunshine Laws: New York's Open Meetings Law and Freedom of Information Law. Albany: New York State Conference of Mayors, 1992.

Thompson, Dennis F. *Political Ethics and Public Office*. Cambridge: Harvard University Press, 1987.

Yutang, Lin, ed. and trans. *The Wisdom of Confucius*. New York: Carlton House, 1938.

Weeks, Kent M. *Ombudsmen Around the World: A Comparative Chart*, 2d ed. Berkeley: Institute of Governmental Studies, University of California, 1978.

A Whistle-Blower's Guide to the Federal Bureaucracy. Washington, D.C.: Institute for Policy Studies, 1977.

Winter, Ralph K., Jr. *Watergate and the Law: Political Campaigns and Presidential Power*. Washington, D.C.: American Enterprise Institute for Public Policy Research, 1974.

PUBLIC DOCUMENTS

Access to the Ballot in Primary Elections: The Need for Fundamental Reform. New York: New York State Commission on Government Integrity, 1988.

Access to Governmental Records. Carson City: Nevada Legislative Commission, 1982.

The Albany Money Machine: Campaign Financing for New York State Legislative Races. New York: New York State Commission on Government Integrity, 1988.

Annual Report. Albany: New York Temporary State Commission on Lobbying, 1991.

Annual Report for Fiscal Year 1991. Washington, D.C.: United States Merit Systems Protection Board, 1991.

Annual Report of the Ombudsman: Ireland 1991. Dublin: The Stationery Office, 1993.

Annual Report of the Ombudsman Northern Ireland, 1992. Belfast: The Ombudsman, 1993.

ATF Internal Control Evaluation System. Washington, D.C.: Bureau of Alcohol, Tobacco, and Firearms, United States Department of the Treasury, 1986.

Attorney General's Manual on the Administrative Procedure Act. Washington, D.C.: United States Department of Justice, 1947.

Becoming a Judge: Report on the Failings of Judicial Elections in New York State. New York: New York State Commission on Government Integrity, 1988.

Bid-Rigging in the Competitive Bidding Process. Albany: New York State Department of Law, 1985.

Blowing the Whistle in the Federal Government: A Comparative Analysis of 1980 and 1983 Survey Findings. Washington, D.C.: United States Merit Systems Protection Board, 1984.

Brock, Jack L., Jr. *Computer Security: Hackers Penetrate DOD Computer Systems.* Washington, D.C.: United States General Accounting Office, 1991.

Campaign Finance Law 92. Washington, D.C.: Federal Election Commission, 1992.

Campaign Finance Reform: The Public Perspective. New York: New York State Commission on Government Integrity, 1988.

Campaign Financing: Preliminary Report. New York: New York State Commission on Government Integrity, 1987.

Classified Information: Volume Could be Reduced by Changing Retention Policy. Washington, D.C.: United States General Accounting Office, 1993.

The Commissioner's Interim Report on Integrity Within the Internal Revenue Service. Washington, D.C.: Internal Revenue Service, 1990.

Committee on Government Operations, United States House of Representatives. *A Citizen's Guide on Using the Freedom of Information Act and the Privacy Act of 1974 to Request Government Records.* Washington, D.C.: United States Government Printing Office, 1991.

Committee on Government Operations, United States House of Representatives. *Misconduct by Senior Managers in the Internal Revenue Service.* Washington, D.C.: United States Government Printing Office, 1990.

Committee on the Judiciary, United States House of Representatives. *The INSLAW Affair.* Washington, D.C.: United States Government Printing Office, 1992.

Committee on Standards of Official Conduct. *Ethics Manual for Members, Officers, and Employees of the United States House of Representatives.* Washington, D.C.: United States Government Printing Office, 1987.

Commodity Programs: Should Farmers Grow Income-Supported Crops on Federal Land? Washington, D.C.: United States General Accounting Office, 1992.

Computer Security: DEA Is Not Adequately Protecting Sensitive Drug Enforcement Data. Washington, D.C.: United States General Accounting Office, 1992.

Computer Security: Hackers Penetrate DOD Computer Systems. Washington, D.C.: United States General Accounting Office, 1991.

Conflict-of-Interest Policy: Defense Logistics Agency Employees Whose Spouses Work for Contractors. Washington, D.C.: United States General Accounting Office, 1992.

Constitutional Documents of Sweden. Stockholm: The Swedish Riksdag, 1989.

Fresner, Sykes, Jordan & Townsend, Incorporated. *Campaign Finance Reform: The Public Perspective.* New York: New York State Commission on Government Integrity, 1988.

Employee Conduct Standards: Some Outside Activities Present Conflict-of-Interest Issues. Washington, D.C.: United States General Accounting Office, 1992.

Energy Management: DOE Needs to Better Implement Conflict-of-Interest Controls. Washington, D.C.: United States General Accounting Office, 1990.

Ethics: The Department of Justice's Ethics Program. Washington, D.C.: United States General Accounting Office, 1988.

Ethics Enforcement: Process by Which Conflict-of-Interest Allegations are Investigated and Resolved. Washington, D.C.: United States General Accounting Office, 1987.

Ethics Enforcement: Results of Conflict-of-Interest Investigations. Washington, D.C.: United States General Accounting Office, 1988.

Ethics Handbook. Phoenix: City of Phoenix, 1991.

Ethics Manual for Members, Officers, and Employees of the United States House of Representatives. Washington, D.C.: United States Government Printing Office, 1992.

Ethics: Office of Government Ethics' Policy Development Role. Washington, D.C.: United States General Accounting Office, 1988.

Executive Order No. 91: Annual Financial Reporting of Income, Assets, and Liabilities of City Officials. New York: Office of the Mayor, 1986.

Executive Order No. 346. Boston, Mass.: Executive Department, December 2, 1992.

Expanding Drug Treatment: The Need for Fair Contracting Practices. New York: New York State Commission on Government Integrity, 1989.

Fair Information Practices Acts in Utah, Minnesota, and Massachusetts. Madison: Wisconsin Legislative Council Staff, 1976.

Federal Records: Document Removal by Agency Heads Needs Independent Oversight. Washington, D.C.: United States General Accounting Office, 1991.

Federal Records: Removal of Agency Documents by Senior Officials Upon Leaving Office. Washington, D.C.: United States General Accounting Office, 1989.

Final Report of the Special Commission Established to Make an Investigation of an Act Establishing a Code of Ethics to Guide Employees and Officials of the Commonwealth in the Performance of their Duties. Boston: Wright & Potter Printing Company, 1962.

Financial Audit: Expenditures by Nine Independent Counsels. Washington, D.C.: United States General Accounting Office, 1992.

Financial Disclosure: Legislative Branch Systems Can be Further Strengthened. Washington, D.C.: United States General Accounting Office, 1989.

Financial Management: DOT's Accounting and Financial Information System Should be Improved. Washington, D.C.: United States General Accounting Office, 1992.

Financial Management: Poor Internal Control has Led to Increased Maintenance Costs and Deterioration of Equipment. Washington, D.C.: United States General Accounting Office, 1993.

Financial Management: Weak Accounting Controls Leave Commodity Assets Vulnerable to Misuse. Washington, D.C.: United States General Accounting Office, 1992.

Fletcher, Thomas; Gordon, Paula; and Hentzell, Shirley. *An Anticorruption Strategy for Local Governments*. Washington, D.C.: Law Enforcement Assistance Administration, 1978.

For Merit and Honesty in Government: The Role of the Special Counsel. Washington, D.C.: United States Office of the Special Counsel, 1980.

Freedom of Information: FDA's Program and Regulations Need Improvement. Washington, D.C.: United States General Accounting Office, 1992.

Garcia, Rogelio. *Government in the Sunshine: Public Access to Meetings Held Under the Government in the Sunshine Act, 1979-1984*. Washington, D.C.: Congressional Research Service, 1986.

Gardiner, John A.; Lyman, Theodore R.; and Waldhorn, Steven A. *Corruption in Land Use and Building Regulation*. Washington, D.C.: Law Enforcement Assistance Administration, 1978.

General Services Administration: Actions Needed to Improve Protection Against Fraud, Waste, and Mismanagement. Washington, D.C.: United States General Accounting Office, 1992.

General Services Administration: Actions Needed to Stop Buying Supplies from Poor-Performing Vendors. Washington, D.C.: United States General Accounting Office, 1993.

Getzeis, Judith, and Thurow, Charles. *An Analysis of Zoning Reforms: Minimizing the Incentive for Corruption*. Washington, D.C.: Law Enforcement Assistance Administration, 1978.

Gomez, Barney L. *Alcohol, Tobacco, and Firearms: Bureau's Handling of Sexual Harassment and Related Complaints*. Washington, D.C.: United States General Accounting Office, 1993.

Government in the Sunshine Act: History and Recent Issues: A Report of the Committee on Governmental Affairs, United States Senate. Washington, D.C.: United States Government Printing Office, 1989.

Guide to the Conflict of Interest Law. Boston: Massachusetts State Ethics Commission, 1983.

Guide for Evaluating and Testing Controls Over Sensitive Payments. Washington, D.C.: United States General Accounting Office, 1993.

Health Insurance: Medicare and Private Payers are Vulnerable to Fraud and Abuse. Washington, D.C.: United States General Accounting Office, 1992.

HUD Reforms: Progress Made Since the HUD Scandals but Much Work Remains. Washington, D.C.: United States General Accounting Office, 1992.

In the Matter of Representative Geraldine A. Ferraro, Report of the Committee on Standards of Official Conduct, United States House of Representatives. Washington, D.C.: United States Government Printing Office, 1985.

Information Disclosure: Government in the Sunshine Act Compliance at Selected Agencies. Washington, D.C.: United States General Accounting Office, 1988.

Inspectors General: Issues Involving the Farm Credit Administration's Chairman and IG. Washington, D.C.: United States General Accounting Office, 1992.

Inspector General Semiannual Report to the Congress: April 1, 1991–September 30, 1991. Washington, D.C.: United States Department of Transportation, 1991.

Internal Controls and Accountability over Meter Revenue (New York City). New York: Office of the State Comptroller, 1992.

Internal Control Guidelines. Washington, D.C.: United States Office of Management and Budget, 1982.

Internal Control Review Handbook. New York: Metro-North Commuter Railroad, n.d.

Investigation of the Agency for International Development Administrator's Compliance with Ethical Standards: A Staff Report. Washington, D.C.: Committee on Government Operations, United States House of Representatives, 1992.

Kidera, David J., and Fletcher, Stephen M. "New York Takes the Pulse: Internal Control in State Government." *Government Finance Review* VII (August 1991), 7–10.

Kingsbury, Nancy. *Federal Employment: Sexual Harrassment at the Department of Veterans Affairs.* Washington, D.C.: United States General Accounting Office, 1993.

Kleeman, Rosslyn S. *Agency Compartmentalizations and Senior Employee Designations Under the Ethics in Government Act.* Washington, D.C.: United States General Accounting Office, 1987.

Lyman, Theodore R.; Fletcher, Thomas W.; and Gardiner, John A. *Prevention, Detection, and Correction of Corruption in Local Government.* Washington, D.C.: United States Department of Justice, 1978.

Major Oversight Initiative: Hearings before the Committee on Ways and Means, House of Representatives, May 8 and 9, 1991. Washington, D.C.: United States Government Printing Office, 1992.

Managing Internal Controls. New York: Metro-North Commuter Railroad, 1991.

Manikas, Peter, and Protess, David. *Establishing a Citizens' Watchdog Group.* Washington, D.C.: Law Enforcement Assistance Administration, 1978.

Mayor's Office of Contracts: Contract Award Hearings. New York: Office of the State Comptroller, 1992.

Medicare: HCFA Monitoring of the Quality of Part B Claims Processing. Washington, D.C.: United States General Accounting Office, 1992.

Medicare: One Scheme Illustrates Vulnerabilities to Fraud. Washington, D.C.: United States General Accounting Office, 1992.

The Midas Touch. New York: New York State Commission on Government Integrity, 1989.

The Municipal Conflict of Interest Act, 1983. Toronto: Ontario Ministry of Municipal Affairs and Housing, 1983.

New York Ethics: A Guide to the Ethics Law. Albany: New York State Ethics Commission, n.d.

Office of Government Ethics' Oversight Role. Washington, D.C.: United States General Accounting Agency, 1990.

Office of Inspector General. *Report of the Audit of Supervision and Regulation Conflicts of Interest.* Washington, D.C.: Board of Governors of the Federal Reserve System, 1993.

Office of the Inspector General. *Review of the NRC Staff's Responses to Congressional Inquiries Regarding Joseph Wampler and the Welding Program at Seabrook Nuclear Station.* Washington, D.C.: Nuclear Regulatory Commission, n.d.

OMB's High Risk Program: Benefits Found But Greater Oversight Needed. Washington, D.C.: United States General Accounting Office, 1992.

Open Local Government. Toronto: Ministry of Municipal Affairs, n.d.

Opinions of the Attorney General for the Year Ending December 31, 1989. Albany: New York State Department of Law, 1990.

Peach, J. Dexter. *Federal Contracting: Cost-Effective Contract Management Requires Sustained Commitment.* Washington, D.C.: United States General Accounting Office, 1992.

Post-Employment Lobbying Restrictions: Hearings Before the United States Senate Subcommittee on Oversight of Government Management. Washington, D.C.: United States Government Printing Office, 1988.

A Practical Guide to the Conflict of Interest Law for Municipal Employees. Boston: Massachusetts State Ethics Commission, n.d.

The President's Ethics Proposals. Washington, D.C.: United States General Accounting Office, 1989.

Private Interest Over Public Trust: An Investigation into Certain Improprieties by the Leadership at the Division of School Safety. New York: City of New York Special Commissioner of Investigation for the New York City School District, 1992.

Public Officials Handbook. St. Paul: Ethical Practices Board, 1991.

The Public Service: Issues Affecting Its Quality, Effectiveness, Integrity, and Stewardship. Washington, D.C.: United States Government Printing Office, 1989.

The Quest for an Ethical Environment. New York: State-City Commission on Integrity in Government, 1986.

Questions and Answers on Circular A-123 (Revised) "Internal Control Systems." Washington, D.C.: United States Office of Management and Budget, 1984.

Questions & Answers About Whistleblower Appeals. Washington, D.C.: United States Merit Systems Protection Board, 1991.

A Report to Congress from the U.S. Office of Special Counsel, Fiscal Year 1991. Washington, D.C.: United States Government Printing Office, 1992.

Report of Investigation Concerning Operation of the New York State Labor Relations Board. Albany: Office of Inspector General, 1989.

Report on a Bill on Campaign Financing and Public Funding of Election Campaigns. New York: State-City Commission on Integrity in Government, 1986.

Report of Investigation Concerning Awarding of No-Bid Consulting Contracts and Related Contracting Matters. Albany: New York State Office of Inspector General, 1992.

Report of Investigation Concerning Improper Exercise of Authority by the Board of Directors of the Hudson River–Black River Regulating District and Other District Management Practices. Albany: New York State Office of Inspector General, 1993.

Report and Recommendations on Conflict-of-Interest and Financial Disclosure Requirements. New York: State-City Commission on Integrity in Government, 1986.

Report and Recommendations on Whistleblowing Protection in New York. New York: State-City Commission on Integrity in Government, 1986.

Report of the Special Committee on Ethics. Albany: The Legislature of the State of New York, 1964.

1991 Report to the Governor and the Legislature. Albany: New York State Committee on Open Government, 1991.

Royal Commission on the Electoral System. *Report.* Wellington: New Zealand Government Printer, 1986.

Rules of the House of Representatives. Washington, D.C.: 1993.

Rules of Conduct. Washington, D.C.: Internal Revenue Service, 1986.

Select Committee on Ethics, United States Senate. *Interpretative Rulings of the Select Committee on Ethics.* Washington, D.C.: United States Government Printing Office, 1989.

Select Committee on Ethics. *Investigation of Senator Alan Cranston.* Washington, D.C.: United States Senate, 1991.

Semiannual Report to the Congress: April 1, 1992 to September 30, 1992. Washington, D.C.: Department of Defense Inspector General, 1992.

Staff Report on Conflict of Interest and Financial Disclosure Law in New York. New York: State-City Commission on Integrity in Government, 1986.

Standards of Ethical Conduct for Employees of the Executive Branch. Washington, D.C.: United States Office of Government Ethics, 1992.

Standing Rules of the Senate. Washington, D.C.: United States Government Printing Office, 1992.

Streamlining Internal Control Processes: Strengthening Management Controls with Less Effort. Washington, D.C.: President's Council on Management Improvement, 1985.

Strengthening Ethical Standards in Rhode Island Government. Providence: Governor's Committee on Ethics in Government, 1986.

Subcommittee on National Policy Machinery, United States Senate. *The Private Citizen and National Service.* Washington, D.C.: United States Government Printing Office, 1961.

Subcommittee on Reorganization, Research, and International Organizations, United States Senate. *Government in the Sunshine: Responses to Subcommittee Questionnaires.* Washington, D.C.: United States Government Printing Office, 1974.

The Swedish Secrecy Act. Stockholm: Ministry of Justice, 1986.

A System Like No Other: Fraud and Misconduct by New York City School Custodians. New York: Special Commissioner of Investigation for New York City Schools, 1992.

Tax Administration: Examples of Waste and Inefficiency in IRS. Washington, D.C.: United States General Accounting Office, 1993.

Tax Administration: Improvement in IRS' Telephone Assistor Accuracy. Washington, D.C.: United States General Accounting Office, 1992.

Tax Administration: IRS Can Improve Controls Over Electronic Filing Fraud. Washington, D.C.: United States General Accounting Office, 1993.

Tax Administration: IRS Should Expand Financial Disclosure Requirements. Washington, D.C.: United States General Accounting Office, 1992.

Tax Systems Modernization: Concerns Over Security and Privacy Elements of the Systems Architecture. Washington, D.C.: United States General Accounting Office, 1992.

Treasury and Civil Service Committee, House of Commons. *Civil Servants and Ministers: Duties and Responsibilities*. London: Her Majesty's Stationery Office, 1986.

Unfinished Business: Campaign Finance Reform in New York City. New York: New York State Commission on Government Integrity, 1988.

Ungar, Bernard L. *Office of Government Ethics: Need for Additional Funding for Regulation Development and Oversight*. Washington, D.C.: United States General Accounting Office, 1992.

——— . *Office of Government Ethics' Oversight Role*. Washington, D.C.: United States General Accounting Office, 1990.

——— . *The President's Ethics Proposals*. Washington, D.C.: United States General Accounting Office, 1989.

United States Merit Systems Protection Board. *Sexual Harassment in the Federal Workplace: Is It a Problem?* Washington, D.C.: United States Government Printing Office, 1981.

What You Should Know. . . . New York: City of New York, n.d.

Whistleblowing and the Federal Employee. Washington, D.C.: United States Merit Systems Protection Board, 1981.

Whistleblowing in the Federal Government: An Update. Washington, D.C.: United States Merit Systems Protection Board, 1993.

Whistleblower Protection: Agencies' Implementation of the Whistleblower Statutes Has Been Mixed. Washington, D.C.: United States General Accounting Office, 1993.

Whistleblower Protection: Determining Whether Reprisal Occurred Remains Difficult. Washington, D.C.: United States General Accounting Office, 1993.

Whistleblower Protection: Employee's Awareness and Impact of the Whistleblower Protection Act of 1989. Washington, D.C.: United States General Accounting Office, 1993.

Whistleblower Protection: Impediments to the Protection of Military Members. Washington, D.C.: United States General Accounting Office, 1992.

Whistleblower Protection: Survey of Federal Employees on Misconduct and Protection from Reprisal. Washington, D.C.: United States General Accounting Office, 1992.

ARTICLES

Alexander, Herbert E. "Hidden Costs of Campaign Reform." *State Government News* XXXIII (April 1990), 16-18.

Amirrezvani, Anita. "The Data Game." *Governing* III (February 1990), 42-45.

Archibald, Sam. "The Early Years of the Freedom of Information Act—1955 to 1974." *PS: Political Science & Politics* XXVI (December 1993), 726-31.

——— . "The Freedom of Information Act Revisited." *Public Administration Review* XXXIX (July-August 1979), 311-18.

Assaf, R. James. "Mr. Smith Comes Home: The Constitutional Presumption of Openness in Local Legislative Meetings." *Case Western Reserve Law Review* (No. 1, 1989-90), 227-69.

Bagdikian, Ben. H. "The Press and Freedom of Information." *The Bureaucrat* I (Summer 1979), 122-26.

Balford, Thomas S., and Adams, Bruce. "Conflict of Interest Legislation and the Common Cause Model Act." *The Municipal Year Book 1975.* Washington, D.C.: International City Management Association, 1975, 170-79.

Ballou, Eric E., and McSlarrow, Kyle E. "Plugging the Leak: The Case for a Legislative Resolution of the Conflict Between the Demands of Secrecy and the Need for an Open Government." *Virginia Law Review* LXXI (June 1985), 801-68.

Baran, Andrew. "Federal Employment—The Civil Service Reform Act of 1978—Removing Incompetents and Protecting 'Whistle Blowers'." *Wayne Law Review* XXVI (November 1979), 97-118.

Barrett, David A. "Facilitating Government Decision Making: Distinguishing Between Meetings and Nonmeetings Under the Federal Sunshine Act." *Texas Law Review* LXVI (May 1988), 1194-228.

Berger, Joseph. "Report Details School Fraud by Custodians." *The New York Times* (November 13, 1992), B1-B2.

"Beyond the Letter of the Law." *Georgia County Government* XXXVII (September 1985), 76.

Bigelow, Judith A. "Meeting the Agency Burden under the Confidential Source Exemption to the Freedom of Information Act." *Washington Law Review* LX (September 1985), 873–87.

Blumenthal, Ralph. "New Weapons Used in Drive on Corruption." *The New York Times* (November 7, 1984), B1 and B3.

Bowman, James S. "Ethics in Government: A National Survey of Public Administrators." *Public Administration Review* L (May/June 1990), 345-53.

Boyle, Robert D. "A Review of Whistle Blower Protections and Suggestions for Change." *Labor Law Journal* XLI (December 1990), 821-30.

Brown, Bruce A. "The Current State of Federal Law on Post-Government Employment Restrictions." *Federal Bar News and Journal* XXXV (December 1988), 434-39.

Burke, Fran, and Benson, George. "Written Rules: State Ethics Codes, Commissions, and Conflicts." *The Journal of State Government* LXII (September/October 1989), 195-98.

Caher, John. "Zumbo Revealed Coyne Tie to Crozier." *The Times Union* (Albany, New York), August 7, 1992, pp. 1 and A-8.

Carter, Colin L. "A Nine-Step, Key Result Audit Approach." *Internal Auditor* XLIV (December 1987), 34-38.

Chi, Keon S. "Financing State and Local Elections: Trends and Issues." *The Book of the States 1992-93.* Lexington, Ky: The Council of State Governments, 1992, 283-91.

———. "State Campaign Finance Reform: Options for the Future." *State Trends Forecasts* II (April 1993), 1-35.

Clement, Daniel G. "The Rights of Submitters to Prevent Agency Disclosure of Confidential Business Information: The Reverse Freedom of Information Act Lawsuit." *Texas Law Review* LV (March 1977), 587-644.

Cleveland, Harlan. "Government is Information (But Not Vice Versa)." *Public Administration Review* XXXXVI (November/December 1986), 605-7.

Clines, Francis X. "President Says He Wouldn't Let Meese Withdraw His Nomination." *The New York Times* (March 22, 1984), B7.

Coffin, Tristram J. "The New York State Ethics in Government Act of 1987: A Critical Evaluation." *Columbia Journal of Law and Social Problems* XXII (Summer 1989), 169-305.

Collier, Timothy W. "Freedom of Information Act—Investigatory Records Exemption—Summarized or Reproduced Information Retains Exemption." *Wayne Law Review* XXIX (Spring 1983), 1269-284.

Collis, Cheri. "State Inspectors General: The Watchdog Over State Agencies." *State Government News* XXXIII (April 1990), 12-14.

"Conflict-of-Interests of Government Personnel: An Appraisal of the Philadelphia Situation." *University of Pennsylvania Law Review* CVII (May 1959), 985-1026.

"Conflict of Interests: State Government Employees." *Virginia Law Review* XXXXVII (October 1961), 1034-77.

"Conflicts of Interest of State Legislators." *Harvard Law Review* LXXVI (April 1963), 1209-232.

"Conflicts of Interest of State and Local Legislatures." *Iowa Law Review* LV (December 1969), 450-64.

Cooper, Melvin G. "Administering Ethics Laws: The Alabama Experience." *National Civic Review* LXVIII (February 1979), 77-81 and 110.

Cooper, Phillip J. "The Supreme Court, the First Amendment, and Freedom of Information." *Public Administration Review* XXXXVI (November/December 1986), 622-28.

Cooper, Terry L. "Hierarchy, Virtue, and the Practice of Public Administration: A Perspective for Normative Ethics." *Public Administration Review* XXXXVII (July/August 1987), 320-28.

Cox, Gloria. "Implementation of the Routine Use Clause of the Privacy Act." *Policy Studies Review* X (Winter 1991/92), 42-50.

Czapanskiy, Karen. "Time Limits Under the Freedom of Information Act: Another Problematic New Property Reform." *Maryland Law Review* XXXXIV (No. 1, 1985), 38-64.

Davis, C. J. "Controlling Administrative Corruption." *Planning and Administration* XIV (Autumn 1987), 62-66.

Davis, Evan A. "Election Law Reform in the State of New York." *Albany Law Review* LI (Fall 1986), 1-18.

Deck, Glenn E., and Thompson, Raymond. "Auditing the Use and Management of Consultants." *Internal Auditor* XLIII (February 1986), 41-45.

Dellay, Patrick J. "Curbing Influence Peddling in Albany: The 1987 Ethics in Government Act." *Brooklyn Law Review* LIII (1988), 1051-85.

Denhardt, Kathryn G. "Ethics and Fuzzy Worlds." *Australian Journal of Public Administration* L (September 1991), 274-78.

———. "The Management of Ideals: A Political Perspective on Ethics." *Public Administration Review* IL (March/April 1989), 187-93.

Devine, Thomas M., and Alpin, Donald G. "Abuse of Authority: The Office of Special Counsel and Whistleblower Protection." *Antioch Law Journal* I (Summer 1986), 5.

Dillon, Sam. "Fighting Police Department Corruption Amid Distrust." *The New York Times* (December 7, 1992), B1 and B8.

Dittenhofer, Mortimer A. "Internal Control and Auditing for Fraud." *The Government Accountants Journal* XXXII (Winter 1983-84), 24-28.

Dobel, J. Patrick. "Integrity in the Public Service." *Public Administration Review* L (May/June 1990), 355-66.

Dworkin, Terry M., and Near, Janet P. "Whistleblowing Statutes: Are They Working?" *American Business Law Journal* XXV (Summer 1987), 241-64.

Edmondson, June E. "And Gifts and Travel for All." *Federal Bar News and Journal* XXXVII (September 1990), 402-6.

Edwards, Matthew. "Are Privacy and Public Disclosure Compatible?: The Privacy Exemption to Washington's Freedom of Information Act—In re Rosier, 105 Wn 2d 606, 171 P.2d 1353 (1986)." *Washington Law Review* LXII (April 1987), 257-75.

Eisenberg, Ralph. "Conflicts of Interest Situations and Remedies." *Rutgers Law Review* XIII (Summer 1959), 666-700.

Embry, Charles R. "Ethics and Public Administration." *News for Teachers of Political Science* (Summer 1984), 1 and 9.

"Ethics Board Criticizes Philadelphia's Mayor." *The New York Times* (February 26, 1986), A18.

"Ethics and Internal Auditors." *Internal Auditor* XXXXVI (April 1989), 12-21.

Farrell, John A. "Campaign Says Dentist Solicitation Improper." *The Boston Globe* (October 28, 1987), 9.

"FEC Imposes Civil Penalties for Violations of the $25,000 Annual Limit." *Record* (Federal Election Commission) XIX (April 1993), 1 and 3.

Feigenbaum, Edward D. "State Campaign Finance Law: 1990-91 Activity." *Campaign Finance Law 91*. Washington, D.C.: Federal Election Commission, 1992, 1-8.

Feinberg, Lotte E. "Managing the Freedom of Information Act and Federal Information Policy." *Public Administration Review* XXXXVI (November/December 1986), 615-21.

Ferrick, John D. "Do We Really Want Ethical Government?" *New York State Bar Journal* (January 1992), 8-10.

"The Fiduciary Duty of Former Government Employees." *Yale Law Journal* XC (November 1980), 189-215.

Flynn, John M. "Internal Control Reform." *The Bureaucrat* XII (Fall 1983), 11-18.

"FOIA Exemption 7 and Broader Disclosure of Unlawful FBI Investigations." *Minnesota Law Review* LXV (July 1981), 1139-168.

Foster, Gregory D. "Law, Morality, and the Public Servant." *Public Administration Review* XLI (January/February 1981), 29-34.

Frederickson, H. George. "Public Administration and Social Equity." *Public Administration Review* L (March/April 1990), 228-36.

Frederickson, H. George, and Hart, David K. "The Public Service and the Patriotism of Benevolence." *Public Administration Review* XXXXV (September/October 1985), 547-53.

Frederickson, Ted P. "Letting the Sunshine In: An Analysis of the 1984 Kansas Open Records Act." *University of Kansas Law Review* XXXIII (Winter 1985), 205-68.

Freilich, Robert H. and Larson, Thomas M. "Conflicts of Interest: A Model Statutory Proposal for the Regulation of Municipal Transactions." *UMKC Law Review* (University of Missouri, Kansas City) XXXVIII (Spring 1970), 373-420.

Fuerbringer, Jonathan. "17 Big Underwriters Bar Campaign Gifts Aimed at Bond Sales." *The New York Times* (October 19, 1993), 1 and D3.

Furby, Tommy E. "The Freedom of Information Act: A Survey of Litigation Under the Exemptions." *Mississippi Law Journal* XXXXVIII (September 1977), 784-817.

Gavison, Ruth. "Privacy and the Limits of the Law." *The Yale Law Journal* LXXXIX (January 1980), 421-71.

Gawthrop, Louis C. "Ethics and Democracy: The Moral Dimension." *The Journal of State Government* LXII (September/October 1989), 180-84.

Gazarek, Jo Anne. "Would Macy's Tell Gimbel's: Government-Controlled Business Information and the Freedom of Information Act, Forwards & Backwards." *Loyola University Law Journal* VI (Summer 1975), 594-621.

Gerety, Tom. "Redefining Privacy." *Harvard Civil Rights-Civil Liberties Law Review* XII (Spring 1977), 233-96.

Gerlach, Wendy L. "Amendment of the Post-Government Employment Laws." *Arizona Law Review* XXXIII (Spring 1991), 401-26.

Gerth, Jeff. "Ferraro Opens Her Tax Figures and Husband's." *The New York Times* (August 21, 1984), 1 and B8.

Gerth, Jeff, and Werner, Leslie M. "Meese's Tax Returns Vary from Disclosure Forms." *The New York Times* (March 22, 1984), 1 and B7.

Giuliani, Rudolph W. "How to Return Ethics to New York." *The New York Times* (April 16, 1986), A27.

Graham, John M. "Fair Administration of the Freedom of Information Act After the Computer Revolution." *Computer/Law Journal* V (Summer 1984), 51-76.

Griswold, Erwin N. "Government in Ignorance of the Law—A Plea for Better Publication of Executive Legislation." *Harvard Law Review* XXXXVIII (November 1934), 198-215.

Gross, Kenneth A. "The Enforcement of Campaign Finance Rules: A System in Search of Reform." *Yale Law & Policy Review* IX (No. 2, 1991), 279-300.

Grubiak, James F. "Ethics, Conflicts-of-Interest, and Abuse of Office." Georgia County Government. XLIV (November 1992), 12-14, and 16-17.

Gunner, Burton. "Committing the Truth: Whistleblowing, Organizational Dissent, and the Honorable Bureaucrat." *Administration in Social Work* IX (Winter 1985/86), 89-102.

"Hansen Faces Inquiry by House Ethics Panel." *The New York Times* (April 4, 1984), B9.

Hart, David K. "The Virtuous Citizen, the Honorable Bureaucrat, and 'Public' Administration." *Public Administration Review* XLV (March 1984), 111-20.

"Hartnett Prohibited from Lobbying before Legislature." *Times Union* (Albany, New York) (December 29, 1992), B-2.

Harvey, Gordon W., and Find, Harold R. "A Comprehensive Staff Training and Development System for Inspector General Audit Staff." *The Government Accountants Journal* XXXIII (Spring 1984), 7-19.

Hays, Steven W., and Gleissner, Richard R. "Codes of Ethics in State Government: A Nationwide Survey." *Public Personnel Management* X (1981), 48-58.

Hejka-Ekins, April. "Teaching Ethics in Public Administration." *Public Administration Review* XLVIII (September/October 1988), 855-91.

Helm, Frederick A., Jr., and Steinberg, Harold. "Implementing the Internal Control Evaluation, Improvement and Reporting Process in the Federal Government." *The Government Accountants Journal* XXXII (Winter 1983-84), 1-22.

Herbers, John. "Demand for Ethics in Government has Outstripped Supply." *The New York Times* (June 19, 1988), E4.

Hernandez, Efrain, Jr. "State Curbs Private Hiring of Its Workers." *The Boston Globe* (December 3, 1992), 1 and 43.

Hill, George E. "Codes of Ethics—The Connecticut Municipal Experience." *Connecticut Government* XXXII (Winter 1980), 5-8.

Hochman, Joseph I. "Post-Employment Lobbying Restrictions on the Legislative Branch of Government: A Minimalist Approach to Regulating Ethics in Government." *Washington Law Review* LXV (October 1990), 883-902.

Hook, Janet. "Passion, Defiance, Tears: Jim Wright Bows Out." *Congressional Quarterly Weekly Report* XXXXVII (June 3, 1989), 1289-394.

Hosch, Heyward C., III. "The Interest in Limiting the Disclosure of Personal Information: A Constitutional Analysis." *Vanderbilt Law Review* XXXVI (January 1983), 139-97.

Howard, John L. "Current Developments in Whistleblower Protection." *Labor Law Journal* XXXIX (February 1988), 67-80.

Hunter, J. Stewart. "Freedom of Information Act: An Appraisal." *The Bureaucrat* I (Summer 1972), 131-35.

"ICMA Code of Ethics with Guidelines." *Who's Who in Local Government Management 1992-1993*. Washington, D.C.: International City Management Association, 1991, 3-4.

"ICMA Code of Ethics: Rules of Procedure for Enforcement." *Who's Who in Local Government Management 1992-1993*. Washington, D.C.: International City Management Association, 1992, 5-7.

Isikoff, Michael. "Information Brokers a Threat to Privacy." *The Times Union* (Albany, New York) (December 28, 1991), A-9.

Jacobs, Theodore J. "The Federal Sunshine Act is Paying Off." *The New York Times* (June 7, 1980), 22.

Janison, Dan. "Public Resources, Private Campaigns." *The Times Union* (Albany, New York) (October 29, 1992), B-2.

————. "Whistle-Blower Wins $300G." *The Times Union* (Albany, New York) (June 7, 1991), 1.

Jehl, Douglas. "Lobbying Rules for Ex-Officials at Issue Again." *The New York Times* (December 8, 1993), 1 and 22.

Jenkins, Frank E., III. "New Disclosure Mandates for County Commissioners." *Georgia County Government* XXXIX (October 1987), 36-37.

Johnson, Robert A., and Kraft, Michael E. "Bureaucratic Whistle Blowing and Policy Change." *Western Political Quarterly* XXXXIII (December 1990), 849-74.

Jos, Philip H.; Tompkins, Mark E.; and Hays, Steven W. "In Praise of Difficult People: A Portrait of the Committed Whistleblower." *Public Administration Review* IL (November/December 1989), 552-61.

Kalo, Joseph J. "Deterring Misuse of Confidential Government Information: A Proposed Citizens' Action." *Michigan Law Review* LXXII (August 1974), 1577-610.

Kaplan, Milton, and Lillich, Richard B. "Municipal Conflicts of Interest: Inconsistencies and Patchwork Prohibitions." *Columbia Law Review* LVIII (1958), 157-82.

Kaufmann, Dan, and Widiss, Alan I. "The California Conflict of Interest Laws." *Southern California Law Review* XXXVI (1963), 186-207.

Kernaghan, Kenneth. "Codes of Ethics and Public Administration: Progress, Problems, and Prospects." *Public Administration* LVIII (Summer 1980), 207-23.

Kerr, Peter. "Campaign Donations Overwhelm Monitoring Agencies in the States." *The New York Times* (December 27, 1988), 1 and B2.

Knapp, Elaine S., ed. "Ethics in Government." *State Government* LXII (September/October 1989), 170-201.

————. "What's Fair and Foul." *State Government News* XXXIII (April 1990), 6-9, and 28.

Kristol, Irving. "Post-Watergate Morality: Too Good for our Good?" *The New York Times Magazine* (November 14, 1976), 35, 50-51, 53, and 55.

Lambert, Joyce C., and Hubbard, Thomas D. "Internal Auditors' Changing Responsibilities for Fraud Detection." *Internal Auditor* XXXXVI (June 1989), 13-16.

Lane, Robert P. "Disclosure." *Georgia County Government* XXXIX (November 1987), 36, 38, and 47-50.

Lavelle, Marianne. "Inspectors General Want Respect." *The National Law Journal* XII (September 11, 1989), 1 and 52.

Lipman, Harvy. "Campaign Ignores Filing Deadlines." *Times Union* (Albany, New York) (November 8, 1993), A-5.

Lively, Don. "Catch 7(A): The Plaintiff's Burden Under the Freedom of Information Act." *Villanova Law Review* XXVIII (No. 1, 1982-93), 75-100.

Locy, Toni. "Tobacco Firms Pay $4.5m to Fight Tax." *The Boston Globe* (September 5, 1992), 1 and 24.

Loftus, Tom, and Cross, Al. "Lies, Bribes, and Videotape." *State Legislatures* XIX (July 1993), 42-43, 45, and 47.

Lowi, Theodore J. "The Intelligent Person's Guide to Political Corruption." *Public Affairs* (University of South Dakota) (September 1981), 1-6.

Mahar, Maggie. "Beneath Contempt: Did the Justice Department Deliberately Bankrupt INSLAW?" *Barron's* (March 21, 1988), 16-18, and 58.

————. "Rogue Justice: What Really Sparked the Vendetta Against INSLAW?" *Barron's* (April 4, 1988), 6-7, and 36-40.

Malan, Roland M. "Traps on the Path to Audit Credibility." *Internal Auditor* XLIII (June 1986), 29-35.

Malin, Martin H. "Protecting the Whistleblower from Retaliatory Discharge." *University of Michigan Journal of Law Reform* XVI (Winter 1983), 277-318.

Marini, Frank. "The Uses of Literature in the Exploration of Public Administration Ethics: The Example of Antigone." *Public Administration Review* LII (September/October 1992), 420-26.

Markey, Edward J. "Telephone Consumer Privacy Protection Act of 1993." *Congressional Record* (November 3, 1993), E-2745-746.

Martenas, Sharleen J. "Beyond Scandals & Statutes: Ethics in Public Administration." *University of Virginia Newsletter* LXVII (July/August 1991), 1-8.

McBride, Ann. "Ethics in Congress: Agenda and Action." *George Washington Law Review* LVIII (February 1990), 451-87.

Means, Kathryn M., and Kazenski, Paul M. "Improved Internal Controls Can Cut Audit Costs." *Management Accounting* LXVIII (January 1987), 48-51.

Meislin, Richard J. "Panel Urges Money Curbs in Campaigns." *The New York Times* (April 30, 1986), B1-B2.

Menzel, Donald C. "Ethics Attitudes and Behaviors in Local Government: An Empirical Analysis." *State and Local Government Review* XXIV (Fall 1992), 94-102.

Michael, James. "The Cult of Secrecy." *The Bureaucrat* I (Summer 1972), 127-30.

Miller, Arthur S. "Executive Privilege: Its Dubious Constitutionality." *The Bureaucrat* I (Summer 1972), 136-41.

Mohl, Bruce. "Inspector General Criticizes Rules for Consultants." *The Boston Globe* (March 1, 1988), 17 and 24.

Moran, James P. "Legislation to Protect Privacy and Safety of Licensed Drivers." *Congressional Record* (November 3, 1993), E-2747-748.

Moss, John E. et al. "The Freedom of Information Act: A Collage." *Public Administration Review* XXXXVI (November/December 1986), 608-14.

Murdock, Eric J. "Finally, Government Ethics as if People Mattered: Some Thoughts on the Ethics Reform Act of 1989." *George Washington Law Review* LVIII (February 1990), 502-25.

Murphine, Ralph. "Negative Campaigns, Big Money: Political Ethics Up to Voters." *State Government News* XXXIII (April 1990), 20-22.

Nicholson, Marlene A. "Basic Principles or Theoretical Tangles: Analyzing the Constitutionality of Government Regulation of Campaign Finance." *Case Western Law Review* XXXVIII (No. 4, 1987-88), 589-607.

Nigro, Lloyd G., and Richardson, William D. "Between Citizen and Administrator: Administrative Ethics and 'PAR'." *Public Administration Review* L (November/December 1990), 623-35.

Niner, David. "Legislative Oversight & the Role of the New York State Legislative Commission on Expenditure Review." *Comparative State Politics* XIII (December 1992), 15-30.

Nolan, Beth. "Regulating Government Ethics: When It's Not Enough to Just Say No." *George Washington Law Review* LVIII (February 1990), 495-516.

O'Brien, David M. "Freedom of Information, Privacy, and Information Control: A Contemporary Administrative Dilemma." *Public Administration Review* XXXIX (July/August 1979), 323-28.

Olmstead, Larry. "2 Managers Held in Bidding Scheme at School Agency." *The New York Times* (April 21, 1993), 1 and B9.

O'Looney, John. "Fractured Decision Making: Sunshine Laws and the Colliding Roles of Media and Government." *National Civic Review* LXXXI (Winter-Spring 1992), 43-56.

Paddock, Richard C. "California's Tough New Ethics Law." *State Legislatures* XVI (August 1990), 9.

Parliaman, George. "Protecting the Whistleblower." *Personnel Administrator* XXXII (July 1987), 26-32.

Pear, Robert. "Judge Lifts Honoraria Ban on Federal Workers." *The New York Times* (March 21, 1993), A19.

Perlez, Jane. "House Panel Reports Ferraro Violated Ethics Law." *The New York Times* (December 5, 1984), 1 and A20.

Persson, Gert. "Computerised Personnel Registers and the Protection of Privacy." *Current Sweden* CCCXXXXIV (February 1986), 1-10.

Petersen, James C. "Protecting Whistleblowers." *Citizen Participation* IV (January-February 1983), 5-6, and 19.

Points, Ronald J., and Michelson, Bruce. "Internal Control Standards for the Federal Government." *The Government Accountants Journal* XXXII (Summer 1983), 9-14.

Precious, Tom. "Democrats at Odds over Anti-Ferraro Ads." *The Times Union* (Albany, New York) (September 10, 1992), 1 and 6.

————. "Panel Limits Lobbying by Former Cuomo Aide." *The Times Union* (Albany, New York) (January 29, 1993), 1 and A-9.

Raby, Vivian R. "The Freedom of Information Act and the IRS Confidentiality Statute: A Proper Analysis." *University of Cincinnati Law Review* LIV (No. 2, 1985), 605-29.

Radburn, William F. "Legislated Internal Audit: Canada's New Provisions." *Internal Auditor* XLIII (June 1986), 18-24.

"Raise Safety Board Ethics." *The Times Union* (Albany, New York) (April 12, 1993), A-6.

Regan, Priscilla M. "Privacy, Government Information, and Technology." *Public Administration Review* XXXXVI (November/December 1986), 629-34.

Reinstein, Alan, and Weirich, Thomas R. "Ethics and Fraud: Opening Doors for Internal Auditing." *Internal Auditor* VL (October 1988), 43-47.

Relyea, Harold C. "Access to Government Information in the Information Age." *Public Administration Review* XXXXVI (November/December 1986), 635-39.

"Rhode Island Panel Fines Ex-Governor." *The Times Union* (Albany, New York) (December 21, 1991), A-10.

Richardson, William D., and Nigro, Lloyd G. "Administration Ethics and Founding Thought: Constitutional Correctives, Honor, and Education." *Public Administration Review* XXXXVII (September/October 1987), 367-76.

Rimmer, Stephen J. "Competitive Tendering, Contracting Out, and Franchising: Key Concepts and Issues." *Australian Journal of Public Administration* L (September 1991), 292-302.

Riso, Gerald R., and Kendig, William L. "Strengthening Federal Management Controls with Less Effort." *Public Administration Review* XXXXVI (September/October 1986), 438-46.

Roberts, Robert N. "Public Service and Private Hospitality: A Case Study in Federal Conflict-of-Interest Reform." *Public Administration Review* LII (May/June 1992), 260-70.

Roberts, Steven V. "House Reprimands Idaho Republican in Financial Disclosure Case." *The New York Times* (August 1, 1984), A14.

Roffman, Howard. "Freedom of Information: Judicial Review of Executive Security Classifications." *University of Florida Law Review* XXVII (Winter 1976), 551-68.

Rosenbloom, David H. "The Constitution as a Basis for Public Administrative Ethics," in Madsen, Peter and Shafritz, Jay M., eds. *Essentials of Government Ethics*. New York: Penguin Books, 1992, 48-64.

Rosenfeld, Frank A. "The Freedom of Information Act's Privacy Exemption and the Privacy Act of 1974." *Harvard Civil Rights-Civil Liberties Law Review* XI (Summer 1976), 596-631.

Rothschild, Joseph. "Evaluating Internal Controls: Are the Auditors as Good as the Audit Standards?" *The Government Accountants Journal* XXXV (Summer 1986), 1-8.

Rourke, Francis E. "Bureaucratic Secrecy and Its Constituents." *The Bureaucrat* I (Summer 1972), 116-21.

Russo, Philip. "The Patronage Police." *Empire State Report* XV (November 1989), 13-14 and 17-19.

Sack, Kevin. "The Great Incumbency Machine." *The New York Times Magazine* (September 27, 1992), 47-49, 52, 54, and 62.

Schick, Allen, ed. "The Short and Sad History of Freedom of Information." *The Bureaucrat* I (Summer 1972), 116-60.

Schmidt, Warren H. and Posner, Barry Z. "Values and Expectations of Federal Service Executives." *Public Administration Review* XXXXVI (September/October 1986), 447-54.

Semmens, John. "Public Policy Debate: The Rigged Game." *The Freeman* XXXVIII (October 1988), 395-97.

"Senate Select Committee on Ethics." *Congressional Record* (February 16, 1993), S1648-659.

"Shameful Shakedown." *The Keene (New Hampshire) Sentinel* (September 15, 1987), 4.

Simmons, Charlene W. "Thoughts on Legislative Ethics Reform and Representation." *PS: Political Science and Politics* XXIV (June 1991), 193-200.

Sluzar, Joseph. "New York Abandons a Commitment to Open Meetings." *Albany Law Review* L (Spring 1986), 613-35.

Smolka, Richard G. "Election Legislation, 1990-91." *The Book of the States 1992-93*. Lexington, Ky.: The Council of State Governments, 1991, 258-64.

Smothers, Ronald. "M.A.C. Employees Exempt on Assets." *The New York Times* (June 18, 1976), D12.

Sobczak, Dean M. "A Survey of Recent Developments Under the Freedom of Information Act." *Administrative Law Journal* (Spring 1989), 183-213.

Sourwine, Darrel A. "How Are Your Internal Controls?" *Internal Auditor* XLIV (June 1987), 41-44.

Stark, Andrew. "Public Sector Conflict-of-Interest at the Federal Level in Canada and the U.S.: Differences in Understanding and Approach." *Public Administration Review* LII (September/October 1992), 427-37.

Stephens, Jack H. "Hawaii's Ombudsmen." *National Civic Review* LIX (February 1970), 81-84, and 105.

Stewart, Debra W. "Managing Competing Claims: An Ethical Framework for Human Resource Decision Making." *Public Administration Review* XXXXIV (January/February 1984), 14-22.

Storozynski, Alex. "The Ethics Cycle." *Empire State Report* XIX (November 1993), 13-15, and 17.

Stroud, Michael A. "Administrative Law—Freedom of Information Act—Law Enforcement Exemption May Prevent Disclosure of Records Not Compiled for Law Enforcement Purposes." *Tulane Law Review* LVII (June 1983), 1564-576.

"The Swedish Ombudsmen." *Fact Sheets on Sweden.* Stockholm: The Swedish Institute, 1978, 1-2.

Taylor, Paul. "Boston Mayor Off the Cakewalk." *Newsday* (January 10, 1983), 7.

Terapak, Richard G. "Administering Ethics Laws: The Ohio Experience." *National Civic Review* LXVIII (February 1979), 82-84.

Tessitore, Aristide. "Making the City Safe for Philosophy: 'Nicomachean Ethics'." *The American Political Science Review* LXXXIV (December 1990), 1251-262.

Thomas, Larry W. "The Courts and the Implementation of the Government in the Sunshine Act." *Administrative Law Review* XXXVII (Summer 1985), 259-79.

Thompson, Dennis F. "The Possibility of Administrative Ethics." *Public Administration Review* XLV (September/October 1985), 555-61.

Tibbetts, Donn. "Merrill Raps Burling on Conflict-of-Interest Issue." *The Union Leader* (Manchester, New Hampshire) (March 18, 1993), 11.

Tolchin, Martin. "10 Pay Fines for Exceeding Campaign Donations." *The New York Times* (March 18, 1993), A17.

Tomlinson, Edward A. "Use of the Freedom of Information Act for Discovery Purposes." *Maryland Law Review* XXXXIII (1984), 119-202.

Topper, Gary. "State Conflict of Interest Laws: A Panacea for Better Government?" *DePaul Law Review* XVI (Spring-Summer 1967), 453-64.

Tyrer, Thomas J. "Corruption Still Haunts Lake County." *City & State* VI (January 2, 1989), 3 and 20.

Uhr, John. "The Ethics Debate: Five Framework Propositions." *Australian Journal of Public Administration* L (September 1991), 285-91.

Van Slyke, Leonard, and Rushing, Terryl. "Sunshine in Mississippi: The Open Meetings Act." *Mississippi Law Journal* LX (Fall 1990), 283-309.

Vaughn, Robert G. "Administrative Alternatives and the Federal Freedom of Information Act." *Ohio State Law Journal* VL (1984), 184-214.

Verhovek, Sam H. "Incumbent Legislators Face Few Primary Challenges." *The New York Times* (September 15, 1992), B6.

Virtanen, Pekka V. "Unethical Land Use." *Planning and Administration* XIV (Autumn 1987), 7-13.

Waldron, Gerard J., and Israel, Jeff A. "Developments Under the Freedom of Information Act—1988." *Duke Law Journal* MDCCCCLXXXIX (June 1989), 686-737.

Walter, J. Jackson. "The Ethics in Government Act, Conflict of Interest Laws, and Presidential Recruiting." *Public Administration Review* XLI (November/December 1981), 659-65.

Warren, Samuel D., and Brandeis, Louis D. "The Right to Privacy." *Harvard Law Review* IV (December 15, 1890), 193-220.

Watkins, John J. "The Arkansas Freedom of Information Act: Time for a Change." *Arkansas Law Review* XXXXIV (No. 3, 1991), 535-628.

West, Jonathan P.; Berman, Eva; and Cava, Anita. "Ethics in the Municipal Workplace." *The Municipal Year Book 1993.* Washington, D.C.: International City Management Association, 1993, 3-16.

Woodward, J. David. "Ethics and the City Manager." *The Bureaucrat* XIII (Spring 1984), 53-57.

Zimmerman, Joseph F. "Ethics in Local Government." *Management Information Service Report* VIII (1976), 1-11.

———. "Ethics in Local Government." *Planning and Administration* IX (Spring 1982), 33-45.

———. "Ethics in the Public Service." *State and Local Government Review* XIV (September 1982), 98-106.

———. "Ethics and the MPA Curriculum," in Birkhead, Guthrie S. and Carroll, James D., eds. *Education for Public Service: 1980.* Syracuse: Maxwell School of Citizenship and Public Affairs, Syracuse University, 1981, 53-65.

———. "Freedom of Information and Privacy—The U.S. Experience." *Seirbhis Phoibli* (Public Service, Dublin) IX (March 1988), 20-24.

———. "The Office of Ombudsman in Ireland." *Administration* XXXVII (1989), 258-72.

———. "Preventing Unethical Behavior in Government." *Urban Law and Policy* VIII (1987), 335-56.

UNPUBLISHED MATERIALS

"Address of Arnold I. Burns, Deputy Attorney General, Executive Development Workshop, President's Council on Integrity and Efficiency, Federal Home Loan Bank Board, Washington, D.C., November 24, 1986."

Bernstein, Marver H. "A Perspective on Ethical Problems in State and Local Government." Paper presented at the National Conference on Government, Atlanta, Georgia, November 15, 1971.

"Conflict of Interest Legislation in the United States." Paper prepared by Common Cause, Washington, D.C., 1991.

Cooper, Melvin G. "Administering Ethics Laws—Effective Balance or Overkill?" Paper presented at the National Conference on Government, Louisville, Kentucky, November 12-15, 1978.

_____. "The Alabama Ethics Act: Its Scope and Implementation." Paper presented at the National Conference on Government, Chicago, Illinois, November 17, 1975.

"The Inspectors General Use of Contractors: Report of the Majority Staff to the Chairman of the Subcommittee on Federal Services, Post Office, and Civil Service, United States Senate Committee on Governmental Affairs." Washington, D.C., 1991.

Johnson, Graham E. "The Public Official and the Public Trust." Paper presented at the National Conference on Government, Williamsburg, Virginia, November 9, 1976.

"A Kingdom All Their Own: New York State's Industrial Development Agencies." Report issued by New York State Senator Franz S. Leichter, January 14, 1992.

Kreutzer, S. Stanley. "How Can We Secure the Public Trust: A Federal Ethics Commission." The Ramsen Bird lecture presented at Occidental College, Los Angeles, California, May 13, 1975.

Matthews, Mark S. "Ethics in Government." Paper presented at the National Conference on Government, Atlanta, Georgia, November 15, 1971.

Mavrinac, Albert. "On the Value of the Concept of Political Neutrality of the Civil Servant in the Contemporary American Democracy." Paper presented at a national conference on ethics and morality in the public service today, Key Biscayne, Florida, April 18-19, 1974.

"Remarks of William F. Weld, Assistant Attorney General, Criminal Division, United States Department of Justice at the Morning Newsmaker, the National Press Club, Washington, D.C., March 8, 1988."

"Statement of William J. Anderson, Assistant Comptroller General, on the Filing and Review of the Attorney General's Financial Disclosure Report before the Subcommittee on Human Resources, House of Representatives, August 5, 1987."

"Statement of Carol E. Dinkins, Deputy Attorney General, before the Subcommittee on Government Information, Justice, and Agriculture, House of Representatives, Concerning Freedom of Information Act Amendments, on August 9, 1984."

"Statement of Deputy Assistant Attorney General James Knapp before the Subcommittee on Patents, Copyrights and Trademarks, United States Senate, concerning S. 1667, Electronic Communications Privacy Act, on November 13, 1985."

"Statement of Janet Reno, Attorney General, before the Committee on Governmental Affairs, United States Senate, concerning S. 24, The Independent Counsel Reauthorization Act, presented on May 14, 1993."

"Statement of Marcy C. Lawton, Counsel for Intelligence Policy, United States Department of Justice before the Subcommittee on Criminal Law, United States Senate on S. 2669—to Prohibit Government Employees from Secretly Taping Conversations with Others, June 13, 1984."

"Statement of Deputy Assistant Attorney General Stuart E. Schiffer before the Subcommittee on Civil Service, United States House of Representatives, concerning H.R. 4033, Whistleblower Protection Act, on February 20, 1986."

"Statement of A. Mary Sterling, Inspector General, U.S. Department of Transportation before the Committee on Ways and Means, U.S. House of Representatives, concerning operations of the Highway Trust Fund, the Airport and Airway Trust Fund, the Oil Spill Liability Trust Fund, the Boat Safety Account of the Aquatic Resources Trust Fund, and the Harbor Maintenance Trust Fund, on May 9, 1991."

"Statement of Victoria Toensing, Deputy Assistant Attorney General before the Subcommittee on Criminal Justice, House of Representatives, concerning Financial Bribery and Fraud, April 26, 1984."

"Suggestions for Anticipating Requests under Freedom of Information Act." Prepared by the National Aeronautics and Space Administration, November 20, 1989.

Zimmerman, Joseph F. "A Code of Ethics in Town Government." Paper presented at the annual meeting of the Association of Towns of the State of New York, New York City, February 16, 1976.

———. "A Commentary on Municipal Codes of Ethics." A paper presented at a public hearing held by the New York State Senate Special Committee on Ethics and Guidance, New York, New York, March 13, 1975.

Index

About the Author

JOSEPH ZIMMERMAN is Professor of Political Science at the Graduate School of Public Affairs, State University of New York at Albany, and Research Director of the New York State Legislative Commission on Critical Transportation Choices. Dr. Zimmerman is author of *State-Local Relations: A Partnership Approach* (Praeger, 1983), *Participatory Democracy: Populism Revived* (Praeger, 1986), *Federal Preemption: The Silent Revolution* (Praeger, 1992), and *Contemporary American Federalism* (Praeger, 1992).